The Essential
Best Foods
Cookbook

225
Irresistible Recipes
Featuring the Healthiest
and Most Delicious Foods

Dana Jacobi
Author of 12 Best Foods Cookbook

RODALE

Printed in the United States of America

Photographs © Mitch Mandel/Rodale Images
Food styling by Diane Vezza

Book design by Joanna Williams

ISBN-13 978–1–59486–668–5   paperback
ISBN-10 1–59486–668–6   paperback

To Muriel Sholin Miller and the treasures of family

To: Klárika love Eva
with

One more into her
drop
"Sea of knowledge"
of cooking.
etc. etc.
2011

Contents

Acknowledgments v

Introduction. 2

Chapter One: The Essentials 7

Chapter Two: Hors d'Oeuvres and Starters 69

Chapter Three: Soups. 92

Chapter Four: Salads. 121

Chapter Five: Poultry and Meat 142

Chapter Six: Fish and Seafood 165

Chapter Seven: Pasta, Whole Grains, and Rice. 188

Chapter Eight: Eggs, Beans, and Soy 213

Chapter Nine: Vegetables and Side Dishes 229

Chapter Ten: Desserts. 259

Chapter Eleven: Breakfasts and Drinks 309

Index 347

Conversion Chart 362

Acknowledgments

Writing this book, I was reminded that the scientific and health care communities are as generous and articulate as the authorities in the worlds of food and agriculture. Thank you to the host of experts and to everyone else who contributed to the cooking and production of this information-filled feast, and to my blessed support network.

For deep background, specifics regarding agriculture or individual foods, and for sometimes supplying products (even out of season): Amy Barr, Beans For Health Alliance; Karen Brux, Zespri International North America; Gloria Chillon, Driscoll Strawberry Associates; Mary Cleaver, The Cleaver Company; Jane DePriest, The Cherry Marketing Institute; Amy Farges, Marché Aux Delices; Tim Fitzgerald, Environmental Defense Fund; Dorie Greenspan and Michele Scicolone on almond paste; Staci Haaga, U.S. Apple Commission; Randy Hartnell and Craig Weatherby, Vital Choice; Mike Hawes, Belovo Inc.; Pamela Holmgren, PomWonderful; Ron Jacobs and Kent Jacobson, Jacobs Farm Herbs; David Karp, The Fruit Detective; Patricia Kearny, The Peanut Institute; Caryl Levine, Lotus Foods; Ruth Lowenfeld, Lewis & Neale; Antonios Maridakis, FageUSA Corp.; Theresa Marquez, Organic Valley; Courtney Allan Nathan, Vann's Spices Ltd.; Sophie Newcomb, Oceanspray Cranberries; Nevia No, Yuno's Farm; Oldways Preservation Trust; Packaged Facts; Jay Ragan, Martek Biosciences Corporation; Kim Reddin, National Onion Association; Frederick Schiller, Dagoba Chocolate; Elizabeth Schneider on vegetables; Jan-Marie Schroeder, Oregon Raspberry and Blackberry Commission; Sat Shakti, Cascade Fresh; William Shurtleff, SoyInfo; Marie Simmons on rice; Robert Schueller of Melissa's World Variety Produce; Karla Stockli, California Raisin Marketing Board; Thomas Stone, Bell & Evans; and the whole gang at the Walnut Marketing Board. Last but not least, to all the experts whose contributions to *12 Best Foods Cookbook* are the underpinning for this one, thank you again.

For nutritional information and guidance, thanks to David Alberts, MD, director of the Arizona Cancer Center, The University of Arizona; Jeffrey Blumberg, PhD, Antioxidant Research Laboratory, Jean Mayer USDA Human Nutrition Center on Aging, Tufts University; Mary Ellen Camire, PhD, Department of Food Science and Human Nutrition, University of Maine; Annemarie Colbin; Karen Collins, MS, RD, CDN at the American Institute for Cancer Research; Roberta Lee, MD, Medical Director, Continuum Center for Health and

Healing, Beth Israel Medical Center, New York City; Riu Hai Liu, MD, Associate Professor of Food Science at Cornell University, Ithaca, New York; The George Mateljan Foundation; and to Lani Bloom Ragan, RD, for vetting the nutritional information.

For recipe development and testing, Jillian Cristofalo, Tina DeGraff, Ellen Fried, Judy Marshall (at long last!), Renee Marton, and the indispensable Liliana Scali (bless you Suzen O'Rourke and Lila Gault for finding this culinary talent). Lani, thanks for your personal culinary passion and bless you Sheila Darnborough, Joan Emery, Jay Ragan, and the mah jongg crew for your healthy appetites. Hilary Maler, thanks for once again turning recipes into manuscript, and to Sheila and Joan for thoughts on tightening words into smart text.

To everyone at Rodale who saw the wisdom of enlarging *12 Best* and making this book even more valuable: Shea Zukowski, who edited, pondered, blue-penciled, and diplomatically shepherded the project; Lois Hazel, Sharon Sanders, and Deri Reed for meticulous copy editing and saintly patience; JoAnn Brader for nutritional analysis; Joanna Williams who met the challenge to make this look even better than *12 Best*; Diane Vezza and Pam Simpson for food and prop styling with taste and patience galore; and to Mitch Mandel, your photography brings it all deliciously alive. Beth Tarson, for smartly spreading the word to the world. Also to the Rodale cafeteria for garden-fresh, beautiful lunches.

Thank you, Margot Schupf for launching this project and to Beth Shepard for your devotion, invaluable wisdom and more, all along the way. Angela Miller, your persistence and expertise as my agent make this all possible. No author could wish for more.

Finally, writing is an isolating process you get through with support from understanding friends and peers like Elizabeth Andoh, Eileen Guastella, Molly Katzen, Alexandra Leaf, Pam Levine, Meryl Rosofsky, Barney Stein, and Muriel Sholin Miller, my godmother.

Introduction

Add a decade or more to your life. If you get the right vitamins, minerals, antioxidants and other phyotchemicals, good protein, fats, and carbohydrates, provided you also exercise and do not smoke, this can be your reward. But when we read one day that pomegranates have the highest antioxidant power of any fresh fruit, on another day an article mentions that dark chocolate can improve cardiovascular health, and perhaps a week later a study praises the benefits of omega-3 fatty acids, how do you make the right choices? *The Essential Best Foods Cookbook* provides dishes that let you enjoy optimal benefits without thinking about it. Together its 61 foods and 225 recipes let you sustain delectable, smart eating every day.

START WITH SUPERIOR VALUE

We live in an age of multitasking. In foods, this has led to orange juice fortified with omega-3s, calcium-enriched soy milk, and other so-called functional foods. The Best Foods, from avocados and apples to winter squash, to walnuts, yogurt, and citrus zest, are all terrific multitaskers you can count on for multiple benefits thanks to the array of nutrients and phytochemicals nature packs into them. Yogurt, prized for its beneficial bacteria that strengthen the immune system, is also a good source of calcium and protein. Strawberries, rich in key vitamins and phytonutrients, are a good source of fiber, too. Even chocolate, proven to help reduce bad cholesterol and boost the good kind, contributes to keeping your vascular system supple and can also provide fiber.

ADD SYNERGY

If following scientific definitions, like synergy—the interaction or cooperation of two or more substances to create a combined effect—is not your cup of tea, simply enjoy a juicy, ripe tomato drizzled with olive oil. While the fat in the oil helps your body better absorb the lycopene in the tomato, don't call this synergy—just call it scrumptious.

You do not even need to orchestrate combinations of the Best Foods to enjoy synergy in their benefits. Most have it solo thanks to the interactivity of substances they contain. For example, a strawberry's cancer-fighting powers seem to include interactions between ellagic acid and its other anthocyanins, plus vitamin C and more, according to Gary Stoner, chair of environmental health sciences at the School of Public Health at Ohio State University.

"Different plants contain more than 8,000 phytochemicals in unique combinations," according to Rui Hai Liu, an associate professor in the Department of Food Science at Cornell University in Ithaca, New York. These combinations of biologically active phytochemicals, including flavanoids and phenolic acids found in fruits and vegetables—especially when you eat them with their skins—are what reduce our risk of heart disease, cancer, stroke, diabetes, and Alzheimer's disease Liu explains. "Each function acts differently in the body: Some are antioxidant, some antiallergenic, some anticarcinogenic, others anti-inflammatory, antiviral, or antiproliferative." *The Essential Best Foods Cookbook* shows how to make your table a delicious banquet of dishes that provide the greatest health benefits.

Synergy applies to more than the antioxidants and phytochemicals in what we eat. It also explains why calcium included in foods appears to do more to protect your bones than taking calcium supplements. So serve those juicy tomatoes with mozzarella cheese and look for other ways to eat calcium-rich foods abundantly and often. Serving Turkey Waldorf Salad provides a different synergy as the protein in the turkey and the fat in the nuts and dressing help to slow down the rate at which the sugars in the apples and grapes are metabolized. Short term, this helps avoid blood sugar levels that spike, then drop. Evening out this seesawing is equally important, long term, as it reduces the risk of developing insulin resistance, a precursor to type 2 diabetes.

MAKE IT SUSTAINABLE

To sustain a Best Foods lifestyle by sticking to high-value choices requires enough variety to keep meals interesting and enough pleasure to make you look forward to them. I know this from personal experience. Providing variety is easy because many of the foods taste so good. Take berries, which are so beneficial that eating them every day is a good idea. Blackberries, blueberries, raspberries and strawberries, all health powerhouses, give you four alternatives. Each one them, good alone, is also versatile enough to combine with other foods, like blueberries in a savory sauce served with pork, strawberries blended with orange juice in a smoothie, and blackberries and blueberries together in Black Bean and Two-Berry Soup.

Variety also means including foods you like but are not the Best. Zucchini, for example, provides far fewer health benefits than spinach. But I believe there is a place for everything, especially if you "Better" it. Better ways to eat zucchini include Green and Yellow Squash Ribbons showered with phytochemical-rich oregano and basil, and Apple Ratatouille, where the squash is partnered with five Best Foods. If you like shrimp, Four Pepper Shrimp, which includes roasted red peppers, tomatoes, and paprika, is another dish with Better value.

Good taste is another way to make healthy eating more sustainable. I like many different foods because my mother was an adventurous and excellent cook who taught me how to make everything taste good. So if you do not like some Best Foods, perhaps kale, whole wheat, and soy, check out Michel's Kaleslaw, whole wheat Fusilli With Broccoli Bolognese, and Black and White Hoppin' John, which may change your mind and get you to enjoy them, too. Since the supermarket is where most of us do our shopping, I have made sure every dish here tastes superb using ingredients bought there. That said, farmers' markets are one of my favorite places to buy the Best. (This also contributes to sustainability in its more common meaning, since most local and small producers practice good agricultural practices to protect the land and environment, including organic methods.) For me, the visual feast and community spirit at farmers' markets increases the enjoyment of the Best Foods lifestyle.

To keep the Best Foods lifestyle sustainable, time counts, too. Many dishes are ready in 30 minutes or less. Look for the recipes with the clock. There are breakfasts to take along, and dishes using only a few ingredients, like Corn With Cilantro and Chives, to save shopping time.

Celebrating holidays and special occasions and comforting yourself on a bad day usually means falling off the sensible-food wagon. You *can* have it all, though. See for yourself in Marshmallow Yams for Grown-Ups, Ginger Cranberry Relish, Cocoa-Crusted Beef Filet with Pomegranate Sauce, instantly gratifying Macaroni And Cheese With Broccoli, and the decadent Black Bean Brownies.

FEAST ON SUCCESS

Since I wrote the *12 Best Foods Cookbook*, studies have proven the benefits from additional foods. So have diets based on research indicating how eating the right choices may turn back your body's clock, improve cardiovascular health, give you better energy, glowing skin, and most important, reduce the inflammation that can be the precursor to many disease and chronic conditions, from cancer and Alzheimer's disease to asthma and arthritis. Wanting these benefits, I have followed the excellent advice in books by Mehmet C. Oz, MD, Nicholas Perricone, MD, Michael C. Roizen, MD, Andrew Weil, MD, and Walter C. Willett, MD, concentrating on creating dishes inspired by their wisdom. I also heard from friends and students equally committed to eating wisely and unhappy with available recipes. The recipes in this cookbook are the result, crammed with what health experts want us to eat. Let them help you easily make delicious meals and snacks in a food lifestyle that is a powerfully health-supporting feast.

CHAPTER ONE

THE ESSENTIALS

Enjoying healthy eating should be easy. After all, many of the foods that are good for us taste good. Think of tomatoes, sweet potatoes, strawberries, even olive oil and chocolate.

Many medical and scientific studies prove that specific foods help reduce your risk for chronic diseases and help maintain optimal wellness, while nutritional guidelines from respected sources tell us how much of them to eat and how often. Yet working these good-for-you foods into real everyday eating still challenges most of us.

That is where this chapter comes in. Here is an overview of all the Essential Best Foods. If a recipe includes one you are not used to preparing, here is all the information you need to be comfortable using it. Along with its health benefits, here also are many ways to fit the food in with what you already like to eat, including how to use it in your own favorite recipes, and practical advice on buying and storing it.

As you see their benefits, plus the numerous ways to enjoy these Essential Best Foods, eating them regularly will become so effortless and delicious that without realizing it you will find yourself following a health-enhancing food lifestyle far too pleasurable to be called a diet.

VEGETABLES • Avocado • Broccoli • Kale and Collard Greens
• Mushrooms • Onions • Spinach • Sweet Bell Peppers • Sweet Potatoes • Tomatoes
• Winter Squash

Vegetables, along with fruits, are our richest source of essential vitamins, minerals, and phytochemicals, particularly carotenoids, polyphenols, and chlorophyll. They are also the best source of water-soluble vitamins such as folic acid and other B vitamins, many of which our bodies store minimally if at all, but which we need every day. Eating vegetables is also important for reaching the recommended goal of 25 to 35 grams of fiber a day for adults.

Most Americans fall short in eating the 2½ to 3 cups a day of vegetables recommended in the USDA's diet guidelines issued in 2005. Our rates of chronic disease, from cancer to heart disease to type 2 diabetes, may be a result of this reluctance to embrace eating vegetables. In Asia, Latin America, and the Mediterranean, where a diet rich in vegetables and grains has traditionally been the foundation of life, people who follow it also benefit by having significantly lower rates of these diseases.

Avocado

Once, avocados were an exotic luxury served stuffed with shrimp at ladies' luncheons. Now, we enjoy them year-round and to our heart's content in salads, sandwiches, wraps, guacamole, and salsas, as well as in elegant entrées, thanks to abundant cultivation in California, Mexico, and Florida.

Why It's Best • Rich in heart-healthy monounsaturated fats that lower LDL and raise HDL levels in the blood • Contains beta-sitosterol, a plant sterol, helps lower cholesterol • Their cholesterol-free fat helps your body absorb more of the nutrients in other foods, including lycopene in tomatoes.

What to Look For • Avocados do not ripen on the tree so plan ahead in order to serve them at peak ripeness. Select unblemished avocados that feel heavy relative to their size. They are ready to use when the skin turns black-brownish green and the fruit yields slightly when gently squeezed. According to growers, there is no way to predict which ones will be fibrous inside.

How to Store • Keep on the counter at room temperature to ripen. Rub cut avocado with citrus juice, cover with plastic wrap, and refrigerate, using as soon as possible.

How to Enjoy • Serve avocado slices with grilled and sautéed fish, poultry, and meat. (Note that avocado can be warmed slightly, but do not cook it, or it will turn bitter.) • Puree together with broth for a chilled soup or sauce. Mash for a sandwich spread, alone (aka "green butter") or mixed with mayonnaise or salsa • Include in salsas.

Good to Know • Avocados harvested from June to November are richer and more oily • In Asia and Latin America, avocado is used in ice cream, sorbet, milkshakes, and other desserts. Pebble-skinned Hass avocados are richest in healthy fat.

Broccoli

One of the most important Essential Best Foods, broccoli beats cabbage, kale, cauliflower, and other cruciferous vegetables nutritionally because it contains two types of potent, detoxifying cancer-fighters and loads of antioxidants. Plus, it is so versatile that eating it often is easy. Broccoli sprouts are even more powerful, containing up to 50 times the amount of preventive substances found in mature broccoli.

Why It's Best • Rich in sulfur compounds that protect against the formation and proliferation of cancer cells • Protects against heart disease • Protects against the *H. pylori* bacteria that cause ulcers and play a role in stomach cancer.

What to Look For • Compact, firm, dark green crowns with small, tightly closed buds. Blue-green leaves and unblemished stems. Avoid yellowed florets, flowers, and a cabbage-like odor. Shop where broccoli is displayed refrigerated or on ice.

How to Store • In a loose plastic bag in the vegetable bin for up to 3 days.

How to Enjoy • For sweetest flavor, steam or blanch broccoli. Also sauté, stir-fry, or roast. • Include in salads, frittatas, pasta dishes, chili, and casseroles • Enjoy on baked potatoes and as crudités • Puree cooked broccoli for soups • Season with oregano, curry powder, garlic, onions, and red chile peppers.

Good to Know • Buying crowns is smart because most of broccoli's phytochemicals are in the florets • To preserve nutritional value, broccoli should be constantly kept just above freezing from field to cooking • Frozen broccoli may provide more nutrition than fresh because it is mostly florets and processed quickly after picking.

Kale and Collard Greens

These dark leafy greens are forms of headless cabbage, but they provide more health benefits than cabbage. For people who avoid them because of their strong flavor, quick-cooking brings out the natural sweetness of these powerhouse vegetables, emphasizing their good-tasting side.

Why They're Best • Kale has seven times more beta-carotene than broccoli, plus vitamin K and loads of heart- and eye-protecting lutein • Collards are one of the top nondairy sources of calcium • Both are rich in cancer-protecting and antioxidant compounds.

What to Look For • Full-bodied leaves with prominent veins and firm, unblemished stems. Collards should be hazy dark green, kale an even, intense bluish green, almost black, or with a purple-red to mauve tinge, depending on the variety. Smaller, younger leaves are more tender and sweet. Avoid wilted or yellowed leaves and brown spots.

How to Store • In the coldest part of refrigerator, in a loose plastic bag, for up to 3 days. Keep away from apples.

Ways to Enjoy • Remove the tough stems, then steam or blanch for the sweetest flavor • Sauté cooked greens in olive oil with garlic • Braise chopped greens in broth or water • For smoky flavor, sauté kale with sliced sausage and collards with bacon or ham • Combine with carrots, corn, potatoes, sweet potatoes, red bell pepper, or tomatoes.

Good to Know • Wait until after cooking kale and collards before chopping to better retain nutrients • Adding a squirt of lemon or splash of vinegar just before serving brightens the flavor of any dark leafy greens.

Mushrooms

Mushrooms contain phytochemicals not found in other produce. Perhaps it was these benefits that made the ancient Egyptians believe that eating mushrooms could confer immortality. In Asia, to this day, many members of this fungus family, including shiitakes, are used medicinally to boost the immune system.

In taste and texture, mushrooms are often described as meaty. One of the few vegetables rich in protein, some of their amino acids contribute to *umami*, that pleasing aspect of their flavor which some experts call the fifth taste. And even though supermarkets sell shiitakes and other so-called exotic varieties, their silken texture and full flavor still make mushrooms seem luxurious.

Why They're Best • Selenium helps repair DNA and protect against prostate cancer • Antioxidants protect against UV radiation • Lentinan, a form of polysaccharide, helps boost the immune system • Antioxidants, including eritadenine, lower cholesterol.

What to Look For • Firm, dry caps and gills. Creamy white button mushrooms and brown creminis should have light-colored gills covered by a "cape" membrane and stems that are firm. Portobellos should have dark, dry gills and an unbroken rim on the cap. Avoid wet, slimy mushrooms or those with or dark spots or dried out or woody stems • Slightly dried-out white and cremini mushrooms with darker, exposed gills have more flavor.

How to Store • Remove mushrooms from plastic-wrapped packages and store loose in a paper bag. Use a mushroom brush or wipe with a damp paper towel just before using. Do NOT wash.

How to Enjoy • Sauté, stir-fry, grill, or roast mushrooms • Marinate in vinaigrette and serve as hors d'oeuvres • Add to sautés, sauces, stews, soups, stuffings, kebabs, pasta dishes, and veggie burgers • Season with thyme, rosemary, garlic, shallots, leeks, onions, wine, or soy sauce.

Good to Know • The dried mushrooms frequently used in Chinese cooking are shiitakes • Portobellos are overgrown cremini mushrooms.

Onions

Onions are more than "the other allium." Frequently used along with garlic in cooking, they provide so many health benefits that we should eat them liberally, which is far easier to do with onions than with garlic.

The more colorful and stronger an onion, the more beneficial. Yellow ones are rich in quercetin and other flavonoids. A particularly potent yellow variety developed at Cornell University in Ithaca, New York, has excelled in studies evaluating anti-cancer benefits. Red onions get their color from anthocyanins, which are potent antioxidants.

Raw onions provide the most benefits, so enjoy them finely chopped in salads, salsa, and to garnish soups. In cooking, being heavy handed with onions helps compensate for what heat destroys; in chili, soups, and other dishes, I often increase the amount recipes call for by 50 percent. Also grill sliced onions in a dry skillet until lightly charred in spots and crunchy-tender.

How onions are cooked affects their taste and texture. Using higher heat produces firmer, browned onions with a bitter edge, while gentle heat caramelizes their sugar more slowly, turning them melting and sweet.

Why They're Best • Onions contain fructooligosaccharides, prebiotic forms of sugar which nurture the good bacteria in your gut that help to strengthen your immune system • Quercetin, and other flavonoids, help protect against cancer and reduce the inflammation associated with asthma • Animal studies showed increased bone mineral content, suggesting possible protection against osteoporosis • Sulfur compounds protect us against heart disease by reducing blood pressure and bad LDL cholesterol levels, raising good HDL cholesterol, and thinning the blood.

What to Look For • See "Onion Primer" on page 107.

How to Store • See "Onion Primer" on page 107.

How to Enjoy • Grill slices in a dry skillet or on a grill; roast or sauté • Serve raw in salads and sandwiches, and sprinkled on other vegetables • Use cooked onions in soups, stews, casseroles, chili, sautéed main dishes, side dishes, pasta, and pizza; serve as a side dish accompanying roasts, chops, and pot roast.

Good to Know • A pinch of salt added when sautéing brings out juices and helps speed cooking • Cooking onions slowly (sweating), covered and over low heat, enriches the flavor of soups and sauces.

Spinach

Eating spinach does more than help make Popeye's strong muscles. It also contributes to good cardiovascular health, youthful eyes, and strong bones.

Wildly versatile, spinach is good raw or cooked, in dishes from hors d'oeuvres and soups to salads and sides, seasoned simply with olive oil and garlic, or seasoned in many ethnic or elegant ways. Fresh baby leaves and frozen chopped spinach are easiest to use. You can even juice and drink your spinach.

Why It's Best • Folate protects against birth defects and reduces the risk of heart disease • Carotenoids protect against age-related macular degeneration and cataracts • Chlorophyll helps inhibit cancer • Vitamin K is important for strong bones.

What to Look For • Whether buying dark, thick-leaved curly or Savoy spinach with thick stems, paler green flat-leaf spinach with slender stems, or tender baby spinach, select evenly green, fleshy, perky leaves and crisp stems. Avoid limp or yellowed leaves, slimy spots, and browned stem tips.

How to Store • In the original package or in a loose plastic bag in the vegetable bin for up to 3 days.

How to Enjoy • Serve spinach raw in salads and sandwiches and mixed into meat loaf • Enjoy raw or cooked spinach in dips, soups, pasta, rice, and casseroles; on pizza; with eggs; in baked potato • Use thawed frozen chopped spinach in cooked dishes, first squeezing out as much moisture as possible and then fluffing it with your fingers.

Good to Know • One 10-ounce bag of spinach yields 1½ cups cooked; 1 bunch (about 12 ounces) yields 1½ to 1¾ cups cooked • Prewashed baby spinach saves time and eliminates stems • Commercially grown spinach is heavily sprayed so the Environmental Working Group recommends using organic to avoid possible residues • Fresh citrus juice makes the iron in spinach easier for your body to use • Pressing cooked or thawed frozen spinach in a potato ricer makes removing their moisture easier.

Sweet Bell Peppers

All bell peppers start off stiff, immature, and green, with a bitter flavor. Time allows them to ripen into a rainbow of red, orange, yellow, and more, with sweet flavor and increased health benefits. The benefits in bell peppers vary by their hue. So, while green bells are a good source of vitamin C, ripe red ones contain twice as much, and up to nine times the amount of vitamin A. Depending on their color, mature bells are also loaded with a variety of antioxidant carotenoids.

Why They're Best • Carotenoids help protect against cancer, heart disease, and stroke • Potassium helps maintain healthy blood pressure • Antioxidants, including vitamin C, help neutralize the formation of free radicals that damage DNA and cause inflammation.

What to Look For • Bright intense color, shiny skin, firm flesh, a firm green stem, and heavy weight relative to size. Avoid overly hard flesh (which indicates immaturity), soft spots, wrinkled, flabby, or dull-looking peppers, and brown or moldy stems.

How to Store • In the vegetable bin of the refrigerator for up to 5 days

How to Enjoy • Serve peppers raw with dips, in salads, and on sandwiches • Sauté with eggs, poultry, meat, and vegetables • Include roasted peppers in main and side dishes, pastas, sandwiches, and bruschetta • Season with olive or sesame oil, citrus juice, or ginger.

Good to Know • Thick-walled orange and red hothouse peppers taste the sweetest. Domestic field-grown, thinner-walled red bells have some of the bitterness found in green peppers • The white veins inside peppers are rich in flavonoids.

Sweet Potatoes

Great-tasting and easy to cook, sweet potatoes deserve a place on your table not just between the first frost and the last snowmelt, but all year long because they are loaded with antioxidants and are a good source of fiber. (A cousin to the morning glory, they are botanically unrelated to other potatoes, which are nightshades.)

Sweets have a moderate glycemic index of around 50, versus about 90 for other potatoes.

They range in color from ivory white to deep red-orange. The orange, moist-fleshed varieties, sometimes called yams, are richest in nutrition.

Why They're Best • Beta-carotene helps reduce oxidation of LDL cholesterol and its build-up in arteries • Fiber helps stabilize blood sugar and reduce insulin resistance • Antioxidant phenols, chlorogenic and caffeic acids, help protect the brain from free radicals.

What to Look For • Smooth, unblemished skin and weight that is heavy relative to size. Avoid shriveled or broken ends, brown or sunken spots, cracks, and woody striations on the skin.

How to Store • In a cool, dark place with some humidity for up to 5 days. Do not refrigerate.

How to Enjoy • Whole, sliced, diced, or shredded, then baked, braised, stir-fried, or steamed • Include in soups, dips, casseroles, and salads; pancakes and waffles; cookies, pies, and cakes • Serve with pork, turkey, black beans, broccoli, apples, or pears.

Good to Know • Baking sweet potatoes caramelizes their sugars and cooling them slightly before serving makes them taste sweeter • After harvesting, commercial growers cure sweet potatoes in a hot, humid room or in the sun for 3 to 5 days. This process protects the potato by thickening its skin and also brings out its buttery, sweet flavor.

Tomatoes

For the best taste, fresh tomatoes should be locally grown and enjoyed in season. Along with their great taste comes useful substances, particularly lycopene, which we must eat daily to maintain their benefits. All tomatoes provide lycopene, but fortunately for most of the year when appealing fresh tomatoes are not available, the lycopene in cooked tomatoes is even easier for the body to absorb.

Any form of processed tomatoes—a generous blop of ketchup, a well-sauced pizza slice, or a glass of tomato juice—can provide lycopene's benefits. Pizza, lasagna, and chili are also ideal because the fat in olive oil or cheese helps our bodies absorb lycopene.

Lycopene gives tomatoes their rich red color, combats cancer, helps keep blood platelets from aggregating, protects against cardiovascular disease, guards your eyesight, and offers all the other benefits gained from neutralizing free radicals. A result can be staying vigorous into old age.

Why They're Best • Lycopene protects against prostate, breast, lung, and other cancers • Vitamin C and other antioxidants protect against heart disease • Carotenoids protect eyes against age-related macular degeneration and also provide very mild sun protection, equal to about an SPF of 3.

What to Look For • Firm feel, with at least some red blush but preferably a deep, even color. Avoid soft spots and bruises.

How to Store • ALWAYS at room temperature in a shady place, stem end up to avoid bruising delicate shoulders.

How to Enjoy • Let less-than-ripe tomatoes sit until deep red to improve both their flavor and nutritional content • Season so-so tomatoes with salt and let sit 20 minutes • Serve sliced tomatoes with a sliced orange or mango as a salad • Serve grape and cherry tomatoes as appetizer dippers • Enjoy cooked tomatoes with kale, collards, or brown rice.

Good to Know • Only red tomatoes contain lycopene • Most phytonutrients are in the skin, so eating small tomatoes provides more per serving • Out of season, plum and grape tomatoes taste best • Organic brands of processed tomatoes may contain less sodium • So-called *vine-ripened* supermarket tomatoes may simply be picked under-ripe, then gassed with ethylene before shipping. Buy local or organic tomatoes to avoid gassed tomatoes.

Winter Squash

Along with beans and corn, winter squash is one of the trio of foods, called *The Three Sisters*, that provided a nutritionally complete diet for Native Americans. Varieties like buttercup and delicata that turn sugar-sweet when cooked are golden comfort food.

Why It's Best • Alpha-lipoic acid, a "superantioxidant," protects against stroke and cataracts • Thiamine helps maintain the nervous system • Alpha-carotene is even more effective at stopping cancer cells than beta-carotene.

What to Look For • Dull skin, firm, and with a stem and a hollow sound when tapped. Avoid blemishes, cuts, and bruises.

How to Store • In a dry, dark, cool place for up to 1 month.

How to Enjoy • Dice, cut into rings, or stuff. Bake, steam, or stir-fry • Mash or puree, glaze, or use in soups and stews • Bake into pie, cookies, and muffins • Season with rosemary, thyme, ginger, cinnamon, citrus, curry, sherry, or cheese.

Good to Know • Frozen pureed butternut squash can be excellent by itself or with a pat of butter and dash of nutmeg • Mashed butternut squash can replace pumpkin in recipes and, in fact, is often what you get when buying canned pumpkin.

FRUITS • **Apples** • **Blackberries** • **Blueberries** • **Citrus** • **Cranberries** • **Kiwifruit** • **Mango** • **Raisins** • **Raspberries** • **Sour Cherries** • **Strawberries** • **Watermelon**

Many of the same pigments that give fruits their vibrant golden, orange, deep red, intense blue, and purple hues also provide a rich harvest of phytochemicals, especially antioxidant polyphenols, phenolic acids, and carotenoids. Fruits are also a major source of vitamin C, folate, and other water-soluble vitamins, as well as an important source of mostly soluble fiber that helps lower cholesterol.

While fruits have many elements in common, each also includes unique phytochemicals—like mangifluene in mangos, tangeritin in tangerines, and naringenin in grapefruit—that scientists are finding contribute to the synergy that is the basis for optimal health benefits.

Eating fruit raw is ideal because heat destroys valuable enzymes and some vitamins.

Since most fruit is portable, consuming the 1½ to 2 cups a day recommended in the USDA's dietary guidelines is easy.

Apples
Apples are the most concentrated food source of flavonoids, a major group of antioxidant polyphenols.

Today, good apples are available year-round as supermarkets import them from Chile, New Zealand, and other countries where the seasons are the reverse of those in the Northern Hemisphere. Still, most of the best tasting apples are locally grown and picked ripe during a season that may extend from August through December. Also, apples grown commercially above the equator are often picked before they are fully ripe and then stored in a controlled atmosphere. Studies indicate this storage does not affect their phytochemical content.

Why They're Best • The combination of phenolic acids and soluble fiber in apples appears to maximize their ability to lower blood cholesterol and LDL lipids • Quercetin helps decrease the risk of cancer and the inflammation associated with asthma • Insoluble fiber helps control weight and promotes regularity.

What to Look For • Firm fruit that is heavy for its size with shiny skin and bright color. Avoid soft fruit, bruised spots or holes, and a fermented aroma.

How to Store • At room temperature for 1 to 2 days, in a perforated plastic bag in the vegetable bin of refrigerator for 1 week. (Flavor diminishes with longer storage.) Keep away from lettuce, collards, and kale to avoid brown spots or yellowing.

How to Enjoy • Slice, shred, or chop apples and use in salads, salsa, and pancakes • Cook in sautés, soups and stews, apple sauce, pies and other baked goods, chutney and other condiments • Make applesauce.

Good to Know • Apple peel contains far more phytochemicals than the flesh • Fuji and Red Delicious are highest in phytonutrients • If you are concerned about possible pesticide residue and gas processing, choose organic apples.

Blackberries

You can pick wild blackberries from rambling thickets growing along rural byways around much of the United States. In May, just look for billows of pink-white blossoms covering dense, thorny bushes and make a note to return in late July, making sure to avoid big roads where exhaust fumes concentrate.

This fiber-rich berry tops some rankings for antioxidants in fresh produce. When fully ripe, its complex taste is sweet with a slightly bitter finish. Once exclusively a fragile and uncultivated summer treat, durable blackberries are now grown commercially in California, Mexico, and Chile, making the fresh fruit available in supermarkets most of the year. They include new strains producing more succulent fruit.

In addition, loose-packed frozen blackberries grown mainly in Oregon are available year round.

Why They're Best • 1 cup provides 50 percent of the RDA for vitamin C and 30 percent of fiber • Anthocyanins, catechins, and ellagic acid all protect against cancer • Insoluble fiber in blackberry seeds protects against colon cancer and promotes regularity.

What to Look For • Slightly dull looking, firm fruit that gives slightly when pressed. Avoid shiny, hard berries, reddish color, and crushed, bruised, or moldy fruit.

How to Store • In one layer on a plate loosely covered with a plastic bag in the refrigerator for up to 2 days.

How to Enjoy • Cook fresh or frozen blackberries in desserts and savory or dessert sauces • Enjoy fresh in fruit salad and soups, on spinach salad, as a snack, and use to make jam.

Good to Know • Dark red loganberry and Marionberry are blackberry–red raspberry hybrids now sold commercially • Most frozen and processed blackberries are Marionberries. Olallieberry and dewberry are varieties found on the West Coast • Choose organic if you are concerned about possible chemical residues, particularly for blackberries grown outside the United States.

Blueberries

Big or little, cultivated or wild, fresh, frozen, or dried, blueberries are crammed with so much goodness that it is hard to believe it all fits in. They rank highest in antioxidant levels of all fresh fruits, and studies indicate blueberries could be called brain food because of their antioxidant benefits. They are also the hardiest berry, requiring less pesticides during cultivation than other types.

Why They're Best • Resveratrol and other phytochemicals give blueberries the highest antioxidant power of any fresh fruit • Animal studies indicate benefits for short- and long-term memory • Polyphenols, including chlorogenic acid, help protect against cancer.

What to Look For • Fresh: Firm blueberries with a powdery "bloom." Buy fresh berries from a refrigerated case, if possible, as their antioxidants are highly heat sensitive. Avoid those with a reddish color, shriveled, moldy, or crushed fruit, or juice stains on the box • Frozen: Look for packages where the berries move loosely. Avoid frozen packages that are solid or contain chunks.

How to Store • Spread fresh berries in a single layer on a plate, cover loosely with a plastic bag, and refrigerate for up to 2 days. Or freeze on a baking sheet, transfer to a resealable plastic bag, and keep for up to 3 months.

How to Enjoy • Serve raw blueberries with cereal, in pancakes, and mixed with yogurt • Use fresh or frozen fruit in baked goods. Puree frozen berries to make sorbet • Add dried to trail mix and granola • Dip fresh blueberries in melted chocolate.

Good to Know • Size does not affect the sweetness of cultivated blueberries • Look for dried blueberries sweetened with fruit juice, not corn syrup • Whole and dried blueberries have more benefits and are lower on the glycemic index than blueberry juice.

Citrus

An orange contains 170 phytochemicals, including 60 flavonols, so its benefits are myriad. Other citrus fruits offer many of these same substances, plus ones that are unique to each variety. Eat an assortment of citrus fruits, including sweet and bitter oranges, lemons, limes, kumquats, mandarins, yellow and red grapefruit, and various citrus permutations like the Mineola and you will help your heart and entire cardiovascular system, your brain, eyes, gut, and most of the rest of you.

Eating the fruit is more beneficial than drinking even freshly squeezed citrus juice because you get their fiber along with some of the flavonoid-rich white pith. Citrus zest, the colorful outer skin, is so good for you that it counts as a separate Essential Best Food (page 59).

Why It's Best • Antioxidants, including glutathione, lower cholesterol and discourage clotting to reduce the risk of stroke, heart attack, and atherosclerosis • Vitamin C boosts the immune system and, together with hesperetin, has enhanced antiviral activity • Limonene and other polyphenols in citrus help fight the formation of cancer • Potassium helps to stabilize blood pressure.

What to Look For • Fruit heavy for its size with shiny skin that yields with gentle pressure. Avoid spongy or relatively lightweight fruit, dull skin, thick skin on lemons and most oranges, brown spots on limes, and oranges that look dyed.

How to Store • On a plate at room temperature in a single layer for best flavor • Citrus fruits rot when crowded together • Loose in the vegetable bin of the refrigerator for up to 2 weeks. Always refrigerate limes.

How to Enjoy • Serve "smiles," a whole juice orange cut into quarters • Squeeze your own juice to get the best flavor and most benefits, including the oils in the zest (see page 122) • Include in salad dressings, sauces, marinades, and baked goods • Add to tea and other cold drinks; combine with club soda for a fizzy refresher.

Good to Know • Roll citrus fruit on the counter before squeezing to extract the most juice • When buying juice, select the kind with pulp • Mail-order companies offer premium quality fruit and unique varieties of citrus with limited availability.

Cranberries

Mainly associated with holiday meals and juice drinks, finally cranberries are getting the attention they deserve as an important choice all year long. Famously good for preventing urinary tract infections, cranberries also provide a long list of other benefits, thanks mainly to their high antioxidant content.

Including cranberries in meals is easy because they are surprisingly flexible. Use them fresh, frozen, dried, or as juice, in sweet and savory dishes, from morning to night.

Why They're Best • Cranberries are rich in anti-inflammatory antioxidants • Antibacterial properties help prevent urinary tract infections and also the buildup of dental plaque. They can discourage *H. pylori* bacteria that cause stomach ulcers • They protect against heart disease by helping to thin the blood.

What to Look For • Shiny, firm, plump berries with an intense red to black-red color. Avoid pale, translucent, soft, or dented berries.

How to Store • Store fresh berries in the vegetable bin of the refrigerator for 2 weeks or more, or freeze in their bag for 3 months or more.

How to Enjoy • Grind fresh or frozen cranberries with an orange for the classic relish • Cook in soups, stews, and sauces, and with Brussels sprouts or red cabbage • Bake in pies, crumbles, and other baked goods • Enjoy dried cranberries as a snack, in salads, on cereal, in trail mix and granola, and in baked goods • Add juice to soups, drinks, and desserts.

Good to Know • Natural food stores sell frozen cranberries all year • Make sure dried cranberries are juice-sweetened, not coated with corn syrup • Heat brings out bitterness so cook only until the berries pop.

Kiwifruit

The contrast between a kiwi's drab fuzzy brown exterior and its sparkling, juicy green flesh is as striking as the decorative ring of tiny seeds and radiating lines inside. Its tart, distinctive flavor becomes sweeter and gains tropical nuances when the fruit is fully ripe. Golden varieties also have a hint of ginger and higher nutritional content than green-fleshed kiwis.

Why It's Best • One kiwi contains more vitamin C than an orange • Antioxidants help reduce LDL cholesterol, triglyceride levels, and blood pressure • Kiwis reduce the risk for cataracts and age-related macular degeneration.

What to Look For • A greenish or golden tinge and fruit that yields slightly to pressure. Cut fruit should have translucent flesh. Avoid rock hard, dark brown fruit, soft or mushy spots, and shriveled ends. In cut fruit, avoid cloudy flesh.

How to Store • On the counter until fully ripe (the fruit yields slightly when squeezed).

How to Enjoy • Add kiwi to fruit salads, puree in sauce for fish, including halibut and grouper.

Good to Know • Prepare kiwis just before eating to avoid loss of vitamin C • To peel kiwi, slice off the top and bottom. Holding the fruit, use a serrated swivel-blade vegetable peeler to remove the skin. Or stand on one end on work surface and slice away skin like peeling an orange • Use an egg slicer to cut even rounds • Watch for red-fleshed kiwis, which are in commercial development.

Mango

Eat a tree-ripened mango in the tropics and this lush fruit overwhelms you with fragrance and bathes you in creamy, sweet flesh, creating an almost out-of-body ecstasy. A few commercially grown varieties, particularly Alphonso and Ataulfo or champagne mangoes, can sometimes equal this experience.

Why It's Best • Mango is rich in carotene that is good for the eyes • Beta-cryptoxanthin, a carotenoid, is important for heart health • Fiber helps protect against heart disease, cancer, and type 2 diabetes.

What to Look For • Yields to gentle pressure; black spots may indicate sweetness. Avoid squishy fruit or shriveled skin.

How to Store • On the counter until fully ripe. Do not refrigerate.

How to Enjoy • Let a mango sit at room temperature until fully ripe, then eat it over the sink • Add diced mango to fruit salads; puree it in smoothies, sorbet, and for a sauce for halibut, grouper, and other seafood • Use unripe mangoes in salads and chutney.

Good to Know • Color may not indicate ripeness because some varieties remain green when ripe • To avoid chemicals used on some imported mangoes, choose organic.

Raisins

Grapes are great and turning them into raisins makes them even better. Drying, either in the sun or using warm air, concentrates their vitamins, minerals, and antioxidants, including resveratrol, creating one of nature's most nutrition-packed portable, and deliciously versatile foods.

Raisins contain inulin, a fiber-like prebiotic that supports good bacteria in the gut. They also contain substances that help reduce the bacteria in your mouth that cause plaque and tooth decay, making them a sweet that is actually good for your teeth—and possible more since poor dental health contributes to overall, systemic inflammation that is a factor in heart disease, diabetes, and other chronic diseases.

Most raisins, dark and light, are sun-dried green Thompson grapes. Golden raisins, though, are air-dried indoors and treated with sulfur dioxide, to which some people are allergic. Flame and Monuka raisins are made from red and black grapes, respectively, so they may contain the same phytochemicals found in dark-skinned grapes. Currants are made by sun-drying tiny red champagne grapes.

Why They're Best • Antioxidants and other phytochemicals reduce LDL cholesterol and prevent the formation of arterial plaque • Inulin promotes good intestinal flora and encourages lower cholesterol • Antibacterial oleanolic acid helps protects teeth and gums.

What to Look For • Raisins that are plump and soft • Avoid those that are hard or musty.

How to Store • In an airtight container in a cool, dry place away from light.

How to Enjoy • Snack on raisins out of hand and add to trail mix, cereal, and yogurt • Add to stews, chili, salad, and grain dishes • Cook in baked goods, fruit compotes, and chutneys • Use raisins on the stem found in specialty stores around holiday time, to decorate fruit bowls and cheese plates.

Good to Know • Buying organic raisins lets you avoid possible chemical residues • Because raisins are high in sugar and calories, measure out a portion and stick with it.

Raspberries

One of the most delicate of foods, this tender fruit packs an iron punch because each fragile berry is packed with 50 percent more cancer-preventing ellagic acid than a strawberry, and twice the fiber, too.

Luscious red raspberries balance sweetness and acidity nicely. Golden ones are sweeter. Black raspberries, which you may find at farmers' markets or growing wild, are less juicy and have crunchier seeds. Their colors also signal some differences in phytochemical content from red raspberries. In clinical studies, freeze-dried black raspberries have demonstrated significant anti-cancer powers.

Fresh raspberries, including those commercially grown, are costly because they are always hand-picked. Frozen berries, which are mechanically harvested, make a good alternative to puree for sauces, drinks, or other dishes.

Why They're Best • Ellagic acid, by preventing carcinogens from binding to DNA, helps inhibit cancer • Anthocyanins can inhibit COX compounds associated with inflammation • Flavonoids, including quercetin, reduce oxidation of LDL cholesterol.

What to Look For • Fresh: Select plump, rounded, velvety-looking berries. Avoid soft, moldy, or mushy fruit and containers with stains • Frozen: Look for berries that move loosely in the package. Avoid packages that are solid or contain chunks.

How to Store • On a plate in one layer, covered with a paper towel, in a loose plastic bag in the refrigerator. Fresh berries keep 2 to 3 days but are best when used within 24 hours. Rinse just before using, under gentle spray. Or freeze fresh berries in one layer on a baking sheet, then store in resealable plastic bags in the freezer.

How to Enjoy • Serve fresh or frozen raspberries in fruit salad and desserts, and at breakfast • Puree and strain frozen berries for an instant dessert sauce • Macerate in vinegar.

Good to Know • The Environmental Working Group names raspberries as consistently contaminated with pesticides, so consider buying organic.

Sour Cherries

Why are sour cherries, sometimes called *pie cherries*, an Essential Best Food? While dark sweet cherries also offer good amounts of vitamins A, C, various carotenoids, and some omega-3 fatty acids, measure for measure, thin-skinned Montmorency and Morello sour cherries give you 26 times more vitamin A and beta-carotene, double the vitamin C, and more than double the omega-3s than sweet cherries. In addition, they are being studied for anti-inflammation benefits that act like the COX-2 inhibitors in medications which help people with rheumatoid arthritis.

Fresh tart cherries are extremely delicate and appear for just a few weeks in farmers' markets, mainly in New York, Michigan, and other areas where they grow in abundance. Fortunately, dried and canned fruit and sour cherry juice are always widely available. Most cherry jam is also made from these tart-sweet cherries.

Why They're Best • Antioxidants provide cardiovascular protection by reducing oxidation of LDL cholesterol • Perillyl alcohol is a powerful cancer fighter • Demonstrate anti-inflammatory activity like the COX-2 inhibitors in painkillers in laboratory tests and in anecdotal testimony from consumers.

What to Look For • Fresh: Select firm, shiny and glowing cherries with green stems. Avoid dull-looking, soft fruit and soft brown or moldy spots • Dried and canned: Look for dried fruit sweetened with fruit juice and canned cherries with minimal sugar added. Avoid corn syrup–sweetened dried cherries treated with sulfites.

How to Store • Fresh sour cherries keep on a plate in one layer, loosely covered with a plastic bag, for 2 days. Or pit and freeze in one layer, then store in a resealable plastic bag. Keep dried fruit in an airtight container in a dark, dry, cool place for 6 months.

How to Enjoy • Bake fresh or canned sour cherries in pies and cobbler; add to fruit salad; make into a sauce for pork and poultry • Enjoy dried cherries in granola, with cereals, as a snack, in biscotti and other baked goods, and on spinach salad • Add juice to iced tea and other drinks.

Good to Know • Unsweetened sour cherry juice provides valued health benefits • Pitted fruit imported in jars from Europe can be excellent and reasonably priced.

Strawberries

Each kind of berry provides a unique combination of health-enhancing phytochemicals. That is why so many of them are Essential Best choices. Strawberries in particular are effective against inflammation and, along with blueberries, for protecting the brain against the effects of aging. In animal studies, they especially supported short-term memory.

Botanically unrelated to other berries, strawberries belong to the rose family and are unique in bearing their seeds on the outside. An edible barometer, they taste sweetest when it is dry and sunny, watery after it rains. Outside of California and Florida, their season is about 4 weeks, essentially the month of June, except for day-neutral varieties that fruit all summer.

Commercially grown strawberries are bred for looks and durability, with great taste a distant third. Driscoll's, a widely distributed brand, is a notable exception. This company's proprietary varieties are naturally bred to have a rotund shape and meaty flesh plus a reliable and distinctive strawberry flavor.

Why They're Best • One cup of strawberries contains 140 percent of the RDA for vitamin C • Antioxidant anthocyanins in strawberries help protect against age-related decline in brain function • Anti-inflammatory phytochemicals lessen activity of COX enzymes that play a role in osteoarthritis, rheumatoid arthritis, and asthma • Soluble fiber helps lower cholesterol levels.

What to Look For • Fresh: Select firm, shiny, fragrant, evenly red berries with bright green, perky caps. Avoid berries with white or green tips, dull or limp caps, or mold. Inspect the bottom of the container for bruised or crushed fruit • Frozen: Look for fruit that moves loosely in the package. Avoid packages with lumps or contents in a solid block.

How to Store • Refrigerate on a plate in one layer, covered with paper towel and a loose plastic bag, for 1 day. Wash with caps on, just before using.

How to Enjoy • Drizzle fresh berries with balsamic vinegar and serve with bowls of sour cream and brown sugar for dunking • Slice or chop to enjoy with cereal, fruit salad, shortbread, ice cream and other desserts, pancakes, and yogurt and honey • Puree fresh or frozen strawberries for dessert sauce, or as a topping for pancakes, French toast, and waffles • Add dried strawberries to trail mix, granola, or yogurt • Use frozen berries in smoothies.

Good to Know • Fresh strawberries taste best when served at room temperature • Sliced strawberries sprinkled with sugar make their own syrup when set aside for 20 minutes • Dried strawberries are loaded with fiber • The Environmental Working Group cites strawberries as a food most likely to have chemical residues. To avoid this, you may prefer organic.

Watermelon

Cubed watermelon, now available most of the year, is convenient to eat at your desk and even at a picnic. But in hot weather, nothing beats the messy ritual of burying your face in an icy melon wedge. So-called personal or icebox melons, about the size of a large cantaloupe, let you do this while avoiding the pits found in older varieties.

Red watermelon is rich in lycopene, the same red pigment that colors tomatoes. The more recently popular and often sweeter yellow-fleshed melons lack lycopene but do include this juicy food's other benefits.

Why It's Best • Watermelon contains more cancer-fighting lycopene than tomatoes • Provides citrulline, an amino acid important for keeping your vascular system healthy • No fruit beats watermelon for keeping you hydrated.

What to Look For • Lustrous skin, a hollow sound when thumped, and a yellow "ground spot" on the bottom of the melon. Avoid white or pale green ground spots or dull-sounding melons • In cut melon, look for a fresh, sweet aroma and deep color without white streaks. Avoid cut melon with a fermented smell, or shiny or transparent-looking flesh.

How to Store • Maintain a melon at the same temperature as when bought, i.e., if chilled, keep refrigerated, if at room temperature, store on counter • Whole melons keep at room temperature for 2 to 3 weeks, cut melon in the refrigerator up to 1 week.

How to Enjoy • Spritz watermelon with lime juice and add a dash of cayenne pepper or sea salt for a zesty dessert • Include in fruit salad with other melons, or blueberries and mango • Alternate slices with tomato slices and sprinkle with crumbled feta cheese for salad • Puree and freeze into a granita.

Good to Know • Wash or wipe a whole melon before cutting to remove any bacteria on the rind. Afterward, wash work surfaces with hot, soapy water • Seedless varieties are hybrids, not genetically engineered • Eating watermelon with foods containing fat, such as feta cheese, improves the absorption of lycopene and lowers the glycemic load from the sugar in the melon.

WHOLE GRAINS • Buckwheat • Oats • Quinoa • Rice
• Whole Wheat

Eating whole grains reduces your risk of stroke, heart disease, and type 2 diabetes and helps keep your body trim. Yet many people resist eating more than a morning bowl of oatmeal. Whole wheat bread they eat only grudgingly, telling me they do not like its flavor and the extra chewing. But if you are truly intent on eating well, whole grains are worth exploring. I was lucky to grow up eating many kinds of whole grains and learned how to make their earthy flavor and texture good enough to savor every bite.

Fiber and protein were long considered the key reasons to eat whole grains. Now, we know they are rich in important phytochemicals, too. I chose buckwheat, oats, quinoa, rice, and whole wheat because they rate well, plus they are easy to cook, enjoyably light, and versatile. For storage information, see page 198.

Buckwheat

For me, buckwheat is soul food thanks to my mother's buckwheat griddle cakes. This distinctive grain is also used to make Japanese soba noodles, Italian pizzoccheri pasta, and Russian blini.

Buckwheat is an Essential Best choice because it is one of the few grains that is high in protein and also contains all the essential amino acids that make a complete protein. Research shows that this soluble fiber, like oats, it contains soluble fat that can help lower blood pressure and reduce cholesterol—plus buckwheat contains quercetin and other anti-inflammatory phytochemicals.

Why It's Best • Rutin, a flavonoid, helps lower cholesterol and LDL levels • In animal studies, eating buckwheat lowered blood sugar levels • Allows gluten-sensitive people to enjoy the benefits in whole grain.

How to Enjoy • Cook buckwheat with broth, milk or soymilk, cider, or fruit juice • Use like bulgur in tabbouleh and salads, in chili, to stuff peppers or onions, for poultry stuffing, in casseroles, and in place of rice in baked pudding • Serve as a hot breakfast cereal • Use buckwheat flour in pancakes, crepes, and blini • Sweeten gingerbread and spice cake with dark buckwheat honey.

Good to Know • In Russia and Eastern European countries, kasha means any grain cooked as porridge, while to Americans it specifically means toasted buckwheat • Simply boiled like rice, buckwheat makes a soupy mush. To avoid this, traditionally cooks stir in a beaten egg before the liquid is added, and stir until each grain has a dry coating. However, pan-toasting the groats has the same effect and is much easier.

Oats

The health benefits oats provide are simple—their fiber lowers cholesterol, antioxidants neutralize free radicals, and minerals help lower blood pressure.

Good-quality oats taste nutty and sweet, especially in porridge and baked goods. How you cook oatmeal for hot cereal affects its texture. Preparing it with milk, in a covered pot, produces the most soft and creamy porridge. Using water and cooking it uncovered makes it nicely chewy.

Why It's Best • Soluble fiber helps reduce cholesterol levels • Antioxidants unique to oats called *avenanthramides* prevent LDL cholesterol from oxidizing to aid in maintaining cardiovascular health • Complex carbohydrates in oats help stabilize blood sugar levels.

How to Enjoy • Cook oatmeal with cider or berry juice, plus raisins, dates, or shredded apple, and top with brown sugar, maple syrup, dried fruits, or preserved ginger • Add oats to meat loaf, soups, baked goods, pancakes, and waffles • Soak uncooked oats in milk then whirl into smoothies.

Good to Know • Toasting oats in a dry pan adds even more flavor • Steel-cut oats soaked overnight cook in 15 minutes • Quick-cooking oats have the flavor and fiber of thicker flakes, yet cook in 5 minutes • Instant oats contain only 1 gram of fiber per serving.

Quinoa

The light texture, mild flavor, and short cooking time of quinoa make it a perfect introduction to whole grains. Resembling a round sesame seed, quinoa (KEEN-wah) can be ivory beige, rusty red, deep purple, or black. It is an Essential Best choice because it provides complete protein, i.e., all eight essential amino acids, a rarity among grains.

Nature protects the seeds of this plant, which is related to Swiss chard and spinach, with a coating of saponin. Too much of this soapy substance leaves a bitter taste, so the grain is milled or washed to remove most of it. Still, always rinse quinoa well before cooking. Quinoa is unique in another way—its germ curls out as a little comma-like tail when the grain is cooked.

Why It's Best • High-quality protein helps the body build tissue and strength • Iron is essential for healthy blood • Contains as much fiber as oats.

How to Enjoy • For pilaf, cook quinoa with broth, juice, or water • Toast before cooking (as in the Popped Quinoa Pilaf recipe on page 196) • Season with cinnamon, cumin, turmeric, leeks, onions, or scallions • Combine with chopped vegetables or fruits and nuts for salad • Mix cooked quinoa into pancake and muffin batter.

Good to Know • Beige quinoa cooks in 15 to 20 minutes, red and black varieties in 20 to 25 • Quinoa flakes make an almost instant hot breakfast cereal • Quinoa flour boosts protein in baking and helps reduce gluten • Quinoa pasta is gluten-free.

Rice

Today, whole grain rice comes in colors beyond basic brown, including Bhutanese red, Thai purple, and black Forbidden Rice. And brown rice now comes in an appealing variety of flavors and textures including Lundberg Golden Rose Brown Rice. Although whole grain rices take longer to cook than white, these many varieties make it just as versatile.

Whole grain rices get their rich color from their outer coating, called *husk* or *bran*. For white rice, this coating is polished off, along with the germ, a process that also removes most of the grain's valuable vitamins, minerals, and phytochemicals, and all of its fiber. The resulting rice is digested as a simple carbohydrate, and acts like sugar on your metabolism. The fiber in whole grain rice slows down the absorption of complex carbohydrates so your blood glucose will not spike and drop. Because it is not a complete protein, in meatless dishes combine rice with beans, dairy, or other protein.

Why It's Best • Fiber helps control weight • Selenium helps reduce oxidative stress that damages blood vessels • Ferulic acid, an antioxidant, appears to inhibit formation of cancer-causing substances.

How to Enjoy • Serve whole grain rices the same ways as white rice, with one exception. Brown Arborio makes poor risotto because the hull prevents the release of the starches that give the dish its creamy consistency.

Good to Know • All rice is gluten-free, even kinds called *glutinous* • Most quick-cooking brown rice is bland and mushy, but Trader Joe's frozen organic brown rice is an excellent exception.

Whole Wheat

Until recently, whole wheat has been valued mainly for its fiber, which is mostly the insoluble kind that promotes regularity and a healthy gut. Now though, we also value it for phenols that help prevent cancer, and for having a higher antioxidant content than many other grains.

Buying whole wheat bread and baked goods, cereals, pasta, and pizza and baking with whole wheat flour at home are easy ways to get these benefits, as well as all the others associated with all whole grains. Today's artisanal whole wheat breads and good-quality whole wheat, tomato, and spelt pastas paired with the right sauces are, indeed, appealing.

Why It's Best • Insoluble fiber is good for your gut • Antioxidants help slow buildup of arterial plaque and reduce the risk of heart disease • Complex carbs help protect against type 2 diabetes by reducing insulin resistance.

How to Enjoy • Whole wheat pasta pairs well with mushrooms, dark greens, tomatoes, and other strong flavors • Whole wheat flour gives best results in recipes when combined with refined flour • Bulgur and farro provide ways to eat whole wheat in salads and pilaf.

Good to Know • For whole wheat bread, breakfast cereal, and pizza, read labels to be sure they contain a useful amount of whole wheat. Either whole wheat or whole wheat flour should appear as the first ingredient.

BEANS AND LEGUMES • Black Beans and Kidney Beans
• Lentils • Soy Beans

Legumes are a good choice because they provide cholesterol-free protein. Eating them produces a feeling of fullness and satisfaction that is helpful for weight control. Plus the prebiotic oligosaccharides in beans stimulate the growth of good bacteria in the intestinal tract. These natural sugars are, unfortunately, also what produce flatulence for some people. Often, though, this diminishes and disappears over time when you start with a small serving and eat beans regularly. If not, stick with lentils, which do not contain these sugars.

The USDA recommends eating five servings of legumes a week, but I suggest having them daily since they offer such varied ways to get fiber. As food costs escalate, legumes are also a good source of affordable protein. Even imported Italian lentils, which cost up to $8 a pound, are a good buy since a pound serves eight people. For storage information, see page 228.

Black Beans and Kidney Beans

Black beans and kidney beans are Essential Best Foods for four reasons. First, they rank high in phytochemicals thanks to their dark colors. Second, they rate well nutritionally, providing 8 grams of protein and 7 to 8 grams of fiber per serving. Third, beans are deliciously versatile. Finally, canned black and kidney beans have good texture and in many dishes produce better results than dried.

Why They're Best • Antioxidant lignans may help reduce the risk of heart disease • By lowering estrogen levels, lignans could also lower the risk of breast and other cancers • The resistant starch in beans helps manage blood sugar levels.

How to Enjoy • Include beans in salads, soups, stews (including chili), burritos, and nachos. Black beans are also good in salsa and mashed for refried beans and hummus. Kidney beans make a great dip • Add beans to leftover soups • Black beans are good in dishes with Hispanic, Asian, Caribbean, and Mediterranean flavors, from cumin and cilantro, to ginger and tropical fruits, to herbs like basil and thyme • Kidney beans go well with thyme and other Mediterranean herbs, chile peppers, Middle Eastern and Indian seasonings like cinnamon and curry powder, plus American chili powder.

Good to Know • Canned beans can contain more than 500 milligrams of sodium per half-cup serving. To avoid this, select organic or reduced-sodium brands • Rinsing removes most sodium from canned beans but also much of their flavor so I prefer simply draining brands that are lower in sodium, then using less salt to season • In canned beans, texture varies by brand in canned beans so try different ones. Brands of firmer beans good for soups and salads include Eden, Westbrae, Bush's, Goya, and S&W. Softer ones, like Progresso, Green Giant, and Whole Foods Markets 365 Organic brand, are better for dips and refried beans.

Lentils

Lentils, usually considered a food of the poor, are an essential meatless protein in India and Middle East, and have long been appreciated in Mediterranean countries, too. Recently, this humble legume has also attracted the spotlight in American cooking.

Lentils are an easy legume to eat often because they come in a multitude of sizes and colors, from greenish-beige and red to deep green and black, and every kind has a distinctive flavor. Some kinds do not need soaking and cook in as little as 15 minutes. Lacking the sulfur compounds found in beans, they do not cause flatulence.

I love lentil salads because they need little oil or other dressing and you can add lots of finely chopped vegetables and sautéed shallots, and perhaps pancetta, or canned tuna.

Why They're Best • One cup of lentils provides 17 grams protein and up to 16 grams fiber • By slowing absorption of sugars into the bloodstream, lentils help stabilize blood sugar and prevent type 2 diabetes.

How to Enjoy • Include lentils in soups, salads, and stews. Serve as a side dish for fish or seafood, poultry, pork, and game • Bake in lasagna or stir into rice • Mix with beef for meat loaf or use as a filling for stuffed zucchini and other vegetables.

Good to Know • Canned lentils are mushy and bland, but some canned lentil soups are good • For tasty basic lentils, cook with a carrot and celery rib, each cut in 4 pieces, a halved onion and a bay leaf, then discard before serving the lentils.

Soy

Benefits from eating soy have been significantly reevaluated since the 1990s, when it was proclaimed "the ultimate food." Subsequent research has since revealed that soy protein lowers cholesterol and LDL less than originally thought. Studies also could not pin down how reliably isoflavone, a mild plant form of estrogen, reduces the risk of breast cancer or other cancers. How well soy protects bones from osteoporosis has also eluded conclusive results. Finally, clinical studies on how reliably soy alleviates symptoms of menopause confirm relatively little effect.

Still, soy is an Essential Best Food because of the important benefits it provides. It's best to eat soy like an Asian, especially in meatless meals. This means consuming one or two servings most days, including 1 cup of soy milk or 1 container of soy yogurt, a snack of edamame (green soybeans), a handful of soy nuts, ½ cup of tofu in a stir-fry, or black soybeans in a stew.

Why It's Best • Provides the highest quality, complete and cholesterol-free protein • Soy protein helps reduce blood cholesterol and LDL in people with elevated levels, along with a healthy diet and lifestyle • Isoflavones may help protect against cancers and osteoporosis, although results are not conclusive.

How to Enjoy • Serve soy milk, yogurt, and tofu at breakfast (tofu scrambles nicely with eggs and fresh herbs) • Let soy dairy products replace conventional dairy to cut saturated fat and cholesterol from your diet • Blend tofu into dips and dressings, meatballs, puddings, and other desserts • Combine edamame with other vegetables in salads, soups, stews, grain dishes, and vegetable sides • Use soy milk or tofu in smoothies.

Good to Know • Organic soy products do not use genetically engineered soybeans • Soy products are not consistent in taste and texture from one brand to another. If you do not like one, another brand may please you • If you like tofu, Asian markets offer it in scores of forms, from custard-like *dofu* to serve warm, and dark brown, firm squares seasoned with five-spice and soy sauce, to puffy, golden balls of fried tofu • Fresh Asian soy milk tastes very beany and is not calcium-fortified.

FISH, POULTRY, EGGS, AND DAIRY

• Salmon • Turkey Breast • Eggs • Yogurt

Protein provides the essential building material for our bodies. It is found in every cell and makes up much of our structure, including organs, skin, hair, and enzymes that help cells function. While an optimal diet emphasizes vegetable protein, rich in phytochemicals and low in saturated fat, four of the Essential Best Foods are animal protein, and for good reason.

Salmon is the best food source of omega-3 fatty acids, which combat inflammation in the body, and it is in the form our bodies use most efficiently. Fortunately, it is also the fresh fish Americans consume most.

Turkey breast, another Essential Best choice, is even leaner than chicken. Turkey white meat has other virtues, too, enough that it has almost replaced chicken on my table.

Eggs, including those produced by pasteurized free-range hens and flocks fed a diet that increases their omega-3 content, are another Essential Best Food. With the cost of protein foods increasing, they offer good value as well as smart nutrition and easy eating.

Finally, yogurt represents dairy, a food group vital for its calcium content. It is clearly the Essential Best dairy food because of the health support its live bacteria provide. Plus, it is portable, convenient, and surprisingly versatile in the kitchen.

Salmon

Health experts spotlight salmon as the best source of heart-protecting omega-3 fatty acids, particularly DHA and EPA. In fact, the American Heart Association and other health experts recommend that we eat two or more servings of omega-3–rich fish a week—that means at least 8 ounces (opinions on serving size vary). Salmon ranks third, after shrimp and canned tuna, in per capita seafood consumption, according to statistics from the National Marine Fisheries Service for 2006.

Regarding wild vs. farmed salmon, ecological concerns are valid; but even earth-conscious health experts, declaring the health benefits so significant, urge eating farmed salmon if that gets it on your table. Additionally, PCB levels in farmed salmon are now equal to those in wild fish and mercury levels are lower.

If fresh wild salmon is a budget-buster and you shun farmed, canned and flash-frozen wild are fine choices. Canned skinless and boneless salmon can be used as neatly as canned tuna, although you lose the calcium from the bones. Flash-frozen fish, processed quickly after it is caught, can actually be fresher and have more nutritional integrity than fresh fish channeled through the distribution chain to supermarkets.

Why It's Best • Omega-3 fatty acids reduce the risk of heart disease and stroke • Omega-3s also help reduce symptoms of depression and hypertension • Studies show that omega-3s support the immune system.

What to Look For • Fresh: fillets and steaks with flesh intact • Frozen: preferably flash-frozen fillets or burgers. Avoid fillets and steaks with a fishy smell, torn or split flesh, or a dull look.

How to Store • Fresh salmon must be refrigerated. Ask for ice to pack with it if not heading straight home • Discard store wrapping and set the fish on a plate, cover with plastic wrap, and place in the coldest part of refrigerator for no more than 24 hours, or wrap tightly and freeze (if not previously frozen).

How to Enjoy • Rub salmon fillets with olive oil, dried thyme, oregano, and basil and bake at 350°F • Serve poached fish with light sauces like Dried Tomato–Mint Salsa (page 171) • Serve smoked salmon on whole grain black bread with a lemon slice and chopped dill • Garnish winter squash, sweet potato, or tomato soup with flaked hot-smoked salmon • Combine canned fish with white beans, red onion, and Fresh Herb Vinaigrette (page 141). See Here's the Catch (page 177) for wild salmon information.

Good to Know • Most canned salmon is wild Alaskan fish, but check the label as some companies use farmed Atlantic salmon • When in season, fresh wild salmon drops in price, especially when the catch is good • The USDA has no organic standards for seafood. Some European standards could allow for feeding antibiotics and parasiticides according to the Environmental Defense.

Turkey Breast

White turkey meat is actually leaner than chicken breast, with fewer calories per serving and less saturated fat. This is significant because health experts find saturated fat even more detrimental to heart health then dietary cholesterol.

Turkey breast is also more flavorful than chicken white meat. This makes all the forms it comes in—on the bone, boneless roast, in cutlets, tenders, and ground—delicious both on their own, and used in recipes. Firmer-textured than chicken breast, turkey is also more satisfying, although chicken, which is more refined, is the right choice for some dishes.

An American and Mexican native, turkey pairs well with many spices and other seasonings, making it good in many ethnic recipes.

Why It's Best • Skinless turkey breast has fewer calories than skinless chicken breast and has almost no saturated fat • Zinc is essential for a healthy immune system and helps promote normal cell division • The body uses tryptophan, an amino acid abundant in turkey, to make serotonin, a mood-boosting neurotransmitter.

What to Look For • All fresh turkey, including ground, should have a clean pink or pink-white color. Avoid packages with an off smell. Fresh breast, whole or sliced, should be plump and firm. Skin should be evenly colored without spots. Select turkey with a "Sell By" date as far as possible from date of purchase.

How to Store • Store fresh breast or ground turkey in the original package, or wrap in plastic and set in the coldest part of the refrigerator for 1 to 2 days.

How to Enjoy • Sauté turkey cutlets with white wine and capers for an "instant" gourmet dinner • Add diced roasted or smoked breast to salads, soups, and curries • Cube raw breast and use to make stews, tagines, and curries • The fat in ground turkey that is 93 percent lean makes burgers and meat loaf juicier and more enjoyable than cardboard-dry 99 percent lean • Enjoy turkey cold cuts and uncured meats including bologna, bacon, and hot dogs made without nitrites, and preservative-free fresh turkey sausage.

Good to Know • Fresh turkey is always better than frozen • Turkeys are raised without hormones and do not need antibiotics because they are hardier than chickens. Most companies feed turkeys a vegetarian diet • Fully cooked turkey may still look pink but breast meat should register 160° to 165°F on an instant-read thermometer. Pop-up thermometers are unreliable, so remove them • Slicing fresh turkey breast into cutlets and freezing them in individual portions that thaw quickly is more economical than buying packages of cutlets • For the holiday bird, or a whole turkey breast any time, Bell & Evans is best in the eastern United States and Diestel in the West.

Eggs

Eggs have been called the perfect food and a protein source even better than milk or beef because they contain complete protein plus choline, carotenoids, omega-3s, and other important nutrients. Yet we hear conflicting viewpoints about the health benefits.

While the FDA prohibits heart-health claims in whole eggs because of the cholesterol in egg yolks, medical experts know that cholesterol is essential to key body functions, and that dietary cholesterol affects blood levels far less than other factors, including exercise. Some authorities also assert that fighting inflammation in the body is more important for health than lowering cholesterol. Bottom line: Ask what your doctor advises.

Conventional eggs contain 37 milligrams of these omega-3s according to the USDA, which recommends consuming 1,700 milligrams of omega-3s per day. Hens fed a diet rich in flax or algae produce eggs with 200 to 660 milligrams of omega-3s. One of these eggs provides one-tenth to one-third of the USDA's recommended amount. But please read further to better understand how the omega-3s in eggs can benefit you.

Why They're Best • Omega-3 fatty acids promote brain health, reduce the risk of Alzheimer's disease, and promote heart health • Choline helps protect the liver from toxins and is needed for forming essential neurotransmitters • Riboflavin helps reduce homocysteine levels, protecting against heart disease.

What to Look For • Eggs that are refrigerated and have clean, intact shells. Avoid eggs kept at room temperature. Always check shells for cracks.

How to Store • In the carton, pointed end down, in the bottom of the refrigerator where the temperature is coldest, for 4 to 5 weeks from stamped date.

How to Enjoy • Before scrambling, beat in dried herbs, chopped fresh herbs, a teaspoon of tomato paste, or a big pinch of turmeric • Include chopped leftover cooked broccoli, spinach, onions, or a roasted pepper in scrambled eggs • Cook a beaten egg as a pancake, then fill with ratatouille, chili, or 2 tablespoons of fruit jam and fold into an omelet • Cut an egg pancake into thin strips and use to garnish a salad or bowl of soup • Serve a poached egg on top of beans or lentils.

Good to Know • Brown or white shell color depends on the breed of hen and does not affect nutrition or taste • *Vegetarian* means no animal by-products were fed to the hens • *Cage-free* does not guarantee birds have access to the out-of-doors • *Organic* means organically fed, reducing the likelihood of pesticide, antibiotic, or other residues in eggs • The vitamin E in egg yolk helps protect fatty acids from the effects of heat, so cook omega-3 eggs any way you like • When a fresh egg is hard-cooked it is hard to peel, so use older eggs.

Yogurt

Yogurt was originally a tart-tasting health food, eaten only by health food faddists. Then, to make it more palatable and popular, manufacturers added sugar, jam, thickeners, and all kinds of flavors, turning yogurt into a pudding-like comfort food. Today, happily, serious yogurt is back and alive with health-promoting bacteria.

Yogurt is made by culturing milk with benevolent bacteria, sometimes called *probiotics*, that produce enzymes that thicken the milk and convert its natural sugar to lactic acid. The USDA requires that yogurt contain *Lactobacillus bulgaricus* and *Streptoococcus thermophilus.* It may also contain *L. acidophilus, L casei, bifidus,* or *L. reuteri.* All these live bacteria are beneficial for colonizing your gut to encourage the growth of still more good bacteria and suppress the bad kinds. These good bacteria can improve resistance to colds and other illness, encourage regularity, and reduce the risk of more serious problems, possibly even cancer and the effects of asthma and other inflammation-linked diseases. Since antibiotics wipe out good bacteria along with the bad, many experts recommend eating yogurt when you take them.

Why It's Best • Yogurt provides and supports intestinal flora that strengthen the immune system • Probiotics in yogurt help protect your body against cancer-causing mutations • Beneficial bacteria can suppress the *H. pylori* bacteria that cause ulcers and cancer.

What to Look For • Yogurt should have at least 100 million live active cultures per gram at time of manufacture as certified by the National Yogurt Association's seal.

How to Store • In the original container in the refrigerator up to the "Use By" date in order to get full bacterial benefits.

How to Enjoy • Serve yogurt at breakfast, as a snack, and for dessert • Use plain yogurt, regular or Greek-style, in dips, soups, salad dressings, sauces (savory and sweet), pancakes, baked goods, and cereal • Blend flavored yogurt with cereal, mix it with fruit, and use it in smoothies • If using yogurt in a hot dish, always stir it in at the end to avoid curdling.

Good to Know • Yogurt provides more calcium per serving than milk: 40 percent of daily adult need versus 30 percent for milk • Soy yogurt with live cultures and calcium fortification provides the same health benefits, including calcium, as cow's milk • Flavored yogurts can contain 28 grams of sugar or more, so check the label • Greek yogurt is strained to make it thicker and may contain cream or extra milk solids.

NUTS, SEEDS, AND OLIVE OIL • Almonds

• Peanuts • Walnuts • Pumpkin Seeds • Sesame Seeds • Sunflower Seeds • Extra-Virgin Olive Oil

Health experts recommend eating nuts and seeds because they are crammed with phyto-chemicals, protein, and minerals. Some also provide as much fiber in a serving as a bowl of oatmeal. As the FDA explains, eating $1\frac{1}{2}$ ounces of nuts a day as part of a diet low in saturated fat and cholesterol helps reduce the risk of heart disease and lowers blood cholesterol.

Nuts and seeds offer a range of nutrients varied enough that eating many kinds is a good idea. If their calorie content concerns you, a number of clinical studies, including one based on the Mediterranean Diet and another featuring peanut butter, found subjects actually lost more weight and kept it off better when eating nuts and olive oil every day.

Apparently, the monounsaturated fat in nuts and seeds may increase the breakdown of fats in the body's cells. Plus, fat is satisfying, so you feel less inclined to overeat. The key lies in swapping the calories from nuts and seeds for those in other foods so you do not take in more total calories.

Seeds, in particular, contain unique phytochemicals that can lower cholesterol levels in the liver as well as the blood. Men should eat pumpkin seeds because they contain a substance that helps their prostate. Eating raw nuts and seeds is best because the heat of roasting reduces the benefits of their antioxidant content, although I sometimes dry toast nuts and seeds briefly to bring out flavor.

Olive oil is so valuable that I use it almost exclusively, choosing canola oil only when a more neutral taste is needed.

Almonds

Buttery tasting, almonds are the nut highest in monounsaturated fat and also in fiber. Compar-ing an almond to the kernel inside a peach, apricot, or cherry pit shows how closely they are all related. An almond tree, however, puts more of its effort into the kernel inside the pit rather than the flesh around it.

Why They're Best • An ounce of almonds provides 3 grams of fiber • Most of the fat is unsaturated, two-thirds of it monounsaturated, like olive oil • Phytosterols help reduce LDL cholesterol.

What to Look For • Almonds should smell sweet and fresh. Avoid shriveled or limp nuts, and those with a bitter or sharp smell.

How to Store • In a dry, cool, dark place if using promptly, or in a glass container in the refrigerator for 6 months or the freezer for 1 year.

How to Enjoy • Use chopped almonds to coat fish and chicken breast • Add whole almonds to stir-fries and grain dishes • Check out recipes for Sicilian pesto (with herbs and garlic), Spanish romesco, Greek skordalia, and other sauces • Use almonds—whole, sliced, slivered, or ground—in baked goods from biscotti, nut pie crusts, and nut tortes, to French-style macaroons • Try almond butter, like peanut butter, with fruit for a snack.

Good to Know • Spanish Marcona almonds, which are small, plump, and nearly triangular, have sumptuous flavor that is often enhanced by frying in olive oil • Bitter almonds, which contain cyanide, are used with restraint to flavor some amaretti cookies, almond liqueurs, and good-quality marzipan • Almond milk, which can be bought or made by grinding almonds with water then squeezing out the liquid, can replace dairy milk on cereal and in cooking.

Peanuts

You may know that peanuts are actually a legume, although we eat them like a nut. Widely used in savory dishes in Asia and Africa, peanuts became the all-American snack because of vendors hawking them at baseball games and on the street. Today, they are valued for their unsaturated fat and phytochemical content, including resveratrol, the same antioxidant found in red wine, grapes, and raisins.

Why They're Best • Peanuts contain resveratrol, the same heart-protective antioxidant found in red grapes and red wine • They contain the most protein of all nuts • Half the fat in peanuts is monounsaturated.

What to Look For • A hermetically sealed container is preferable. It reduces the possibility of mold or the risk of carcinogenic aflatoxin, which is produced by a fungus. Avoid nuts with evidence of moisture or insect damage, or with a musty or rancid odor.

How to Store • In a dry, cool, dark place in a brown paper bag if using promptly, or in a glass container in the refrigerator or freezer for 1 year. Do not store in a plastic bag, where moisture can result in the formation of mold.

How to Enjoy • Use peanuts or peanut butter in stir-fries, on noodles, in beef and chicken dishes, salads, and Indonesian Gado Gado • Add to desserts, trail mix, and cookies • Enjoy peanut butter off a spoon, drizzled with maple syrup, or spread on apple slices.

Good to Know • By law, peanut butter is 90 percent peanuts • Natural peanut butter is unsweetened and unhomogenized • Roasting peanuts increases their level of p-coumaric acid • In Africa, peanuts are called groundnuts.

Walnuts

Walnuts are an Essential Best Food because of their omega-3 content, which is the highest among all nuts. They are also the most versatile nut and have a unique, complex, sweet and bitter flavor.

When subjects in a study following the Mediterranean Diet substituted walnuts for olives and olive oil and other foods rich in cholesterol-free fat, they experienced even more improved cardiovascular risk factors and better arterial function.

Why They're Best • They are the only nut containing significant amounts of ellagic acid, a cancer-fighting antioxidant • Walnuts are one of the few plant sources of omega-3 fatty acids whose antiinflammatory activities help protect the heart and brain • Highest of all nuts in polyunsaturated fats, walnuts help reduce LDL cholesterol and increase HDL cholesterol.

What to Look For • Fresh-looking nuts with white meat, tight-fitting skin, and a sweet smell. Avoid nuts with yellow meat, cracked, flaking skin, or a bitter or sharp smell.

How to Store • In a dry, cool, dark place if using promptly, or in a glass container in the refrigerator for 6 months or the freezer for 1 year.

How to Enjoy • Combine walnuts with dried blueberries and goji berries to make super-GORP • Enjoy at breakfast with cereal and yogurt • Serve at lunch, in salads, or with cottage cheese on raisin bread for a sandwich • Chop and use to coat a goat cheese log for an easy hors d'oeuvre • Use in cookies, cakes, and nut pie crust.

Good to Know • Some cookbooks, especially from outside the United States, call for English walnuts. This is simply another name for the nut we know, which actually originated in Persia • Walnut oil is rich in omega-3s. Use it for dressings and as a finishing oil to give pasta and other dishes a luxuriously rich, nutty flavor.

Pumpkin Seeds

An important food for Native Americans and widely used in Mexican cooking, pumpkin seeds deserve attention for everyday eating because ¼ cup provides 8½ grams of protein (more than an egg), along with cholesterol-lowering plant sterols. Their pronounced flavor, with a bitter undertone, makes this challenging. Using them to top muffins and cookies or toasting until they swell up and become crisp helps tame this flavor.

Why They're Best • For men, curcurbitacins, a group of polyphenols, play a role in preventing and controlling a benign enlarged prostate • Pumpkin seeds are rich in minerals • Phytosterols help lower blood cholesterol levels.

What to Look For • Evenly dark olive-green seeds with a nutty and sweet smell from stores where stock turns quickly. Avoid a musty or rancid odor and unevenly colored seeds.

How to Store • In a glass jar in the refrigerator for 6 months or the freezer for 1 year.

How to Enjoy • Use to garnish spinach and other salads • Include in trail mix with dried cranberries, walnuts, and dried apples.

Good to Know • Seeds from your Halloween pumpkin, which are paler in color and from a different variety than the kind sold commercially, contain less phytochemicals.

Sesame Seeds

When it matures, the pod holding sesame seeds suddenly and audibly pops open. This is supposedly how we got the expression "open sesame." To get all their benefits and the most flavor, get sesame seeds with their hull, the crunchy outer layer that gives them a beige or black color. Avoid the hulled seeds, which are white and creamy and are often sold in a jar in the spice section at supermarkets. These taste blander and are less beneficial nutritionally.

Sesame seeds are frequently listed as a source of calcium, but substances in them called *oxalates* mean your body can only utilize some of it.

Why They're Best • Sesame seeds are a good source of copper, which helps the body fight inflammation • Sesamin, a lignan, can lower cholesterol levels in the liver as well as the blood • Lignans also inhibit the formation of inflammatory omega-6 fatty acids.

What to Look For • Choose seeds that smell nutty and sweet, from stores where stock turns quickly. Avoid a musty or rancid odor.

How to Store • In a glass jar in the refrigerator for 6 months or the freezer for 1 year.

How to Enjoy • Sprinkle sesame seeds on stir-fries, cooked green beans, spinach and carrots, salads, and yogurt • Add to granola, muesli, and salad dressings • When baking, use on top of breads and rolls, muffins, and cookies • As tahini, to make hummus, baba ghannouj, Asian sesame noodles, and sauce for falafel.

Good to Know • Gomasio, a seasoning used in Japanese and macrobiotic cooking, is toasted sesame seeds ground with sea salt • The name *benne seeds*, as in the Southern cookie called benne seed wafers, comes from the Nigerian word for sesame.

Sunflower Seeds

Sometimes referred to as birdseed because parrots and other feathered friends enjoy cracking their grey-and-beige striped shells, sunflower seeds have great value as people food. One-quarter cup provides 8 grams protein, 4 grams fiber, and 76 percent of the day's official requirement for vitamin E. Also they are rich in phytosterols, poly- and monounsaturated fats, and a number of minerals.

Raw sunflower seeds taste sweet and a touch earthy. Their creamy texture makes eating just a handful quite satisfying.

Why They're Best • Betaine lowers homocysteine, an indicator for the risk of heart disease • Arginine, an amino acid, plays a role in keeping the cardiovascular system relaxed so blood can flow easily • Vitamin E is an essential antioxidant for the brain, heart, and vascular system.

What to Look For • Select seeds with an even, pale green-gray color and a nutty, sweet smell from stores where stock turns quickly. Avoid a musty or rancid odor and dark or unevenly colored seeds.

How to Store • In a glass jar in the refrigerator or the freezer for 1 year.

How to Enjoy • Sprinkle sunflower seeds on cold cereals and use to top spice muffins, quick breads, and whole grain loaves • Include in trail mix • Use to coat a Cheddar cheese ball.

Good to Know • Snacking on sunflower seeds will increase your energy and satisfy your appetite.

Extra-Virgin Olive Oil

Olive oil is central to the Mediterranean Diet. This qualified claim authorized by the FDA since 2004 explains why:

About 2 tablespoons of olive oil daily may reduce the risk of coronary heart disease due to the monounsaturated fat in olive oil. Since olive oil, like all fats, contains 120 calories per tablespoon, use it to replace a similar amount of saturated fat to maintain the total number of calories you eat in a day.

Specifically, extra-virgin olive oil is an Essential Best Food because it has the highest amount of antioxidant polyphenols and it is one of the great pleasures of healthy eating. This oil comes only from the first pressing of the olives. By law, extra-virgin oil must be cold pressed (mechanically extracted without heat or chemicals) and have less than 1 percent acidity. Thanks to minimal processing, it retains most of the phytochemicals in olives, along with vitamin E, which acts as a natural preservative.

Why It's Best • Monounsaturated fat and vitamin E improve cardiovascular health by protecting LDL cholesterol from oxidizing and helping to keep down triglyceride levels • A study conducted in Greece indicated that olive oil lowers blood pressure • Monounsaturated fat lowers the risk of inflammation.

What to Look For • Flavor and appearance tell you how healthy an olive oil is because polyphenols add a slightly bitter taste and make it grassy green. Golden, milder extra-virgin oils, which are made from riper olives, still offer plenty of benefits • Oil should be packaged in a dark glass bottle or sealed in a can. Avoid oil that smells off or rancid or has been exposed to heat and sunlight.

How to Store • In a dark glass bottle or can in a cool, dark place. Unopened oil, properly stored, can last 12 months. After opening, use within 3 months. Ideally, keep a small amount handy and store the rest in the refrigerator, refilling the smaller container often to minimize air in the container.

How to Enjoy • Drizzle extra-virgin olive oil on vegetables, pasta and grain dishes, and soup for flavoring • Use in salad dressings, marinades, and sauces like Sicilian salmoriglio, a combination of chopped fresh oregano, parsley, lemon juice, and olive oil • Enjoy as a dipping sauce for bread, and brush on foods to be grilled • Look for recipes using it in breads, cakes, and cookies.

Good to Know • Cloudy, unfiltered olive oils contain more phytochemicals than filtered ones • Keep on hand a few oils with various flavors. Use the top-quality ones to flavor dishes but do not cook with them, as heat diminishes their volatile flavors • When sautéing, keep the heat below smoke point, which is about 410°F • For frying, use virgin olive oil, not extra-virgin, for its higher smoke point.

HERBS, SPICES, AND OTHER AROMATIC SEASONINGS Basil • Cilantro • Mint • Oregano • Parsley • Rosemary • Thyme • Cinnamon • Turmeric • Chile Peppers • Citrus Zest • Garlic • Ginger

Until the mid-19th century, medical doctors relied heavily on herbs and spices. Modern scientific research has shown why using them was effective for treating patients. Tested under modern conditions, the essential oils that give herbs and spices their potent aromas have significant antimicrobial, antinausea, and other protective or healing effects.

In cooking, although we use herbs and spices as seasoning in smaller amounts than when doctors and herbalists prescribe them, the abundance and concentration of phytochemicals in them still makes the amounts normally used enough to provide health benefits, especially when they are used regularly. For example, consuming ½ to 1 teaspoon a day of ground cinnamon has a positive effect on stabilizing blood sugar levels, and eating even a tablespoon of citrus zest a week reduces the risk of skin cancer. In India, the low rate of Alzheimer's disease appears to be related to eating turmeric every day. With no official definition of "a serving" for herbs and spices, I simply use a wide variety of them, often and liberally.

Herbs are the green, leafy parts of a plant. Many of them grow best in a Mediterranean climate. Spices are the non-leafy parts (seeds, roots, stems, fruit, bark, and flowers) of plants, including trees. They come mainly from the tropics.

The aromatic essential oils in herbs and spices are quite volatile. When you open a jar, if the aroma has faded, the flavor and health benefits have diminished, too. Throw it out and replace it with fresh, buying an amount you are likely to use up in about 6 months (longer as indicated). Store what you have away from heat with the date of purchase written on it.

To eliminate possible contamination or pests, most spices and dried herbs from major companies like McCormick are treated with ethylene oxide gas. If you wish to avoid this, choose products from organic packagers like Frontier and other small companies, such as Vanns Spices and Penzeys Spices, who do not follow these practices.

When cooking with herbs and spices, if you need to substitute dried for fresh, or vice versa, the rule of thumb is to use one-third or one-half as much dried as you would fresh. To bring out the flavor in dried herbs, rub them vigorously between your palms before using. For spices, dry toasting or heating them in oil has a similar effect.

HERBS • Basil

Basil is indispensable for both the sunny flavor in Italian dishes and the complex taste in Southeast Asian cooking. To create these distinctly different results, Mediterranean cooks rely on the lush leaves of Genovese or sweet basil. Southeast Asian varieties have pointier, smaller leaves and more complex notes of citrus and mint in their anise-tinged flavors.

The many phytochemicals responsible for both the flavor and health benefits in this member of the mint family make both fresh and dried forms of basil an Essential Best choice.

Why It's Best • Antioxidants, including vicenin, protect cells from oxidative damage • Eugenol, a volatile oil, is able to block inflammatory COX enzymes • Antimicrobial volatile oils protect against *Listeria* and other bacteria.

How to Enjoy • Sprinkle chopped fresh basil on tomatoes, mozzarella cheese, pasta, summer squash, salads, fish, seafood, and chicken, or use it dried • Use whole leaves on bruschetta and panini • Mix into stuffing for eggplant, peppers, and other foods • Infuse oil or vinegar with fresh basil • Sprinkle on spaghetti with ricotta, minced raw garlic, citrus zest, and lots of pepper • Use purple and Asian varieties from the garden or farmers' market.

Good to Know • Basil's tender leaves bruise easily and darken quickly when cut. The best method is to stack leaves, roll them into a long tube, then cut the roll crosswise with a sharp knife into fine strips, called *chiffonade*. Do this just before serving.

Cilantro

Cilantro, the leaves of the coriander plant, came to the New World in the 15th century as part of the Columbian Exchange and became a staple for Hispanic cooks. (At the same time, reversing the trip, chile peppers, one of cilantro's perfect partners, traveled in the opposite direction, to Europe, Asia, and Africa.)

Cilantro's scalloped and lobed leaves resemble flat-leaf parsley leaves so closely that it is also called Chinese parsley. Rubbing a leaf to release cilantro's distinctive fragrance, which some describe as fetid or sweaty, is the best way to tell which you have. Its flavor fades with heat, so add fresh cilantro later in cooking. Avoid dried cilantro, which has minimal flavor.

Why It's Best • Rich in antioxidants, including apigenin, kaempferol, and rhamnetin • Dodecanol, an antibiotic compound, may be as effective against Salmonella as some prescribed antibiotics • Vitamin K helps protect against osteoporosis.

How to Enjoy • Use cilantro in salsa and guacamole; with mint and other herbs for Southeast Asia dishes; with coconut, green chiles, and mint in fresh chutney; and in other Indian dishes • Cook with beans, lentils, in rice, and Moroccan tagines • Sprinkle cilantro on cooked carrots, and sliced orange salad, and use to garnish other dishes.

Good to Know • The most intense flavor is in the very bottom of the stem, in the white part resembling the bottom of a tiny celery rib • To save time, include the tender stems between the top leaves and those just below them when chopping or pureeing cilantro.

Mint

What is as refreshing as a glass of iced mint tea on a hot day, or as calming and revitalizing as a cup of hot mint tea with honey? These contrasts demonstrate mint's talent for being both stimulating and soothing.

Mint grows almost everywhere in the world with temperate weather. Spearmint, also called garden mint, has a mellow and slightly sweet flavor that is perfect in most dishes, although commercially grown spearmint often tastes more bitter than minty. Bright green spearmint at the farmers' market may have long, pointy, serrated leaves or more rounded, crinkly ones. Peppermint is darker colored, potently bitter and icy cool. And look for gently flavored pineapple or apple mint, and chocolate mint.

Why It's Best • In lab studies, perillyl alcohol combats the formation of cancer and stops its growth • Volatile oils in mint stop the growth of *H. pylori* and other bacteria • Rosmarinic acid helps reduce inflammation associated with asthma.

How to Enjoy • Sprinkle chopped fresh mint on fruit and fruit salad, beans and lentils, summer squash, or green peas; mix into Asian dipping sauces • Use in green salads, tabbouleh, Indian fresh chutney, and with yogurt in raita • Crush fresh peppermint or spearmint leaves and steep for tea, or add to cocktails and iced tea • Infuse in syrup to use with fruit and in chocolate desserts • Sprinkle dried mint on yogurt and cucumber for a salad, or mix into lamb or beef for meatballs.

Good to Know • Herbal mint tea is simply dried fresh mint. Read labels carefully, as supermarkets also carry mint-flavored black and green teas that contain caffeine.

Oregano

This Mediterranean herb is synonymous with pizza, meatballs, and other Italian red-sauce dishes. It is also essential in all-American chili and many Hispanic dishes.

Oregano grows wild all around the Southern Mediterranean. Its dark green, spade-shaped leaf is tougher than those of other fresh herbs, except for rosemary. The oregano Mexican cooks use comes from a different botanical family. It tastes stronger and less minty, with a more bitter afternote than the Mediterranean kind. Increasingly, you can find it in supermarkets.

On the health side, oregano has the highest antioxidant activity of all herbs, 42 times more than that of apples. Natural products often use oregano oil for its antibacterial properties.

Why It's Best • Carvacrol and thymol make oregano a killer of *E. coli*, *Staphylococcus*, and other harmful bacteria • Quercetin helps prevent cancer by fighting tumor growth • Polyphenol antioxidants, including rosmarinic acid, prevent cancer-causing cell mutations.

How to Enjoy • Use oregano to season Mediterranean dishes, especially those with tomatoes, eggplant, summer squash, onions, or sweet peppers • Add to chili, soups, stews, and egg dishes; sprinkle on beans and lentils, poultry, and baked fish • Sprinkle on pizza and focaccia • Use in stuffing for squash and other vegetables and to flavor marinades.

Good to Know • Dried Greek and wild Italian oregano have more resinous, pungent flavor and a grey-green color. Some ethnic and specialty food stores sell it in a bunch like a bouquet.

Parsley

The ancient Romans, who ate parsley as a breath freshener, understood its power to detoxify. As a chlorophyll addict, I was pleased to learn that it is a good source of this and other antioxidants—and the most popular herb. When using chopped parsley as a garnish, I double what recipes call for, since it adds more than just color.

Parsley can have either flat or curly leaves. I recommend sticking with the flat-leaf kind (aka Italian parsley). Darker green, its phytochemical level is higher, yet it tastes less bitter than curly parsley. Its leaves are also easier to chop and more tender.

Why It's Best • Myristicin, a volatile oil, reduces cancer risk by inhibiting tumor growth • Eugenol neutralizes carcinogens, including those found in smoke from grilling • Antioxidants, including lutein, neutralize free radicals, removing their ability to damage cells.

How to Enjoy • Use parsley to make Italian gremolata (with lemon zest and fresh garlic); salsa verde (a blend of fresh herbs and capers); Argentine chimichurri (a vinegar sauce with lots of garlic); and Moroccan chermoula (cilantro, cumin, garlic, paprika, and lemon juice) • Add to omelets and frittatas, green salads, potato salad, and other vegetable salads. Include in pesto; add to tomato sauce, ricotta, or cottage cheese; and sprinkle over pastas • Simmer parsley stems in soups and stocks for added flavor.

Good to Know • Ignore dried parsley, which has little flavor.

Rosemary

Related to mint, oregano, and thyme, fragrant branches of rosemary were once burned as an air sanitizer. This tenacious and potent herb grows as a shrub with tiny, intensely sky-blue flowers and needle-shaped leaves. Around the Mediterranean and in California, rosemary grows wild and is cultivated as an attractive hedge that also serves the cook.

Rosemary's pungent, piney flavor easily overpowers a dish and it has a bitter aftertaste, so use it with restraint. Eating its tough leaves is pleasant when they are finely chopped. They hold their flavor well, so add rosemary early in cooking.

Why It's Best • Carnosol and rosmanol are polyphenols that prevent carcinogens from binding with DNA • Compounds in rosemary prevent the breakdown of acetylcholine, a neurotransmitter • Rosmarinic acid, an anti-inflammatory, neutralizes free radicals.

How to Enjoy • Use rosemary in marinades for seasoning poultry, lamb, pork, and vegetables • Finely chop and add to frittatas, ratatouille, broccoli soup, carrots, winter squash, sweet potatoes, and beans and lentils • Sprinkle on rustic breads and focaccia • Include in pesto with spinach, parsley, and almonds • Place branches inside a chicken before roasting • Use in syrup to sweeten lemonade and iced tea.

Good to Know • Dried rosemary is too woody to use.

Thyme

I reach for thyme more often than any other herb because warm, faintly minty, and resinous flavors go with many foods, including Cajun dishes, vegetables, eggs, beans, and even some fruits. I also like it in tuna salad, and infuse it in a light syrup to spoon over fresh strawberries.

My mother sweetened mint tea with thyme honey when I had a cough, and French friends brew thyme tea to ease a cold and congestion. We know now that thymol, an essential oil in this herb, is the active ingredient providing this relief. There are 100 plus varieties, including lemon and orange thyme. Its flavor is sturdy enough to last all through cooking.

Why It's Best • Thymol and other compounds help relieve chest and respiratory congestions • Apigenin, a flavonoid, increases its antioxidant capacity • Carvacrol and other essential oils are antimicrobial.

How to Enjoy • Use fresh or dried thyme to season fish, poultry, pork, and lamb • Good with sweet potatoes, winter squash, mushrooms, roasted potatoes, beans and lentils, tomatoes, and eggplant • Use in soups, meat loaf, and marinades, and in Creole and Cajun dishes • Add thyme to stuffings, fillings for vegetables, and savory bread pudding.

Good to Know • Thyme is an important part of the French *bouquet garni* and za'atar, the Middle Eastern seasoning blend including sesame seeds, sumac, and salt.

SPICES • Cinnamon

Thoughts of comfort food and the USDA seldom occur together, but cinnamon brings both to mind. We associate cinnamon's warm fragrance with cozy times and soothing dishes, including apple pie, rice pudding, and hot spiced wine. At the USDA, research reveals that this spice appears to have major medical potential for controlling blood sugar, thanks to MHCP, a chalcone polymer that seems to act like insulin. This may ultimately help people with type 2 diabetes simply and significantly.

In the United States and Europe, cinnamon mainly flavors desserts and baked goods. Cooks in Asia, North Africa, and Mexico use it more often in savory dishes, such as Moroccan tagines and Mexican mole sauce. Using cinnamon as much as possible is a good idea. This is a spice to eat every day.

Why It's Best • Helps balance blood sugar by reducing insulin resistance • Protects cardiovascular health by reducing clumping of blood platelets and blood cholesterol, triglyceride, and LDL levels • Antimicrobial properties help protect against *H. pylori* and *E. coli* bacteria, candida, and other organisms.

How to Enjoy • Sprinkle ground cinnamon on cereal, toast, and yogurt • Use to season beef, pork, and poultry, especially stews • Goes well with spinach, sweet potatoes, tomatoes, and winter squash as well as apples, blueberries, cranberries, oranges, oats, rice, walnuts, almonds, and coffee • Also good with lamb, eggplant, zucchini, and other vegetables, as well as bananas and pears.

Good to Know • Stick cinnamon adds flavor without darkening the color of the dish or adding a grainy look.

Turmeric

This may be the Essential Best Food you know least. Learning to use it is wise since researchers are finding in animal studies that it fights cancer, protects the brain against Alzheimer's disease, and is an anti-inflammatory that may alleviate rheumatoid arthritis, asthma, and other chronic diseases.

Turmeric gets it intense yellow color from curcumin, which is also the beneficial substance in it. Other than ballpark mustard, turmeric is little used outside of curries and other Asian dishes.

A rhizome related to ginger, fresh turmeric is grown in Hawaii and Asia. It looks like a short, slim finger of fresh ginger with browner, orange-tinged skin and bright orange-yellow flesh. If you find it at an Asian market or natural food store, add thin slices to stir-fries, soups, and stews to give them a subtly peppery, earthy, and faintly citrus flavor.

Ground dried turmeric tastes less peppery and more pungent. The darker its brassy color and the deeper its flavor, the higher its curcumin content. A little turmeric goes a long way in flavor and the benefits of frequent use add up, so start out by adding ¼ teaspoon to already strongly flavored dishes.

Why It's Best • Curcumin, a potent anti-inflammatory, appears to relieve arthritis and may lower histamine levels that trigger asthma • Appears to protect against Alzheimer's disease • Shown to have antitumor effects in animal studies on cancer • Provides cardiovascular protection as an antioxidant that inhibits oxidation of LDL cholesterol.

How to Enjoy • Turmeric is good with cauliflower, eggplant, spinach, carrots, potatoes, sweet potatoes, and other root vegetables • Use to season rice, particularly along with ground cumin and coriander • Add to lentils, quinoa, scrambled eggs or frittatas, egg salad, and potato salad • Season broccoli soup and tomato sauce with a pinch.

Good to Know • Peel fresh turmeric and use it thinly sliced, chopped, or finely grated • It goes well with other Asian spices, particularly lemongrass, garlic, and chile peppers, and also marries the flavors of other spices in a dish • Turmeric acts like a dye so anything it touches or splashes on will remain brilliantly colored • Cumin sounds similar but contains no curcumin.

Chile Peppers

If you can stand the heat, eat lots of chile peppers. In addition to their extraordinary variety of flavors, they are loaded with capsaicin. Besides igniting our tastebuds, this fiery substance elevates our mood by stimulating the brain to release feel-good endorphins. And it is credited with preventing stomach ulcers and relieving congestion from colds and flu. Eating chiles may suppress our appetite and speed up our metabolism. In addition, cultures in which chiles are eaten liberally have significantly lower incidences of heart attack and strokes.

Whether fresh, dried, or ground, the chile's heat is in the ribs from which it transfers to the seeds. So for maximum strength, leave in the ribs. If you have a low tolerance for heat, eat only the flesh near the tip where there are no seeds and minimal rib.

The color of a chile pepper depends in part on whether it is picked when green and immature or when a ripe red, yellow, or orange. Ripe chiles have more complex flavors, ranging from acidic to floral or sweet, along with their heat.

Why They're Best • Capsaicin reduces blood cholesterol, LDL levels, and clumping of platelets to reduce the risk of heart attack and stroke • Capsaicin also acts to reduce the risk of stomach ulcers • Eating chile peppers may boost metabolism and suppress appetite • The heat of chiles acts as a decongestant when you have a cold or flu.

How to Enjoy • Use chile peppers in Mexican dishes such as fresh salsa, mole sauce, posole, and other stews • They are good in Asian curries, stir-fries, and soups like Chinese hot and sour • Dried chiles are found in many seasoning blends, condiments, and sauces, including Ethiopian berbere, Indian chaat masala, Jamaican jerk, Japanese shichimi togarashi, Korean kimchi, North African harissa, Thai nam prik, Indonesian sambal, Spanish romesco, and Tunisian tabil.

Good to Know • Capsaicin is soluble in fat and alcohol, so when you're on fire, reach for guacamole, milk, ice cream, or beer, NOT water • Applied topically, capsaicin helps dull the pain of arthritis • The heat in chiles is measured in Scoville heat units (SHU), with rankings from 0 to 1 million SHU. Jalapeños are at the low end with 2,500 to 8,000 SHU, habaneros register 500,000 SHU, and bhut jolokia a million plus • Chile heat and flavor are notoriously variable, so one jalapeño may be tame and the next one surprisingly feisty, while one ancho tastes deliciously complex and another is just plain bitter.

OTHER SEASONINGS • Citrus Zest

Zest—the colorful, outermost layer of citrus fruit skin—deserves to be an Essential Best Food on its own because of the volatile oils, whose fragrance envelops you when you peel the fruit and the antioxidant compounds that color it. To enjoy the flavor in these oils, grate or pare off the zest and use it to season and garnish dishes, much as we do with spices and herbs.

Zest is only the outermost, colored layer of the peel, which also includes the pith, the spongy, white layer underneath the zest. (And which happens to contain other useful and potent phytochemicals.) Consuming just 1 tablespoon a week of citrus zest is enough to reduce the risk of skin cancer, based on a study at the University of Arizona College of Public Health and Arizona Cancer Center.

The zest from each kind of citrus fruit, including tangerines and mandarins, usually contains at least one unique compound, so the more varieties of citrus you consume, the better. However, you will gain important benefits from eating more readily available lemon, orange, and lime zest, so the recipes here help you include them often—in salsa, soups, salads, cookies, and other sweet and savory dishes.

Why It's Best • Stimulates body's detoxification defenses to help prevent cancers from starting • In laboratory studies, flavones in citrus zest helped lower cholesterol levels • Limonoids, including limonene, block DNA damage and the formation of cancer cells.

How to Enjoy • Grate or finely chop citrus zest to use as a garnish or for seasoning fish and poultry, salads and dressings, stuffings, soups, desserts, and drinks • Remove zest in strips and use to flavor syrups and sauces; slice it into shards for garnish • Toss the shells from squeezed lemons or limes into a pitcher of water to add flavor and some phytochemicals.

Good to Know • Even when citrus fruits are organic, they can be coated with wax, so wash them well before zesting • Volatile oils from the skin get into the juice you squeeze at home.

Garlic

"Garlic is good for health, good for vampires, good for everything," claims master chef Jacques Pepin. Much of the world agrees, since cooks use it everywhere, from kimchi in Korea to aioli in Provence and sizzling shrimp in Latin America.

The sulfur compounds that give garlic its pungent, hot taste and lingering aroma have proven powers to protect against heart attack and stroke, cancer, and high blood pressure. In addition, this potent allium also provides anti-inflammatory, antibacterial, antiseptic, and anti-microbial protection. Letting chopped garlic sit for 10 minutes increases its potency.

Garlic's flavor is a chameleon. Crude and hot when raw, it tastes subtle when cloves are roasted until their sugars caramelize. The more it is cut up, the stronger its taste, with pressed garlic the boldest of all.

Why It's Best • Sulfur compounds lower cholesterol, LDL, and triglyceride levels, and blood pressure to help prevent heart disease, heart attack, and stroke • Anticoagulant effect keeps blood platelets from sticking and prevents clotting • Reduces the risk of cancer • Allicin, a sulfur compound, is antibacterial and antiviral.

How to Enjoy • Include garlic when cooking most vegetables, especially tomatoes, egg-plant, sweet peppers, and dark greens; also good with shrimp and other seafood, meats, and poultry • Use raw garlic in sauces such as pesto, aioli, romesco, gremolata, and salad dressings; use cooked garlic in tomato sauce, green sauce, and other sauces • Include garlic in Mexican and Asian dishes with cilantro, chile peppers, ginger, and lemongrass • Roast in foil at 400°F for 50 to 60 minutes, then spread on bread or add to pasta.

Good to Know • Garlic stored in oil can grow botulin, the toxin that causes botulism, unless the mixture is specially processed with the preservatives added to commercially prepared products • Slapping cloves with the side of a heavy knife or "garlic stone" loosens clingy inner skin.

Ginger

Arguably the most functional and multinational spice, ginger is called *universal remedy* in traditional Indian Ayurvedic medicine because it treats so many conditions. Today, Western doctors use it to relieve nausea from pregnancy, motion sickness, anesthesia, and chemotherapy.

Ginger is served with sushi and fish because of its antimicrobial powers. It is also anti-inflammatory, anti-cancer, antiviral, antioxidant, antipyretic, antiparasitic, good for coughs, indigestion, and flatulence, and stimulates circulation to warm the hands and feet. Current research is investigating ginger as a painkiller as well.

Often called *ginger root*, it is really a rhizome, or underground stem. A ginger branch resembles a human hand, which is why large clumps of rhizomes are called *hands* and the many, jointed parts are called *fingers*.

Why It's Best • Gingerol is listed in the USDA database for its antinausea properties • In lab studies, ginger inhibits the production of prostaglandins, chemicals that trigger the pain of arthritis • In animal studies, ginger boosted the immune system.

How to Enjoy • Cook fresh ginger with chicken, beef, fish and seafood, and soy foods • Also good with carrots, sweet potatoes, broccoli, bok choy, and stir-fried watercress • Include in Indian curries and Caribbean dishes • Enjoy in desserts, baked goods, and drinks, including ginger lemonade and ginger tea with lemon and honey or maple syrup.

Good to Know • Never substitute ground ginger when recipe calls for fresh, as they taste quite different. But grated fresh can replace dry in dishes, using about 2:1 ratio • Using ginger in cooking and infused as tea can provide most of its benefits. For ginger tea, steep two ½-inch pieces in a cup of boiling water for 10 minutes • Chocolate-coated preserved ginger is divine • Japanese pickled young ginger, served with sushi, is made from thin-skinned young ginger sold in Asian markets.

NOT JUST TO DRINK • Chocolate and Cocoa • Coffee • Pomegranate • Tea • Red Wine

What do chocolate, coffee, pomegranates, tea, and red wine have in common? We can both drink and eat them all, using cocoa in a seasoning for beef, coffee in a sauce for poached pears, turning pomegranate juice into granita, adding powdered green tea to buttery shortbread, and combining red wine with lentils.

These intensely flavorful foods are known for the pleasure they give, and some for their potentially indulgent cost. They all have a remarkably exotic, mythic, or mesmerizing history, as well. Happily, consuming these surprisingly versatile choices may do you significant good, for each of these Essential Best Foods has among the highest levels of antioxidants and other highly desirable phytochemicals of all foods and beverages.

Chocolate and Cocoa

News about chocolate's health benefits continues to be positive, mainly because of the high level of flavanols in cacao beans. These compounds, including epicatechin, are all part of the larger group of flavonoids and appear to have significant cardiovascular benefits. Cacao, from which chocolate and cocoa are made, also contains proanthocyanins similar to those found in red wine and tea.

The darker the chocolate, the more flavanols it may deliver, but how much is hard to say because processing cacao beans into chocolate and cocoa powder reduces the amount of flavanols you get. Chocolate manufacturers are working hard to change this and make the end result predictable. Already, milk chocolate lovers can get chocolate bars claiming to deliver more antioxidants than some dark chocolate. For now, though, intensely flavored dark chocolate containing 70 percent or more cocoa solids is likely to do the most good.

Chocolate also contains fat, sugar, and caffeine. Fortunately, one-third of its fat is monounsaturated, like the kind in olive oil. The rest is saturated fat, but half of that is stearic acid, which seems to have no effect on cholesterol levels. The darker the chocolate, the less sugar it contains. (Cocoa powder is unsweetened and low in fat.) One ounce of dark chocolate contains 10 to 15 milligrams of caffeine, less than in a cup of green tea.

Chocolate also contains theobromine and other mood-altering substances. Reputable studies have yet to prove an actual biochemical link between consuming them in chocolate and the pleasure we experience, but nothing will diminish the way melting chocolate feels on your tongue, or the seduction of its flavors.

Why They're Best • Various studies have shown eating chocolate increased HDL levels and reduced LDL levels, slowed LDL oxidation, and produced blood thinning resembling the effect of taking baby aspirin • Eating an ounce of flavanol-rich chocolate can increase the level of nitrous oxide in the blood, which helps keep the vascular system supple and can reduce blood pressure • An ounce of unsweetened chocolate contains 4 grams of fiber.

What to Look For • Chocolate should be well-wrapped and not exposed to excessive heat or cold. If chocolate develops *bloom*, a white, powdery effect caused by cocoa butter migrating to the surface, it is not spoiled and can be used in cooking.

How to Store • Wrap chocolate tightly in plastic wrap, then foil, and store in a cool, dry place, ideally around 55°F. Temperatures above 70°F can cause bloom. Keep away from any foods with strong odors • Never freeze chocolate. Refrigeration can make chocolate sweat when it returns to room temperature, but does not affect its taste • Properly stored, dark chocolate keeps for a year or more, milk chocolate for several months • Store cocoa in an airtight container in a cool, dark, dry place for 12 months.

How to Enjoy • For eating, chocolate mini-bars made by Green & Black's, Scharffen Berger, Guittard, Dove, and other brands help you stick to the recommended amount • Add unsweetened or dark chocolate or cocoa powder to chili, tomato sauce, and bean dishes • Sprinkle cocoa nibs on salads or oatmeal, use to garnish soups, beef, and game dishes, and add to baked goods and trail mix • Grate chocolate over the top of cakes and cupcakes just before serving for a garnish • Make a smoothie using cocoa powder, a banana, and milk or apple juice.

Good to Know • Each brand of chocolate has a distinctive taste. Sample a variety and use those you like • Chocolate with 70 percent or more cocoa solids may be too bitter to eat but tastes good in baking or a dessert • The amount of cocoa butter and sugar in chocolate affects how it will perform, so before shopping check what your recipe calls for • Let baked chocolate desserts sit for 8 to 24 hours before serving so the many volatile flavor compounds in the chocolate can settle down and meld.

Coffee

Most Americans get the majority of their antioxidants from coffee. Although its health effects are mixed, coffee has enough plusses to be an Essential Best Food. On the plus side, coffee has been found to reduce the risk of diabetes and Parkinson's disease, and to help prevent cancer, though more research is needed to solidify these claims. It also can help manage asthma and may prevent dental cavities.

Most Americans get most of their antioxidants from coffee. Mehmet C. Oz, MD, Director of the Heart Institute, New York Presbyterian Medical Center, advises that drinking four 6-ounce cups of coffee a day is not harmful, though you should check with your own doctor to determine what is good for you. For one thing, coffee can raise cholesterol levels. Also, it is quite acidic and anyone with gastric reflux or an ulcer should avoid drinking it.

Many people crave the energizing, mood lifting effects of the caffeine in coffee, which contains around 85 milligrams per cup. On the negative side, caffeine is an addictive drug that can interfere with sleep and raise blood pressure, although this may be linked more to the caffeine in soft drinks than in coffee. Drinking decaffeinated coffee can alleviate some of these issues.

Coffee's positive effects come from more than caffeine, with nearly 2,000 compounds in the final beverage, many of them created during the roasting process. Many are antioxidants, which you still get when drinking decaffeinated coffee, although the decaffeinating process decreases their levels.

Why It's Best • Increased blood antioxidant levels in a study with postmenopausal women who drank 4 to 5 cups a day, reducing the risk of heart-related death by 19 percent • Numerous studies have shown that regular coffee drinkers are up to 80 percent less likely to develop Parkinson's disease • Harvard researchers calculated that drinking 1 to 3 cups of caffeinated coffee a day reduces the risk of diabetes.

How to Store • In a cool, dark, dry place, well-sealed or in an airtight container. Do not refrigerate. Freeze only if storing for longer than 1 month as it changes the flavor and affects how the beans grind.

How to Enjoy • Use coffee in cooking as a spice, combining it in dry rubs, and add it to flavor savory dishes and chocolate desserts • For the best iced coffee, freeze freshly brewed coffee in cubes. To serve, pour freshly brewed coffee into a glass filled with the coffee cubes.

Good to Know • Arabica are the best quality beans, with less caffeine and acid than lesser quality robusta coffee • Descriptions of brewed coffee sound like those of wine, including smooth, full-bodied, light, acidic, fruity, spicy, bright, rounded, complex, and syrupy • Espresso is made using deep-roasted beans, specially ground and brewed under pressure. It contains less caffeine than regular brewed coffee because of the shorter brewing time • Three methods are commonly used for decaffeination: a chemical solvent, the Swiss water process, and carbon dioxide, with water processing preferable.

Pomegranate

How pomegranate juice became a supermarket staple and fresh California pomegranates a common sight in produce departments is a marketing success story.

Originating in ancient Persia, now Iran, pomegranates' popularity beyond ethnic markets began in 2002 due mostly to Lynda and Stewart Resnick working hard to teach Americans that Wonderful pomegranates (a botanical variety) have two to three times the level of antioxidants than those in red wine and green tea. Using research they helped finance to create a demand, they made their POM Wonderful juice an easy way to get this beautiful fruit's benefits.

The proven health benefits, also supported by independent experts, led to scores of other brands flooding the market. Some produce sections even offer containers of fresh pomegranate seeds when the fruit is in season.

Why It's Best • Research at University of California at Davis confirms that pomegranates contain two to three times more antioxidants than red wine and green tea • Drinking pomegranate juice reduces oxidation of LDL cholesterol • Probably thanks to anthocyanins and tannins, pomegranate juice prevents formation of arterial plaque and may reduce existing plaque • Consuming pomegranates may help lower blood pressure.

What to Look For • Fresh: Pomegranates should feel heavy, with leathery, shiny, unblemished skin. Avoid fruit with cracked skin or soft spots • Juice: Avoid added sugar.

How to Store • Store fruit at room temperature or refrigerate for several weeks. Seeds keep in a tightly sealed container in the refrigerator for 3 to 4 days, in the freezer for 3 months. Refrigerate pomegranate juice and use within 7 to 14 days. Store pomegranate molasses in the pantry indefinitely.

How to Enjoy • Use pomegranate juice in drinks, salad dressings, marinades, pan sauces, smoothies, and sorbet • Sprinkle pomegranate seeds on salads, desserts, and poultry and meat dishes; use to garnish hummus • Use pomegranate molasses to garnish cooked legumes, in salad dressings, and to accent other dishes.

Good to Know • Every brand of pomegranate juice tastes different. Some are thin and very astringent, others have natural flavor added. My favorite is POM Wonderful, for its intense and balanced combination of sweet, tart, and tannic flavors, with full-bodied texture • You can extract the juice from a pomegranate in several ways: Whirl the *arils* (commonly referred to as seeds) in a blender or food processor, then place in cheesecloth and squeeze. Or, cut off the top of a pomegranate, insert a fork, and squeeze the fruit like an orange. Or, press halves of the fruit in a citrus juicer. Always be gentle to avoid getting bitter juice.

Tea

Observing lower rates of heart disease and cancer in Asian countries where people drink multiple cups of tea every day, researchers have focused on figuring out why. The answer: Leaves from *Camellia sinensis*, the tea plant, are lavishly high in antioxidant polyphenols.

Some benefits from drinking green or black tea regularly appear to be helping to reduce or maintain weight, promoting oral health by inhibiting bacteria related to the formation of plaque and cavities, and having a positive effect on bone mass and mental alertness.

The biggest challenge to Americans who want to experience these benefits is developing a taste for a "cuppa" since you have to drink several cups a day to get significant benefits. The substances that make tea healthy also give it a bitter, astringent flavor. Drinking flavored green tea and white tea, which has a light, slightly sweet-smoky flavor and the highest level of polyphenols of all types of tea, can help.

Why It's Best • Polyphenols, including the catechin EGCG in green and white tea, may lower the risk of cancer by protecting DNA from oxidative changes • Tea appears to reduce the risk of heart disease and stroke through a number of effects that help protect LDL cholesterol from oxidation, reduce blood cholesterol levels, and improve blood flow • Drinking tea is associated with lower blood pressure.

What to Look For • Loose tea and bags should be sealed to protect them from air and light, with a clean fragrance. Look for teabags made from chemical-free materials, if desired. Avoid tea with a musty odor.

How to Store • In the original package or an airtight container in a dry, dark, cool place for up to 1 year.

How to Enjoy • For the most antioxidants, steep tea for 3 to 5 minutes and drink freshly brewed • Use tea as an ingredient in soups, sauces, sorbet and shortbread, as well as in chai and other drinks • Keep a selection of teas for variety, including green and white, some flavored with spices or fruit. My favorites include decaffeinated green tea chai, and white needles, a particularly delicate white tea • Filtered water makes the best tasting tea • Steep green tea in cool water for 30 minutes to produce a brew with less bitter flavor.

Good to Know • Tea contains significantly less caffeine than coffee. How much caffeine you get depends on the type of tea and how it is brewed. White and green teas contain around 15 to 20 milligrams per 8-ounce cup (about the same as in an ounce of dark chocolate), black tea around 45 milligrams, compared to 60 to 120 milligrams in a cup of brewed coffee • Decaffeinating reduces the amount of polyphenols in tea but leaves enough to provide useful benefits • Squeeze the tea bag to extract the most polyphenols • Consuming black pepper along with green tea appears to boost the amount of EGCG your body absorbs.

Red Wine

Red wine first made headlines as an explanation for the French Paradox—the seemingly contradictory phenomenon of French people who ate a diet high in saturated fat and smoked cigarettes, but who also consumed red wine, having a lower risk of heart disease and heart attack than those who followed a healthier lifestyle but did not drink wine. Resveratrol, one of the polyphenols in wine, may be a veritable fountain of youth, with major amounts of this antioxidant prolonging life in fruit flies and mice. It has even maintained healthy function in obese mice.

Resveratrol is abundant in the skin and seeds of red grapes. Red wine has a significantly greater concentration of this antioxidant than the fresh fruit. It also has a 20 to 50 percent higher level of polyphenols than white wine, where the grape skins and seeds are removed early in the fermentation process.

Studies have shown that one glass of red wine a day for middle-aged women, two for men, reduced the risk of heart disease by 30 to 50 percent, and that in older adults, those who consumed one to six drinks a week were less likely to develop dementia.

Why It's Best • Polyphenols in grape skins and seeds, particularly resveratrol, prevent oxidation of LDL cholesterol that contributes to the risk of coronary heart disease • Saponins from grape skins may help prevent the body's absorption of cholesterol from foods • Drinking wine promotes socializing and relaxation, both proven to contribute to better health.

What to Look For • What you enjoy. Select organic wines made without sulfites if you are sensitive to them.

How to Store • In a dark, cool place with stable temperature.

How to Enjoy • Learn to pair wine with foods • Eat and drink together with friends. Benefits of the Mediterranean Diet come from taking time to relax and share leisurely meals as well as from consuming wine and healthy foods • Use red wine as an ingredient in sauces, salad dressings, and desserts.

Good to Know • If you are sensitive to sulfites, which occur naturally in wines as well as being an additive, red wine contains about half the amount found in white. There are also organic wines with no added sulfites.

CHAPTER TWO

HORS D'OEUVRES AND STARTERS

[THREE DIPS WITH CRUDITÉS

Lemon Pesto Dip with Red Pepper and Cherry Tomatoes 70

Feta Dip with Confetti Vegetables 72

Three-Onion Dip with Broccoli 73]

Roasted Red Pepper and Walnut Spread 74, *Hot Bean Dip* 75, *Pita Chips with Dukka* 76,

Rosemary-Marinated Olives 78, *Black Bean and Nectarine Salsa* 80,

Smoked Salmon and Goat Cheese Crostini with Fennel Gremolata 81, *Salmon-Stuffed Eggs* 82,

Chinese Tea Eggs 84, *Black Olive Caviar in Endive* 85, *Citrus-Marinated Shrimp* 86,

Ginger Chicken Meatballs 88, *Spanish Smoked Almonds* 89, *Curried Chickpeas* 90,

Chocolate-Glazed Peanuts 91

Three Dips with Crudités

Dips are a seductive way to encourage eating raw vegetables. They also help you serve lavish amounts of herbs as well as dairy foods we love. Lemon Pesto Dip gives an eternal favorite a sparkling new twist.

Feta Dip and Three-Onion Dip show how to enjoy deliciously creamy ones with remarkably little fat and big flavor.

LEMON PESTO DIP WITH RED PEPPER AND CHERRY TOMATOES

● **FOOD FACT**

Raw spinach gives you more lutein—an antioxidant carotenoid that may help prevent heart disease and cancer—than cooked.

Lemon zest, fresh spinach, and fresh basil make this a sprightly dip. The lemon also helps keep it bright green for a couple of days. It clings nicely to red pepper strips and small tomatoes served on toothpicks.

1½	cups packed basil leaves	½	teaspoon freshly ground pepper
½	cup packed baby spinach leaves	¼	cup extra-virgin olive oil
½	cup walnuts	½	teaspoon grated lemon zest
¼	cup (1 ounce) grated Asiago cheese	1	large red bell pepper, cut into ¾" strips
2	tablespoons soft silken tofu	1	pint cherry tomatoes
½	teaspoon salt		

1. Pulse the basil and spinach in a mini food processor until finely chopped. Add the nuts and cheese. Whirl until the nuts are finely chopped. Add the tofu, salt, and pepper. With the motor running, drizzle in the olive oil. Add the lemon zest, and whirl to blend.

2. Scoop the pesto into a bowl. Set the bowl on a plate and surround it with the pepper strips and the tomatoes. The dip keeps for 2 days, covered in the refrigerator.

Makes 1 cup dip, 8 servings

Per serving: 141 calories, 13 g fat, 2 g saturated fat, 3 g protein, 5 g carbohydrates, 2 g fiber

FETA DIP WITH CONFETTI VEGETABLES

Liptauer, a sheep's milk cheese spread flavored with caraway seeds, paprika, and capers that is sold at Hungarian and Slovakian food stores in my neighborhood, inspired this colorful, thick dip. Strips of crisp vegetables and wedges of warm pita bread go with it nicely.

½	cup reduced-fat feta cheese	1	tablespoon capers, rinsed, drained, and chopped
¼	cup fat-free Greek yogurt		
¼	cup fat-free cream cheese	1	green bell pepper, cut into ¾" strips
2	teaspoons Dijon mustard		
1½	teaspoons sweet or hot Hungarian paprika	1	red bell pepper, cut into ¾" strips
		1	yellow or orange bell pepper, cut into ¾" strips
½	teaspoon caraway seeds		
¼	teaspoon freshly ground pepper	½	pint cherry tomatoes
¼	cup finely chopped roasted red pepper (see page 117)	1	small zucchini, cut into 2" spears

1. Whirl the feta, yogurt, cream cheese, mustard, paprika, caraway seeds, and pepper in a mini food processor until the mixture is just slightly grainy. Scoop the dip into a mixing bowl. Add the roasted pepper and capers and stir to mix. Cover with plastic wrap and refrigerate for 8 to 24 hours.

2. Pack the dip into a serving bowl. Set the bowl on a platter and surround it with the bell peppers, tomatoes, and zucchini, arranging them by color.

Makes 1 cup plus 2 tablespoons dip, 9 servings

Per serving: 43 calories, 1 g fat, 1 g saturated fat, 4 g protein, 5 g carbohydrates, 1 g fiber

THREE-ONION DIP
WITH BROCCOLI

Combining three alliums—red onion, scallions, and shallots—this dip is a fresh take on the classic made from onion soup mix, omitting all of its processed ingredients and load of sodium. Blending sour cream with Greek-style yogurt keeps the dip creamy and indulgent, but with much less fat.

2	tablespoons extra-virgin olive oil	½	cup finely chopped scallions,
½	cup thinly sliced shallots		green and white parts
¾	cup fat-free Greek yogurt		Salt and freshly ground pepper
¾	cup reduced-fat sour cream	1	bunch broccoli
1	small red onion, very finely		
	chopped, ½ cup		

● BEST TECHNIQUE

To avoid its tough neck when slicing a scallion, slice the white bulb, then rotate the scallion 180 degrees, and cut off the dark green top where it branches from the pale green neck. (Discard the neck or add it to stock.) Continue slicing the dark green top.

1. In a small skillet, heat the oil over medium-high heat. Add the shallots and cook, stirring occasionally, until soft and golden, about 8 minutes. Set the shallots aside to cool in the pan.

2. In a mixing bowl, combine the yogurt and sour cream. Add the red onion and scallions. Using a slotted spoon, lift the shallots from the oil and stir them into the yogurt mixture. Season to taste with salt and pepper. Cover and refrigerate to allow the flavors to develop, 2 to 24 hours.

3. Cut the broccoli into long spears, slicing it vertically to give each floret a long, tapered stem. Steam the florets until tender-crisp, about 3 minutes. Immediately drain in a colander and rinse the broccoli under cold running water until cooled. Drain well. The cooled broccoli can be covered and refrigerated for up to 24 hours.

4. Transfer the dip to a serving bowl set in the center of a plate and arrange the broccoli in a ring around the bowl.

Makes 1¾ cups dip, 14 servings

Per serving: 60 calories, 4 g fat, 1 g saturated fat, 3 g protein, 5 g carbohydrates, 1 g fiber

ROASTED RED PEPPER AND WALNUT SPREAD

● **BEST INGREDIENT**

If using jarred roasted peppers, drain them well. Use pomegranate molasses instead of pomegranate juice to balance their higher moisture to keep the dip thick.

● **TOASTING NUTS**

Spread nuts in one layer on a baking sheet. Toast in a 350°F oven until fragrant and lightly colored, 10 minutes, stirring after 3 minutes and after 6 minutes. Spread on a plate to cool.

Alongside hummus and baba ghannouj, many stores now offer muhammarah. Served with pita bread as part of meze, it is also a delicious condiment served with roasted chicken and grilled fish. Pomegranate molasses is a syrupy reduction of pomegranate juice sold in Middle Eastern markets and some supermarkets.

1	red bell pepper, roasted, peeled, and coarsely chopped (see page 117)	1	tablespoon extra-virgin olive oil
		1	tablespoon pomegranate juice or 1 teaspoon pomegranate molasses
1	slice whole wheat bread, crust removed, toasted, and cut into 1" cubes	½	teaspoon ground cumin
		¼	teaspoon red-pepper flakes
½	cup walnuts, toasted (left)		Salt and freshly ground pepper

Pulse the red pepper, toast cubes, walnuts, oil, pomegranate juice or molasses, cumin, and red-pepper flakes in a food processor until the mixture is a rough paste. Season to taste with salt and pepper.

Makes ¾ cup, 6 servings

Per serving (2 tablespoons): 101 calories, 9 g fat, 1 g saturated fat, 2 g protein, 4 g carbohydrates, 1 g fiber

HOT BEAN DIP

Pinto beans are beautifully creamy when mashed. You will also like the way a spoonful of unsweetened chocolate intensifies their flavor. Choose the heat level for this dip by the salsa you add—from mild to spicy. Serve with tortilla chips and green bell pepper strips.

● **ANOTHER WAY**

For breakfast or brunch, nestle a poached or fried egg into ½ cup of this dip.

1	tablespoon canola oil	¼	cup hot or mild prepared salsa
¾	cup finely chopped onion, divided	2	teaspoons fresh lime juice
¼	cup finely chopped green bell pepper	1	teaspoon natural unsweetened cocoa powder
1	(15-ounce) can pinto beans, drained		Salt and freshly ground pepper
		½	teaspoon ground cumin
		¼	cup chopped cilantro leaves

1. In a medium skillet, heat the oil over medium-high heat. Add ½ cup of the onion and the green pepper. Sauté until the onion is soft, 5 minutes.

2. Add the beans to the pan. Using a fork, mash them to the desired texture, from rough to very smooth. Mix in the salsa, lime juice, and cocoa powder. Off the heat, season to taste with salt and pepper. Scoop into a serving bowl.

3. In a small bowl, combine the remaining ¼ cup raw onion with the cumin. Toss to coat. Sprinkle the onion mixture over the dip, then the cilantro. Serve immediately.

Makes 1¾ cups, 14 servings

Per serving (2 tablespoons): 34 calories, 1 g fat, 0 g saturated fat, 1 g protein, 5 g carbohydrates, 1 g fiber

PITA CHIPS WITH DUKKA

● **BE AUTHENTIC**

To enjoy dukka the Middle Eastern way, cut a pita bread into wedges and separate them. Serve with small bowls of olive oil and dukka, dipping the bread first in the oil then the dukka.

I love this aromatic Middle Eastern blend of ground toasted nuts, sesame seeds, coriander, and mint. It is used in Lebanon and Israel to season hummus, cooked carrots, and other vegetables, and as a dip for pita bread (see Another Way). I also bake this spicy blend right onto pita wedges to serve as dippers or on their own as an out-of-the-ordinary bread.

2	8" whole wheat pita breads, quartered	1	tablespoon extra-virgin olive oil
		4	teaspoons Dukka (opposite)

1. Preheat the oven to 350°F.

2. Separate each pita wedge into 2 pieces. Arrange the pieces in 1 layer on a baking sheet, inside sides facing up. Brush with the oil. Sprinkle ¼ teaspoon of the Dukka on each piece.

3. Bake about 5 minutes, or until the pita pieces are crisp at the edges. Cool the chips on the baking sheet on a rack. (The chips will crisp as they cool.) Serve the cooled chips immediately, or store them on a plate, covered with foil, for up to 8 hours.

Makes 16

Per chip: 23 calories, 1 g fat, 0 g saturated fat, 1 g protein, 3 g carbohydrates, 1 g fiber

DUKKA

2	tablespoons blanched almonds	¾	teaspoon crushed dried mint
2	tablespoons raw pumpkin seeds		leaves, optional
2	tablespoons sesame seeds	¼	teaspoon freshly ground pepper,
1	teaspoon coriander seeds		optional

1. In a dry skillet set over medium heat, combine the almonds, pumpkin seeds, sesame seeds, and coriander seeds. Cook, stirring constantly, until the pumpkin seeds puff and the sesame seeds start to pop, 2 to 3 minutes. The almonds will not color. Spread the mixture on a plate and cool completely.

2. Whirl the toasted mixture in a mini food processor until the almonds are mostly ground with some chunks, and the pumpkin seeds are finely chopped. The spices and sesame seeds will be partially ground. Mix in the mint or pepper, if using. Cover and refrigerate any leftover dukka for up to 3 days.

Makes ¾ cup

ROSEMARY-MARINATED OLIVES

Although high in fat, these olives offer such intense garlic, herb, and citrus flavors that you will be content to nibble on them slowly. Spooned into an attractive jar, they make a distinctive hostess gift.

½	cup extra-virgin olive oil	1	teaspoon whole black peppercorns
¼	cup canola oil		
3	cloves garlic, cracked	¼	teaspoon red-pepper flakes, optional
3	strips orange zest, 2" × ½"		
6	sprigs thyme	12	ounces mixed olives
1	tablespoon rosemary leaves		

1. In a medium nonreactive saucepan, combine the oils, garlic, zest, thyme, rosemary, peppercorns, and pepper flakes if using. Set over medium heat until bubbles form a ring around the sides of the pot. Mix in the olives, reduce the heat to low, and simmer for 10 minutes to bring out the flavors in the garlic, zest, and herbs. Set aside for 2 hours.

2. Cover and refrigerate the olives and marinade for 24 hours, or up to 5 days. To serve, place the olives, garlic, and orange strips in a serving bowl. Pour on some of the oil from the marinade, reserving the rest to drizzle over vegetables or serve with bread. Discard the remaining solids. The olives keep well, sealed in a container in the refrigerator, for up to 2 weeks.

Makes about 2 cups, 12 servings

Per serving: 181 calories, 19 g fat, 2 g saturated fat, 0 g protein, 3 g carbohydrates, 1 g fiber

BLACK BEAN
AND NECTARINE SALSA

I like adding this Cal-Mex combination of fruit and beans to the usual salsa ingredients. Serrano chile pepper provides heat and a pronounced floral note. Serve the salsa with pork chops or grilled salmon as well as with tortilla chips.

1	(15-ounce) can black beans, drained	⅓	cup finely chopped red onion
1	nectarine, chopped, about 1 cup	¼	cup chopped cilantro leaves
1	tomato, seeded and finely chopped, about 1 cup	½	teaspoon grated orange zest
1	serrano chile pepper, seeded and finely chopped	1	tablespoon fresh lime juice
			Salt and freshly ground pepper

In a mixing bowl, combine the beans, nectarine, tomato, chile, onion, cilantro, zest, and lime juice. Toss salsa with a fork to mix. Season to taste with salt and pepper.

Makes 3 cups

Per serving (¼ cup): 46 calories, 0 g fat, 0 g saturated fat, 2 g protein, 10 g carbohydrates, 3 g fiber

SMOKED SALMON AND GOAT CHEESE CROSTINI WITH FENNEL GREMOLATA

Smoked salmon goes splendidly with mild fresh goat cheese and my version of gremolata, which combines lemon zest, shallots, dill, and fennel. For a more elegant presentation, if you wish, use slices of black bread instead of the crostini. The extra gremolata goes well with a turkey burger or lamb chops.

4	slices (½" thick) whole wheat Italian bread	¼	teaspoon grated lemon zest
½	cup finely chopped fennel bulb	1	teaspoon fresh lemon juice
2	tablespoons finely chopped scallions, green parts only		Salt and freshly ground pepper
1	tablespoon chopped dill leaves	4	teaspoons goat cheese
1	tablespoon finely chopped shallot	4	thin slices (about 2 ounces) top-quality smoked salmon

1. For the crostini, grill or toast the bread.

2. In a small bowl, combine the fennel, scallions, dill, shallots, zest, and lemon juice. Season to taste with salt and pepper.

3. Spread the cheese to thinly cover each crostini. Arrange one slice of the salmon over the cheese. Spoon one-quarter of the gremolata onto each crostini. Serve immediately.

Makes 4

Per crostini: 117 calories, 4 g fat, 2 g saturated fat, 8 g protein, 14 g carbohydrates, 2 g fiber

SALMON-STUFFED EGGS

● BEST INGREDIENT

Canned red salmon has more flavor than pink.

Chefs use egg yolks to help make dishes creamy. Using this technique, I blend hard-cooked yolk into the filling for these deviled eggs so less mayonnaise is needed to make it smooth and moist.

4	large eggs, hard-cooked and cooled	1	tablespoon minced red onion
½	cup (half a 7-ounce can), skinless, boneless red salmon	1	large pitted green olive, finely chopped
2	tablespoons minced celery	2	teaspoons reduced-fat mayonnaise
1	tablespoon finely chopped flat-leaf parsley	⅛	teaspoon curry powder
			Salt and freshly ground pepper

1. With a sharp knife, halve the eggs lengthwise. Gently remove the yolks and place in a mixing bowl. Add the salmon, celery, parsley, onion, olive, mayonnaise, and curry powder. With a fork, mix until well blended. Season to taste with salt and pepper.

2. Divide the filling into 8 portions. Roll each into a ball and set into the hollow of an egg white half. Cover and refrigerate for at least 2 hours or as long as 24 hours.

Makes 8 egg halves

Per egg half: 62 calories, 14 g fat, 1 g saturated fat, 7 g protein, 1 g carbohydrates, 0 g fiber

CHINESE TEA EGGS

● **BEST TECHNIQUE**

Tapping the shells of the hard-cooked eggs lets the dark liquid seep through all the cracks, creating a lovely marbled pattern on the whites.

● **BEST INGREDIENT**

Constant Comment from Bigelow is a nicely spiced black tea.

Hard-cooked eggs simmered in tea and soy sauce may sound odd but it gives these eggs the cinnamon and pepper flavors of a cup of chai, which tastes quite appealing. Served in China as a snack, these eggs are also excellent for breakfast and picnics.

4	large eggs	3"	cinnamon stick
3	bags spiced black tea	½	star anise
	(see Best Ingredient, left)	4	large Boston lettuce leaves,
2	bags black tea		optional
1	tablespoon reduced-sodium soy sauce		

1. Hard cook the eggs in a pot just large enough to hold them in one layer. Drain and cool under cold running water. Using the back of a tablespoon, crack the eggs all over but do not peel.

2. Return the eggs to the pot, making sure they fit in one layer. Open the 5 tea bags and sprinkle their contents over the eggs. Add the soy sauce, cinnamon stick and star anise. Pour in 5 cups cold water, which should cover the eggs with 1¼". Bring to a boil, reduce the heat, and simmer gently for 1 hour.

3. Drain the eggs and peel immediately. Let them cool to room temperature and serve whole in a small bowl, or halved and arranged cut-side down on a serving plate lined with the lettuce.

Makes 4

Per egg: 74 calories, 5 g fat, 2 g saturated fat, 7 g protein, 1 g carbohydrates, 0 g fiber

BLACK OLIVE CAVIAR IN ENDIVE

Guests will think you hired a caterer when you serve this unexpected finger food. Inspired by tapenade, the Mediterranean olive spread, this chunky version blends the taste of three kinds of olives and finishes with a buzz of hot chili paste. It is also good served on whole wheat crackers.

1	(5¾-ounce) can pitted ripe olives, drained	2	heads Belgian endive
¼	cup pitted kalamata olives	1½	tablespoons reduced-fat sour cream
¼	cup pitted Niçoise olives	1	tablespoon finely minced shallots
1	teaspoon balsamic vinegar		
½	teaspoon Chinese chili paste with garlic	1	tablespoon finely chopped chives
¼	teaspoon freshly ground pepper	1–2	teaspoons very finely chopped kumquat or orange zest

1. Whirl the ripe olives in a mini food processor until they are mostly finely chopped. Transfer to a mixing bowl. Chop the kalamata and Niçoise olives and add to the ripe olives. Mix in the vinegar, chili paste, and pepper. Makes 1 cup caviar.

2. Cut the bottoms off the endives and separate the leaves. Set aside 18 large and medium leaves and reserve the rest for another use.

3. Arrange the endive leaves on a serving platter. Place 2 teaspoons of the caviar near the base of each leaf. Drop ¼ teaspoon of the sour cream on top of the caviar. Sprinkle on a pinch of shallots, then some chives. Add a few bits of zest. Serve immediately.

Makes 18 stuffed leaves

Per stuffed leaf: 26 calories, 2 g fat, 0 g saturated fat, 0 g protein, 1 g carbohydrates, 0 g fiber

● **BEST TECHNIQUE**

To prevent discoloring, refrigerate the separated endive leaves in a bowl of cold water with the juice of ¼ lemon added. Gently dry well before serving.

● **BEST INGREDIENT**

Most canned ripe olives are processed with ferrous gluconate to preserve their color; those from the Santa Barbara Olive Company are not.

CITRUS-MARINATED SHRIMP

● **ANOTHER WAY**

Serve the shrimp on a plate as a light first course or with toothpicks as hors d'oeuvres.

Spanish and Caribbean cooks make escabeche as a way to preserve seafood by first cooking it, then lightly pickling it in wine, vinegar, and olive oil. Here, I substitute citrus juice for the vinegar and add oil just to cover the shrimp.

¾	pound medium (31–40 count) unpeeled shrimp	2	small red onions, halved and thinly sliced
¾	cup fresh orange juice	2	bay leaves
½	cup extra-virgin olive oil	2	cloves garlic, halved lengthwise
¼	cup fresh lemon juice	1	teaspoon black peppercorns
¼	cup dry white wine	⅛	teaspoon red pepper flakes
1	large lemon, cut into 10 very thin slices	8	leaves Boston lettuce
		¼	cup oil-cured black olives

1. Add the shrimp to boiling water, reduce the heat, and simmer until they turn bright red and curl, about 2 minutes. Drain, peel, and devein the shrimp, leaving on the tail. Place in a mixing bowl.

2. In a medium nonreactive saucepan, combine the orange juice, oil, lemon juice, wine, 6 of the lemon slices, onions, the bay leaves, garlic, peppercorns, and red pepper. Bring to a boil over medium heat, then pour the hot mixture over the shrimp. Let cool to room temperature, cover and refrigerate for 24 hours.

3. Bring the marinated shrimp to room temperature. Lift the shrimp and half the onions from the marinade and set aside. For a first course, line each of 4 plates with 2 lettuce leaves. Add one-quarter of the shrimp, an uncooked lemon slice, some onions and olives. For an hors d'oeuvre, line a platter with the lettuce. Top with the shrimp. Arrange the marinated onions, uncooked lemon slices, and the olives around the shrimp.

Makes 4 first-course servings or 8 hors d'oeuvre servings

Per first-course serving: 226 calories, 10 g fat, 1 g saturated fat, 19 g protein, 14 g carbohydrates, 2 g fiber

GINGER CHICKEN MEATBALLS

Fresh ginger plus a maple-soy-sesame glaze makes these oval meatballs a pleasantly pungent appetizer. A touch of tofu blended into the chicken makes them amazingly light and juicy.

1	pound ground chicken breast	3	tablespoons reduced-sodium soy sauce
2	tablespoons pureed soft silken tofu	1	teaspoon canola oil
2	teaspoons grated fresh ginger	1	tablespoon maple syrup
½	teaspoon salt	½	teaspoon toasted sesame oil
½	teaspoon freshly ground pepper		
2	tablespoons mirin (see Best Ingredient, left)		

1. In a mixing bowl, combine the chicken, tofu, ginger, salt, and pepper, mixing with a fork until well blended. Form the mixture into 18 oval patties, each 2" × 1½" × ½", and place on a plate. With a sharp knife, draw 2 diagonal parallel lines across the top of each patty. If desired, cover with plastic wrap and refrigerate for up to 4 hours.

2. In a deep medium skillet, combine the mirin, soy sauce, canola oil, and 1½ cups water. Cook over medium-high heat until bubbles rise. Add the meatballs, scored side up, in one layer and simmer gently for 10 minutes. Turn and cook until the meatballs are no longer pink in the center, 3 to 5 minutes. Transfer the meatballs to a heatproof platter. Cover loosely with foil to keep warm. Cook the patties in 2 batches if necessary.

3. Strain the cooking liquid into a small saucepan. Add the maple syrup and sesame oil. Over medium-high heat, boil the liquid until it is syrupy, about 5 minutes. Spoon enough liquid over the meatballs to glaze them. Pass the remaining glaze as a dipping sauce.

Makes 18

Per meatball: 44 calories, 2.5 g fat, 1 g saturated fat, 4 g protein, 1 g carbohydrates, 0 g fiber

- **BEST TECHNIQUE**

Cover the leftover tofu with cold water and refrigerate for up to 5 days.

- **ANOTHER WAY**

Serve several Ginger Chicken Meatballs as a main course, accompanied by steamed broccoli.

- **BEST INGREDIENT**

Mirin is a sweet rice wine available in natural food stores, Japanese markets, and the Asian or natural foods section of large supermarkets. Alternatively, use 1 tablespoon sake and 1 tablespoon sugar.

SPANISH SMOKED ALMONDS

The Internet makes a world of ethnic ingredients accessible. To compete, now more local food stores also offer imported spices, like the smoked Spanish paprika that gives these almonds intense taste and a deep, earthy color, and Mexican oregano.

● **BEST INGREDIENT**

Mildly hot Turkish Marash pepper flakes have a pleasant, roasted flavor. Many Web sites, including www.zingermans.com, sell them, as well as smoked and sweet or hot Spanish paprika.

1	cup (4–5 ounces) blanched whole almonds
½	teaspoon fine sea salt
½	teaspoon smoked Spanish paprika

1	teaspoon dried Mexican oregano, optional
½–1	teaspoon red-pepper flakes, preferably Turkish Marash
½	teaspoon extra-virgin olive oil

1. Preheat the oven to 350°F.

2. Spread the almonds on a baking sheet and roast for 5 minutes. Stir and continue roasting until lightly colored, 5 minutes longer. Transfer to a small mixing bowl.

3. Sprinkle the salt, paprika, oregano (if using), pepper flakes, and oil over the nuts. Using a fork, toss for 1 minute, or until they are coated evenly and are pale red. Cool to room temperature. Store the almonds overnight in an air-tight container to allow the flavors to mellow. The almonds keep for 5 days, tightly sealed in the refrigerator, after which their flavor fades.

Makes 1 cup, 6 servings

Per serving (2½ tablespoons): 145 calories, 13 g fat, 1 g saturated fat, 5 g protein, 5 g carbohydrates, 3 g fiber

CURRIED CHICKPEAS

● **ANOTHER WAY**

You can also use these seasoned chickpeas like croutons in soup or sprinkle on salads.

● **BEST TECHNIQUE**

When the oil is properly hot, these chickpeas absorb less than 1 tablespoon oil. Measure the oil before and after frying to prove this to yourself.

The dried chickpeas Southern Italians munch on inspired this spicy snack. Firm outside but still creamy inside, they are equally good made with or without salt. To avoid spattering when these chickpeas are fried, they must be very dry.

1	(15-ounce) can chickpeas, rinsed and well drained	½	teaspoon salt, optional
		¼	teaspoon ground ginger
¾	cup canola oil	¼	teaspoon lemon pepper
1	teaspoon curry powder	⅛	teaspoon ground fennel

1. Cover a baking sheet with a double layer of paper towels. Spread the chickpeas in one layer on the towels, picking out and discarding any loose skins or crushed chickpeas. Let the chickpeas sit for 30 minutes. Change the towels, spread the chickpeas out again and dry for 30 minutes longer. Transfer the chickpeas to a bowl. Cover the baking sheet with a triple layer of paper towels and set aside.

2. In a wok with a long handle, heat the oil over medium-high heat until it registers 340°F on a frying thermometer or shimmers in the pan. Wear long, heat-proof mitts while frying the chickpeas and please be careful. Add the chickpeas to the wok, standing back to avoid any spattering. Fry the chickpeas, shaking the wok while keeping the chickpeas moving with a stir-fry paddle, until golden, 3 to 4 minutes. Using a slotted spoon, scoop them out and spread on the prepared baking sheet to drain.

3. Transfer the chickpeas to a mixing bowl. Add the curry powder, salt if using, ginger, lemon pepper, and fennel. Toss with a fork until the chickpeas are well coated. Serve warm or at room temperature.

Makes 8 servings

Per serving: 70 calories, 5 g fat, 0 g saturated fat, 2 g protein, 5 g carbohydrates, 2 g fiber

CHOCOLATE-GLAZED PEANUTS

A light coating of cocoa and spices add flavors that make this bar snack disappear quickly. Make these nuts a day ahead to give the flavors time to meld, but be forewarned—you may have to make a double batch so enough is left to serve after you keep sneaking tastes.

● **BEST INGREDIENT**

Organic corn syrup is made from non–genetically modified corn. It is simple rather than high fructose, so its effect on blood sugar may be less extreme.

1	tablespoon unsalted butter	½	teaspoon ground cinnamon
1	tablespoon organic light corn syrup	½	teaspoon ground cumin
½	teaspoon Dutch-process cocoa powder	½	teaspoon salt
		1	cup unsalted dry roasted peanuts

1. Preheat the oven to 300°F. Line a baking sheet with foil and coat the foil lightly with cooking spray. Set aside.

2. In a small skillet, melt the butter over medium heat. Add the corn syrup and 2 teaspoons water. Mix in the cocoa, cinnamon, cumin, and salt. Bring the mixture to a boil. Off the heat, add the peanuts. Using a wooden spoon, mix and turn the nuts in the glaze for 1 minute to coat them well.

3. Spread the nuts in one layer on the prepared baking sheet. Using 2 forks, separate the nuts as much as possible.

4. Roast the nuts for 10 minutes. Stir and turn them. Bake for 5 minutes and stir again. Bake 5 minutes longer, or until the glaze is mahogany color and the nuts are golden. Slide the foil onto a rack to cool the nuts completely. When the glaze is hard, break the nuts apart to separate them. These nuts will keep in an airtight container for up to 5 days.

Makes 1½ cups, 12 servings

Per serving (2 tablespoons): 85 calories, 7 g fat, 2 g saturated fat, 3 g protein, 4 g carbohydrates, 1 g fiber

CHAPTER THREE
SOUPS

[**A TOMATO SOUP TRIO**
Roasted Tomato Soup 94
Peanut Tomato Soup 96
Manhattan Tuna Chowder 97]

20-Minute Vegetable Soup 93, *Sweet Potato and Shrimp Chowder* 98, *Pear and Root Vegetable Soup* 99,

Red Lentil and Apricot Soup 100, *Red Bean and Walnut Soup* 102, *BBQ Bean Soup* 103,

Tuscan Minestrone with Butternut Squash and Farro 104, *Greens Gumbo with Black-Eyed Peas* 106,

Russian Cabbage and Apple Soup 108, *Wild Mushroom-Barley Soup* 110, *Wild Mushroom Broth* 111,

Beef and Buckwheat Soup 112, *Asian Chicken and Pineapple Soup* 114, *Roasted Red Pepper Gazpacho* 117,

Iced Melon Soup 118, *Black Bean and Two-Berry Soup* 119, *Souped-Up Chicken Broth* 120

20-MINUTE VEGETABLE SOUP

When you have no time to shop or even to cut up vegetables already in your fridge, this soup is a stealthy way to eat your veggies. All its vegetables, except for the potato and onion, go right from the freezer or can into the pot, letting you sit down to a steaming bowl of homemade soup in 20 minutes. And every bowl provides 2½ servings of vegetables and a serving of beans.

● **FOOD FACT**

Yellow-fleshed potatoes contain 50 percent more vitamin C than those with white flesh.

● **ANOTHER WAY**

Use vegetable broth if you prefer a vegetarian soup.

1	tablespoon extra-virgin olive oil		½	cup frozen shelled edamame
1	medium red onion, chopped		½	cup frozen bell pepper strips
3	cups fat-free, reduced-sodium chicken broth		½	cup frozen cut green beans
1	medium yellow-fleshed potato, peeled and cut into ½" pieces		1	teaspoon dried oregano, dried thyme, or finely chopped fresh rosemary
1	(15-ounce) can kidney beans, drained			Pinch of red-pepper flakes
1	cup frozen broccoli florets			Salt and freshly ground pepper
½	cup frozen corn kernels		¼	cup grated Parmesan cheese

1. In a medium Dutch oven or large, heavy saucepan, heat the oil over medium-high heat. Add the onion and sauté until transparent, 4 minutes.

2. Add the broth. When the liquid boils, add the potato. Reduce the heat, and simmer for 3 minutes. Add the kidney beans, broccoli, corn, edamame, bell pepper, green beans, herb, and pepper flakes. Cook until the potato is tender and the vegetables are crisp-tender, 5 minutes. Season to taste with salt and pepper. Divide the soup among 4 wide soup bowls and serve, accompanied by the grated cheese.

Makes 4 servings

Per serving: 269 calories, 6 g fat, 1 g saturated fat, 15 g protein, 38 g carbohydrates, 11 g fiber

A Tomato Soup Trio

Tomato soup is so elemental that limiting the selection here to just three was difficult. Roasted Tomato Soup is fragrant with coriander, cumin, ginger, and lime. Velvety Peanut Tomato Soup tastes like an extra-rich version of old-fashioned cream of tomato soup. Zesty Manhattan Tuna Chowder, studded with fresh fish, is hearty in winter but also a perfect summertime soup supper.

ROASTED TOMATO SOUP

● **FOOD FACT**

Eating cooked tomatoes with some fat helps your body absorb their lycopene.

If you like tomatoes and garlic, you will love the way roasting them deepens their flavor in this intense soup. Its seasonings are a blend of spices used often in Moroccan cooking.

6	medium beefsteak-type tomatoes (2½–3 pounds), halved and seeded	1	teaspoon ground cumin
		½	teaspoon ground coriander
		¼	teaspoon ground ginger
4	large cloves garlic, unpeeled	1	cup fat-free, reduced-sodium chicken broth, or vegetable broth
1	small Spanish onion, halved and cut into ½" slices, divided		
2	tablespoons extra-virgin olive oil, divided		Salt and freshly ground pepper
		1	teaspoon grated lime zest

1. Preheat the oven to 400°F.

2. Place the tomatoes, garlic, and half of the sliced onion on a baking pan with sides. Using 1 tablespoon of the oil, coat the vegetables. Set the tomatoes cut side up. Roast until the tomato tops are golden, about 40 minutes.

3. When the tomatoes are cool enough to handle, over a large bowl, pull off their skins. Discard the skins, tear the tomato flesh into chunks, and drop into the bowl. Coarsely chop the roasted onion and add to the tomatoes. Squeeze

the garlic from the cloves into the bowl. Pour in all the juices from the baking pan. Set the vegetables aside.

4. In a Dutch oven or large saucepan, heat the remaining 1 tablespoon oil over medium-high heat. Sauté the remaining onion until it is soft, about 5 minutes. Mix in the cumin, coriander, and ginger. Cook until the spices are fragrant, 30 to 60 seconds. Add the contents of the bowl to the pot. Pour in the broth. Bring the mixture to a boil, reduce the heat, and simmer the soup, covered, until the onions are soft, 20 to 25 minutes. Let the soup sit, uncovered, to cool slightly.

5. Puree the soup in a blender or using an immersion blender, until it is orange and almost smooth. Divide the soup among 4 deep soup bowls. Garnish with the lime zest and serve. Or, cool the soup and refrigerate it, covered, for up to 2 days. Reheat the soup, covered, in a pot over medium heat, garnish, and serve.

Makes 4 servings

Per serving: 130 calories, 8 g fat, 1 g saturated fat, 4 g protein, 14 g carbohydrates, 4 g fiber

PEANUT TOMATO SOUP

● **ANOTHER WAY**

Add red-pepper flakes or mix in some chopped steamed broccoli.

To transform this soup into a main dish as served in Bénin, add thick fish fillets, chicken breast, or tofu steaks along with the tomato mixture during Step 2. Simmer until they are almost cooked through, then remove carefully. Return to the sauce after adding the peanut butter.

● **FOOD FACT**

Peanut butter provides protein and resveratrol, the same antioxidant found in red wine.

● **BEST INGREDIENT**

Agave is a honey-like natural sweetener made from cactus.

When singer Angelique Kidjo introduced me to a West African dish with a sauce resembling classic tomato soup blended with creamy peanut butter, I realized the sauce on its own would make a great soup. To add some crunch, garnish with a few plantain chips if desired.

2	pounds beefsteak-type tomatoes, seeded and cut into 1" chunks	2	tablespoons tomato paste
1	medium onion, diced	1	teaspoon ground coriander
2	tablespoons fruity extra-virgin olive oil	½	teaspoon dried marjoram
4	teaspoons grated fresh ginger	1	tablespoon agave syrup, or 1–2 teaspoons sugar
2	cloves garlic, grated	¼	cup reduced-fat (2%) milk, optional
½	cup natural smooth peanut butter		Salt and freshly ground pepper

1. Whirl the tomatoes and onion in a food processor, to a pulpy puree. There should be about 4 cups. Set aside.

2. In a large saucepan, heat the oil over medium-high heat. Add the ginger and garlic and cook, stirring constantly and scraping up what sticks, until aromatic and lightly colored, about 1 minute. Add the tomato-onion mixture. When it boils, reduce the heat and simmer, stirring occasionally, until the soup is orange-red and plops from a spoon, about 10 minutes.

3. Off the heat, whisk in the peanut butter, tomato paste, coriander, marjoram, and syrup or sugar. Add the milk, if using. Season to taste with salt and pepper. Return to the heat. Cook until hot but not bubbling. Divide the soup among 4 small bowls and serve.

Makes 4 servings

Per serving: 341 calories, 24 g fat, 3 g saturated fat, 10 g protein, 25 g carbohydrates, 6 g fiber

MANHATTAN TUNA CHOWDER

I grew up in Manhattan, so for me the best clam chowder is red and seasoned liberally with thyme and black pepper. Recently, at a local fish store I saw chowder made with fresh tuna, a smart way to enjoy this fish rich in omega-3s.

¾	pound fresh albacore or yellowfin tuna, cut into ¾" cubes	1	(14½-ounce) can diced tomatoes	
2	cups fat-free, reduced-sodium chicken broth	1	(8-ounce) bottle clam juice	
1	tablespoon fruity extra-virgin olive oil	1	medium boiling potato, peeled and cut into ¾" cubes	
1	medium onion, diced	2	teaspoons chili powder	
1	rib celery, thinly sliced	1	teaspoon dried thyme	
1	small green bell pepper, diced	1	large bay leaf	
¼	cup flat-leaf parsley, chopped	1	teaspoon sugar	
		¼	teaspoon freshly ground pepper	
			Salt	

1. In a medium saucepan over medium heat, combine the tuna and broth. Cook until small bubbles begin to rise, then simmer gently until the fish is opaque in the center, about 5 minutes. With a slotted spoon, remove the tuna and set aside. Pour 1 cup of the broth through a fine strainer into a bowl, and save the rest.

2. In a large saucepan, heat the oil over medium-high heat. Add the onion, celery, and green pepper, and sauté until the onion is translucent, 4 minutes. Add the parsley, tomatoes with their liquid, clam juice, potato, chili powder, thyme, bay leaf, sugar, pepper, and reserved broth. Simmer, uncovered, until the potatoes are tender, 15 minutes.

3. Discard the bay leaf. Add the tuna. Season to taste with salt. When the fish is heated through, divide the chowder among 4 wide, shallow soup bowls.

Makes 4 servings

Per serving: 190 calories, 4 g fat, 1 g saturated fat, 24 g protein, 12 g carbohydrates, 3 g fiber

● BEST TECHNIQUE

Gently poaching the tuna then adding it when the soup is almost done keeps the fish tender and helps protect its heat-sensitive omega-3s. Using chicken broth prevents a fishy flavor.

● FOOD FACT

Small albacore tuna that are line caught off Alaska from July through September contain the lowest levels of mercury and the highest levels of essential fatty acids. Web sites, like www.vitalchoice.com, sell it frozen, making it available year-round.

SWEET POTATO
AND SHRIMP CHOWDER

● BEST INGREDIENT

Spanish chorizo is pork sausage reddened by paprika. Available *picante* (hot) with dried chiles or *dulce* (sweet/mild), it comes in firm links that can be sliced. It is available preservative-free. Mexican chorizo, made with soft ground pork, is the kind most often scrambled with eggs in a breakfast burrito.

● FOOD FACT

Shrimp is a good source of copper, a mineral important for bone health.

Traditional in its combination of seafood, potato, and flavorful pork, this colorful New England–style chowder is made with light coconut milk instead of milk or cream. This keeps the soup rich but dairy-free and lower in calories.

2	teaspoons canola oil
½	link Spanish chorizo sausage (mild or hot), thinly sliced
1	medium green bell pepper, diced
1	medium onion, diced
1	medium orange-fleshed sweet potato, peeled and cut into ¾" cubes
2½	cups fat-free, reduced-sodium chicken broth
4	sprigs fresh thyme
1	bay leaf
1	cup steamed broccoli florets
12	medium (31–40 count) shrimp, peeled and deveined
1	cup light coconut milk
	Salt and freshly ground pepper, preferably white

1. In a large, deep saucepan, heat the oil over medium-high heat. Add the sausage and sauté until lightly browned, 2 minutes. With a slotted spoon, remove the sausage and set aside.

2. Add the green pepper, onion, and sweet potato to the pot. Sauté until the onion is soft, 5 to 6 minutes. Add the broth, thyme, and bay leaf. Bring the liquid to a boil, reduce the heat, and simmer until the potato is almost tender, about 15 minutes. Add the broccoli and return the chorizo to the pot. Cook until they are heated through, 3 minutes.

3. Add the shrimp and coconut milk. Cook until the shrimp are curled and opaque, about 3 minutes. Remove the thyme and bay leaf and discard. Season to taste with salt and pepper. Serve immediately.

Makes 4 servings

Per serving: 203 calories, 10 g fat, 4 g saturated fat, 11 g protein, 19 g carbohydrates, 3 g fiber

PEAR AND ROOT VEGETABLE SOUP

When the temperature drops, serve this warming blend of pear, sweet potato, and other root vegetables. Even kids love its cinnamon flavor. Its crushed vegetable chip garnish is a conversation stopper.

4	teaspoons unsalted butter	1	cup fat-free, reduced-sodium chicken broth
1	medium onion, chopped		
1	medium carrot, chopped	½	teaspoon ground cinnamon
½	small celeriac, peeled and diced	⅛	teaspoon freshly grated nutmeg
1	medium parsnip, peeled and sliced	½	cup reduced-fat (2%) milk
			Salt and freshly ground pepper
1	Bosc pear, peeled and diced	1	cup root vegetable chips
1	medium orange-fleshed sweet potato, peeled and diced		

● **ANOTHER WAY**

In warm weather, use orange juice in place of the milk and serve the soup slightly chilled.

● **FOOD FACT**

A pear contains as much fiber as a bowl of oatmeal.

1. In a medium Dutch oven or large saucepan, melt the butter over medium heat. Add the onion, carrot, celeriac, and parsnip and sauté until the onion is soft, about 8 minutes.

2. Add the pear and sweet potato, broth, cinnamon, and nutmeg. Pour in 2 cups water. When the liquid boils, reduce the heat, cover, and simmer until the vegetables are soft, 20 minutes. Uncover and let the soup cool slightly.

3. Puree the soup until smooth in a blender or use an immersion blender. Blend in the milk. Season to taste with salt and pepper.

4. Divide the soup among 4 deep bowls. Lightly crush the vegetable chips and sprinkle onto the soup just before serving.

Makes 4 servings

Per serving: 184 calories, 5 g fat, 2 g saturated fat, 4 g protein, 32 g carbohydrates, 6 g fiber

RED LENTIL AND APRICOT SOUP

As they cook, red lentils quickly fall apart, making a perfect soup. Dried apricots and chopped tomato add body and tangy flavor. I give this fat-free soup an Indian flourish by swirling in cumin seeds sizzled briefly in hot oil. You can use additional chopped cilantro, if you prefer.

● **GARAM MASALA: AN INDIAN SPICE BLEND IN YOUR PANTRY**

Now sold at many supermarkets, this warm blend is easy to assemble since most of its ingredients are probably in your spice rack right now. Indian cooks make garam masala by grinding whole spices combined to their personal taste. I simply make 2 tablespoons by combining these ground spices: 1¼ teaspoons cardamom, 1¼ teaspoons black pepper, 1¼ teaspoons cumin, 1¼ teaspoons coriander, ½ teaspoon cinnamon, ¼ teaspoon cloves, and ¼ teaspoon nutmeg. Also use this seasoning on chicken, salmon, and with beans and lentils.

1	cup red lentils, picked over and rinsed	½	teaspoon ground turmeric
1	cup finely chopped onion	⅓	cup cilantro leaves, chopped
1	cup canned diced tomatoes		Salt and freshly ground pepper
½	cup chopped Turkish apricots	1	tablespoon canola oil
2	teaspoons grated fresh ginger	1	teaspoon whole cumin seeds
1	clove garlic, minced	1	teaspoon pomegranate molasses or pomegranate juice concentrate
1	teaspoon garam masala		

1. In a large deep saucepan, combine the lentils, onion, tomatoes with their liquid, apricots, ginger, garlic, garam masala, and turmeric. Add 4 cups water. Bring to a boil, reduce the heat, cover, and simmer until the lentils are soft, about 30 minutes. Mix in the cilantro. Season to taste with salt and pepper.

2. Meanwhile, heat the oil in a small saucepan over medium-high heat. Mix in the cumin and cook, stirring, until the oil is bubbling and the seeds start to darken in color, 2 minutes. Immediately, off the heat, mix in the pomegranate molasses or concentrate. Take care, as it will spatter.

3. Divide the soup among 4 deep soup bowls. Drizzle on the cumin mixture and serve.

Makes 4 servings

Per serving: 267 calories, 4 g fat, 0 g saturated fat, 14 g protein, 44 g carbohydrates, 4 g fiber

RED BEAN AND WALNUT SOUP

● **ANOTHER WAY**

Boost the antioxidant content of this soup even higher by adding ¼ teaspoon ground turmeric, if desired.

● **BEST TECHNIQUE**

Adding the herbs and garlic toward the end of the cooking time helps these antioxidant-rich ingredients deliver fullest benefits.

● **FOOD FACT**

Nuts, onions, and beans together provide this soup with over 10 grams of fiber per serving.

Pureed beans and pomegranate juice give this soup a rosy color. Ground walnuts are a familiar thickener in Georgia (the one near Russia). To best enjoy its layered flavors, serve this soup very warm rather than hot.

½	cup walnuts	½	cup pomegranate juice
2	cups fat-free, reduced-sodium chicken broth	3	tablespoons chopped cilantro leaves
2	(15-ounce) cans small red beans, drained, divided	3	tablespoons chopped flat-leaf parsley
1	tablespoon extra-virgin olive oil	1	large clove garlic, minced
1	medium onion, finely chopped		Salt and freshly ground pepper

1. In a blender or mini food processor, chop the nuts until they resemble almond flour. Set aside.

2. In a small Dutch oven or large saucepan, cook the broth with half of the beans, covered, until the beans are very soft, 15 minutes. Puree the soup until smooth in a blender or using an immersion blender. (If using a blender, return the soup to the pot.)

3. Meanwhile, heat the oil in a small skillet over medium-high heat. Add the onion and sauté until golden, 5 to 6 minutes.

4. Add the onion mixture, ground nuts, remaining beans, pomegranate juice, cilantro, parsley, and garlic to the soup. Season to taste with salt and pepper. Let the soup sit for 15 minutes to let its flavors meld, then reheat over medium heat. Divide it among 4 deep soup bowls and serve immediately.

Makes 4 servings

Per serving: 270 calories, 12 g fat, 1 g saturated fat, 11 g protein, 32 g carbohydrates, 8 g fiber

BBQ BEAN SOUP

A Texas chef showed me how to get kickin' good flavor in this bean soup which is ready in just 40 minutes. The secret is sweating the vegetables, then adding intensely flavored ingredients like the barbecue sauce and chile-spiked tomatoes. Collard greens enrich its nutrition and taste terrific with the beans.

1	tablespoon canola oil	1	(14-ounce) can diced tomatoes with jalapeño chile pepper
1	medium onion, chopped	1	(15-ounce) can kidney beans, drained
1	large rib celery, chopped		
1	medium green bell pepper, chopped	1	cup cooked chopped collard greens or 5 ounces (½ package) frozen chopped collards
2	cloves garlic, minced		
2	large or 3 medium chopped scallions, green and white parts	¼	cup barbecue sauce
			Salt and freshly ground pepper
4	cups cold water		

1. In a small Dutch oven or large saucepan, heat the oil over medium-high heat. Add the onion and celery and sauté until the onion is translucent, 4 minutes. Cover, reduce the heat to medium-low, and cook for 10 minutes to draw out the juices.

2. Increase the heat to medium-high. Mix in the green pepper, garlic, and scallions and cook until the vegetables are almost dry, 3 to 4 minutes.

3. Add the water, tomatoes, beans, greens, and barbecue sauce. Bring the liquid to a boil, reduce the heat to medium-low, and simmer until the green are tender, about 15 minutes. Season to taste with salt and pepper.

Makes 4 servings

Per serving: 201 calories, 4 g fat, 0 g saturated fat, 8 g protein, 33 g carbohydrates, 10 g fiber

TUSCAN MINESTRONE WITH BUTTERNUT SQUASH AND FARRO

● **BEST INGREDIENT**

Pancetta is an unsmoked bacon Italian cooks use to flavor dishes. Applegate Farms makes one that is preservative-free.

● **ANOTHER WAY**

The rind of Parmigiano-Reggiano cheese is totally edible. For extra flavor, toss a 3" square of it into the pot. When the soup is done, break up the soft rind and serve a piece in each bowl.

Italian cooks often use a battuto as the flavor base for soups, sauces, and stews. This combination of carrot, celery, onion, and pancetta, chopped almost to a paste then sautéed until golden, is the perfect start to this Tuscan-style soup. The recipe, which includes whole farro, an ancient form of wheat, makes enough to feed a crowd or serve for two meals.

½	cup dried farro
1	medium carrot, chopped
1	medium rib celery, chopped
1	small red onion, diced
½	ounce preservative-free pancetta, coarsely chopped
2	tablespoons extra-virgin olive oil
2	tablespoons chopped flat-leaf parsley
2	cups vegetable broth
1½	cups butternut squash, cut into ¾" cubes

1	cup chopped Swiss chard leaves
1	large plum tomato, seeded and diced
½	cup fresh green beans, cut into 1" pieces
1	teaspoon dried sage
1	(15-ounce) can cannellini beans, drained
	Grated Parmesan cheese
	Salt and freshly ground pepper

1. In a bowl, soak the farro in cold water to cover for 4 to 8 hours. Drain and set aside.

2. Whirl the carrot, celery, onion, and pancetta in a mini food processor until finely chopped.

3. In a small Dutch oven or large saucepan, heat the oil over medium-high heat. Add the battuto and sauté until golden, 3 minutes. Mix in the parsley.

4. Add the broth, squash, chard, tomato, green beans, sage, soaked farro, and 4 cups water. Bring the liquid to a boil, reduce the heat, and simmer, covered,

until the vegetables are al dente and the farro is almost soft, 20 minutes. Add the cannellini beans, cover, and cook until they are heated through, about 10 minutes. Season to taste with salt and pepper.

5. Divide the soup among shallow, wide soup bowls and pass grated Parmesan cheese on the side. Cool any remaining soup, and refrigerate for up to 4 days. Reheat covered.

Makes 8 servings

Per serving: 147 calories, 5 g fat, 1 g saturated fat, 4 g protein, 23 g carbohydrates, 5 g fiber

GREENS GUMBO
WITH BLACK-EYED PEAS

Creole gumbo z'herbes calls for at least seven greens. My version includes four. They look like a mountain of raw greens but cook down to just handfuls.

1	bunch collard greens, stems removed	1	cup drained canned tomatoes
1	bunch curly kale, stems removed	2	bay leaves
1	bunch Swiss chard, stems removed	2	whole cloves
1	(10-ounce) bag spinach, thick stems removed	2	teaspoons dried thyme
		½	teaspoon ground allspice
3	tablespoons canola oil		Cayenne pepper, to taste
1	large onion, chopped	½	teaspoon freshly ground pepper
1	cup chopped scallions, green and white parts	1	cup fresh or frozen corn kernels
		1	(15-ounce) can black-eyed peas, drained
1	rib celery, chopped	2	teaspoons cider vinegar
1	medium green bell pepper, diced		Salt
2	tablespoons long-grain white rice		

● FOOD FACT

Black-eyed peas are rich in magnesium, a mineral needed for strong bones and an active metabolism.

● ANOTHER WAY

Andouille sausage is a popular addition to this traditionally vegetarian dish.

I like this gumbo served over cooked long-grain rice.

1. In a large pot of boiling water, cook the collards and kale 5 minutes. Add the chard and spinach and cook 3 minutes longer. Drain, reserving 6 cups of the cooking liquid. When cool enough to handle, squeeze most of the moisture from the greens, chop them, and set aside.

2. In a large Dutch oven, heat the oil over medium-high heat. Add the onion, scallions, celery, and green pepper. Sauté until the onion is soft, 6 minutes. Add the greens, reserved cooking water, rice, tomatoes, bay leaves, cloves, thyme, allspice, cayenne, and pepper. Bring the liquid to a boil, reduce the heat, cover, and simmer for 30 minutes.

3. Add the corn and black-eyed peas. Cook, uncovered, until the greens are very tender, about 20 minutes. Mix in the vinegar and season to taste with salt.

Makes 6 servings

Per serving: 219 calories, 8 g fat, 1 g saturated fat, 9 g protein, 31 g carbohydrates, 8 g fiber

Onion Primer

Onions fall into two groups, storage and spring onions, based on when they are harvested.

STORAGE ONIONS: Includes most hard red, yellow, or white onions harvested in fall or winter.

- **Spanish:** Large, yellow, and mild.
- **New York Bold:** A dry, particularly pungent variety grown in New York State.
- **Pearl:** Less than 1" to 1¾" in diameter; pearls may be red, yellow, or white.
- **Boilers and creamers:** Mostly white and larger than pearls.

Select hard, dry onions with shiny, papery skin. Avoid sprouting, and soft, moldy, or wet spots. Keep in a dry, airy, cool place in one layer at least 4 weeks. Never refrigerate whole storage onions.

SPRING ONIONS: Includes the mild sweet onions mostly harvested from early spring through summer, and some types found mainly at farmers' markets.

Sweet onions: Their mild flavor comes from high water content and minerals in the soil. Harvested in the US, mainly March through June, look for Georgia Vidalias, Texas SuperSweets and 1015s, Arizona Grand Canyons, Hawaiian Mauis, Washington State Walla Wallas, California Sweet Imperials, and New Mexico Nu-Mexes. Keep for 2 weeks or more wrapped in newspaper and refrigerated, or knotted in legs of panty hose and hung at room temperature.

Bunching onions: Resemble giant scallions, with onion-size bulbs. Sold mostly at farmers' markets, they keep with green tops on for 1 week in the vegetable bin of the refrigerator.

Scallions (aka green onions): An immature onion with brush of roots at the tip and an erect green top. Avoid torn, bruised, limp or yellowed top, spongy whites. Store loosely wrapped in plastic for 3 to 4 days in the vegetable bin.

SHALLOTS: Has flavor between an onion and garlic and contains similar substances. Store like onions.

RUSSIAN CABBAGE AND APPLE SOUP

● BEST TECHNIQUE

To keep hands unstained, insert them into plastic sandwich bags when peeling and cutting beets. To protect your work surface, cover it with waxed paper.

● FOOD FACT

Folic acid in beets helps rid the body of homocysteine, an amino acid whose presence can signal heart disease.

● ANOTHER WAY

Russians sometimes put a whole hard-cooked egg in the bowl, turning this soup into a one-dish meal.

A recipe from a tea company inspired the addition of green tea to this ruby red soup. It adds a gentle smoky touch to the vegetable-crammed mélange. This soup tastes even better served the day after it is made. Slices of buttered whole grain black bread are the perfect accompaniment.

2	tablespoons fruity extra-virgin olive oil	1	tablespoon finely chopped rosemary leaves
½	medium head green cabbage, cut into ½" strips	½"	piece fresh ginger, cut into 2 slices
1	medium carrot, sliced	2	whole cloves
1	rib celery, sliced	1	small Granny Smith apple, peeled and diced
1	small parsnip, sliced		
6	cups cold water	1	medium yellow-fleshed potato, peeled and diced
1	medium beet, peeled and cut into 1½" × ½" pieces	1	cup strong brewed green tea
1	small red bell pepper, chopped		Juice of ½ lemon
1	medium beefsteak-type tomato, seeded and chopped		Salt and freshly ground pepper
		⅓	cup reduced-fat sour cream
1 or 2	large cloves garlic, chopped	⅓	cup chopped dill leaves

1. In a large Dutch oven, heat the oil over medium-high heat. Add the cabbage, carrot, celery, and parsnip. Cook until the cabbage is wilted and translucent, 4 minutes. Cover, reduce the heat to medium-low, and cook the vegetables gently until the cabbage just starts to brown, 8 minutes.

2. Add the water, beet, red pepper, tomato, garlic, rosemary, ginger, and cloves. Increase the heat until the liquid boils. Reduce the heat, cover, and simmer until the vegetables are al dente, 15 minutes.

3. Add the apple, potato, and tea. Cook, covered, until the potato is tender, 10 minutes. Add the lemon juice. Season to taste with salt and pepper. Allow to cool to room temperature.

4. Reheat the soup, covered, over medium heat. Ladle into 6 shallow, wide soup bowls. Add a dollop of sour cream and some dill to each bowl. Or, cover and refrigerate the cooled soup for up to 3 days before reheating and serving.

Makes 6 servings

Per serving: 155 calories, 7 g fat, 2 g saturated fat, 3 g protein, 22 g carbohydrates, 5 g fiber

WILD MUSHROOM-BARLEY SOUP

● **FOOD FACT**

Barley contains both soluble and insoluble fiber, just like oatmeal.

● **BEST INGREDIENT**

A fruity olive oil such as L'Estornell or Nunez de Prado, both from Spain, goes better with the butter than a pungent green one.

For this rustic soup, intensely flavored mushroom broth and a splash of wine add nice back notes. I like this meatless soup as is, but add dill or freshly grated Parmesan cheese, if you like.

1	tablespoon unsalted butter	1	large clove garlic, minced
2	tablespoons extra-virgin olive oil, divided	¼	cup dry vermouth or sherry
		⅓	cup pearl barley
8	ounces cremini mushrooms, sliced	4	cups Wild Mushroom Broth (page 111)
4	ounces shiitake mushrooms, sliced	1	medium potato, peeled and cut into ½" cubes
1	medium onion, finely chopped		Salt and freshly ground pepper
¼	cup finely chopped shallots		

1. In a deep, large saucepan, melt the butter with 1 tablespoon of the oil over medium-high heat. Add the mushrooms and sauté until they release their liquid and about half of it evaporates, about 8 minutes. Transfer the mushrooms to a bowl and set aside.

2. Add the remaining oil to the pot. Add the onion, shallots, and garlic and sauté until they are soft, 5 minutes. Add the vermouth or sherry and boil until it has evaporated, 4 minutes.

3. Mix in the barley, coating it with the oil in the vegetables. Add the mushroom broth and 2 cups water. Return the mushrooms to the pot. Bring the liquid to a boil, reduce the heat, cover, and simmer 15 minutes. Add the potato, cover, and cook until it is tender, 10 minutes. Season to taste with salt and pepper. Serve in wide, shallow soup bowls.

Makes 6 servings

Per serving: 156 calories, 5 g fat, 2 g saturated fat, 4 g protein, 22 g carbohydrates, 4 g fiber

WILD MUSHROOM BROTH

This profound broth adds concentrated flavor to Wild Mushroom-Barley Soup and miso soup. Also use it for cooking rice and other grains. Made with three kinds of mushrooms, the broth is complex enough to serve as a soup on its own, garnished with cooked wild rice and chopped scallions.

2	teaspoons extra-virgin olive oil	1	large rib celery, chopped
1	medium yellow onion, chopped	6	sprigs flat-leaf parsley
8–10	ounces white mushrooms, sliced	½	teaspoon whole peppercorns
¼	ounce dried shiitake mushrooms	10	cups cold water
¼	ounce dried porcini or cèpes mushrooms		

1. In a large saucepan, heat the oil over medium-high heat. Add the onion and sauté until well browned, 10 to 15 minutes. Add the white, shiitake, and porcini mushrooms, celery, parsley, peppercorns, and water. Bring the liquid to a boil, reduce the heat, and simmer for 40 minutes. Remove the pot from the heat and cover. Let steep for 1 hour to develop the flavor.

2. Strain the broth in a strainer or colander, pressing on the solids lightly to extract more of the liquid. Discard the solids. If not using immediately, cool and transfer the broth to a tightly sealed container. Refrigerate for up to 3 days, or freeze for up to 3 months.

Makes about 7 cups

Per serving (1 cup): 37 calories, 1 g fat, 0 g saturated fat, 1 g protein, 5 g carbohydrates, 1 g fiber

BEEF AND BUCKWHEAT SOUP

● **BEST TECHNIQUE**

Hot water added to the pot here helps burnt-on marinade come off easily. Add some baking soda, if necessary.

● **IT'S GLUTEN-FREE**

Contrary to its name, buckwheat is actually the seeds of a Russian herb, not wheat at all. If cooking for someone who is gluten-sensitive, replace the hoisin sauce with gluten-free soy sauce or hatcho miso.

Buckwheat makes this soup so thick it is almost a stew. When you sear the meat, its spicy marinade caramelizes, producing flavor that enriches the soup. This also creates an aroma that warms your home as the soup simmers.

MARINADE AND BEEF

2	tablespoons hoisin sauce
2	tablespoons red wine vinegar
3	cloves garlic, minced
1	teaspoon ground cumin
½	teaspoon salt
½	teaspoon freshly ground pepper
1	pound top round beef, cut into 1" cubes

SOUP

2	tablespoons canola oil, divided
1	cup diced onion
1	cup diced carrots
1	cup diced celery
½	cup diced parsnips
2	cups fat-free, reduced-sodium beef broth
4	sprigs fresh thyme or 1 teaspoon dried
1	teaspoon toasted sesame oil
½	cup whole buckwheat groats
	Salt and freshly ground pepper
4	tablespoons chopped flat-leaf parsley

1. **FOR THE BEEF AND MARINADE:** In a 1-quart resealable plastic bag, combine the hoisin sauce, vinegar, garlic, cumin, salt, and pepper. Add the meat, seal the bag, and massage to coat the pieces. Marinate at room temperature for 1 hour.

2. **FOR THE SOUP:** In a large Dutch oven, heat 1 tablespoon of the canola oil over medium-high heat. Add the marinated meat and brown on at least 2 sides, turning it with tongs and reducing the heat as needed to minimize burning. Transfer the browned meat to a plate and set aside. Add hot water to the pot and scrape up as much of the browned and burnt crust as possible, then wash out the pot.

3. In the clean pot, heat the remaining 1 tablespoon canola oil over medium-high heat. Add the onion and sauté until well browned, about 6 minutes. Mix in the carrots, celery, and parsnips and cook, stirring occasionally, until the vegetables look moist, 3 minutes.

4. Return the meat and any collected juices to the pot. Add the broth, thyme, and 4 cups water. When the liquid begins to boil, reduce the heat. Simmer until the meat is almost fork tender, 45 minutes. Using a large spoon, skim off the foam and fat that rise during the first 15 to 20 minutes.

5. In a small, heavy skillet, warm the sesame oil over medium heat. Stir in the buckwheat until coated, then add the buckwheat to the simmering soup. Cover and cook until the grain is tender but still holds its shape and the meat is tender, 10 to 15 minutes. Season to taste with salt and pepper. Divide among 4 wide soup bowls, sprinkle with parsley, and serve. Thin leftovers with beef broth as needed when reheating.

Makes 4 servings

Per serving: 361 calories, 12 g fat, 4 g saturated fat, 31 g protein, 31 g carbohydrates, 5 g fiber

ASIAN CHICKEN AND PINEAPPLE SOUP

As easy to prepare as a stir-fry, this chunky soup delivers sweet and sour Asian flavor. It is ready to serve in less than 15 minutes once the chicken has marinated. Omit the bean sprouts if you wish, but never the lime. Its flavor pulls the entire dish together.

MARINADE AND CHICKEN

2	teaspoons Asian fish sauce
½	teaspoon sugar
1	tablespoon chopped shallots
1	small clove garlic, minced
¼	teaspoon freshly ground pepper
½	pound boneless, skinless chicken breast

SOUP

2	tablespoons canola oil
1	medium onion, sliced vertically into thin crescents
1	large shallot, halved and thinly sliced vertically
1	large beefsteak-type tomato, cut into 16 wedges
4	ounces fresh pineapple, cut into ½" × ½" pieces
1	tablespoon sugar
3	tablespoons Asian fish sauce
	Salt and freshly ground pepper
1	cup bean sprouts
1	red chile pepper, thinly sliced crosswise
1	lime, cut into 4 wedges
	Cilantro leaves and chopped Thai or purple basil leaves

1. **FOR THE MARINADE AND CHICKEN:** In a resealable plastic bag, combine the fish sauce, sugar, shallots, garlic, and pepper. Cut the chicken with the grain into ½" strips. Cut each strip into ¾" pieces. Add the chicken to the marinade and massage the bag to coat the pieces evenly. Set aside at room temperature for 30 minutes. Remove the chicken from the marinade and pat dry. Discard the marinade.

(continued)

Called *nuoc nam* in Vietnam and *nam pla* in Thailand, fish sauce is the liquid exuded from small fish fermented with salt. Good fish sauce tastes nutty or like fine aged cheese. The best ones are made from anchovies, a fish rich in omega-3s, and are aged for up to 2 years.

Like soy sauce and Parmigiano-Reggiano cheese, fish sauce has *umami*, translated from Japanese as "delicious flavor" and sometimes called the fifth flavor. Besides these protein-rich fermented foods, others naturally rich in the glutamates that stimulate the sensation of umami include walnuts, tomatoes, and mushrooms.

2. **FOR THE SOUP:** In a large Dutch oven or other heavy pot, heat the oil over medium-high heat.

Stir-fry the chicken until it is cooked through, 4 to 5 minutes. With a slotted spoon, remove the chicken to a bowl and set aside.

3. In the same pot, stir-fry the onion and shallot until cooked and lightly browned on the edges, 1 minute. Add the tomato, pineapple, and sugar and stir-fry until the tomatoes soften slightly at the edges, 1 to 2 minutes. Add 4 cups water. Add the fish sauce and bring the liquid to a gentle boil. Reduce the heat and simmer the soup for 5 minutes. Season to taste with salt and pepper.

4. Divide the chicken among 4 large soup bowls and ladle in the hot soup. Add the bean sprouts and chile pepper to taste. Garnish with cilantro leaves and basil, set a lime wedge on the edge of each bowl, and serve immediately.

Makes 4 servings

Per serving: 192 calories, 8 g fat, 1 g saturated fat, 16 g protein, 16 g carbohydrates, 2 g fiber

ROASTED RED PEPPER GAZPACHO

Including roasted red peppers and raw onion in addition to the tomatoes and garlic you expect gives this gazpacho more complex flavor than most. Using whole wheat bread for thickening works beautifully.

2	oven-roasted red bell peppers (see Best Technique, right) or jarred roasted red peppers	1	tablespoon white wine vinegar
		2	tablespoons extra-virgin olive oil
			Salt and freshly ground pepper
2	large ripe beefsteak-type tomatoes, seeded and cut into 1" pieces	½	cup finely diced green bell pepper
		½	cup finely diced red radish
1	small onion, chopped	½	cup finely diced seeded cucumber
2 or 3	cloves garlic, chopped		
2	cups tomato juice	1	hard-cooked egg, chilled and finely chopped
1	slice day-old whole wheat bread, crust trimmed		

1. Whirl the roasted peppers, tomatoes, onion, and garlic in a blender or food processor until pureed. Pass the mixture through a fine strainer into a bowl. Discard the solids. Return to the blender or food processor.

2. Add the juice, bread, and vinegar. Whirl until the soup is smooth. With the motor running, drizzle in the oil until well blended. Season to taste with salt and pepper. Pour the gazpacho into a container, cover, and refrigerate for 8 to 24 hours, to chill and allow the flavors to meld.

3. Divide the soup among 4 bowls. Place the green pepper, radish, cucumber, and egg in individual small bowls and pass them to add to the soup. The gazpacho keeps for 3 days, tightly covered in the refrigerator.

Makes 4 servings

Per serving: 161 calories, 9 g fat, 1 g saturated fat, 5 g protein, 17 g carbohydrates, 3 g fiber

● **FOOD FACT**

This soup provides plenty of beta-carotene from the red pepper and lycopene from the tomatoes. Plus the raw onions and garlic provide benefits that cooking diminishes.

● **ROASTING PEPPERS**

Flame-roasted peppers have smoky flavor, oven-roasted ones are sweeter. Roast whole bell peppers over direct flame, turning with tongs until charred all over. Or halve peppers, brush with oil, and bake in one layer on oiled baking sheet at 425°F until soft, 30 minutes. Place peppers in bowl, cover, and let steam 10 minutes. When cool enough to handle, remove the skin and seed the peppers. Reserve any liquid to use according to the recipe.

ICED MELON SOUP

● **FOOD FACT**

Eating cinnamon may help even out the metabolic response to sugar in melon and other fruit.

● **ANOTHER WAY**

Also serve this soup as dessert or at brunch.

With cubed fresh melon readily available, you can whip up this soup in 5 minutes. A final flourish of freshly ground black pepper enhances its flavor. If you wish, garnish it with fresh mint as well

3	cups diced cantaloupe	1 or 2	tablespoons orange liqueur or
3	cups diced watermelon		fresh lemon juice
¼	cup orange juice	½	teaspoon ground cinnamon
1	tablespoon mesquite or		Pinch of salt
	wildflower honey		Freshly ground pepper

1. Whirl the cantaloupe, watermelon, orange juice, honey, and liqueur or lemon juice in a blender or food processor until pureed. Add the cinnamon and salt. Whirl to blend. Pour the soup into a tightly sealed container and refrigerate until well chilled, 2 to 8 hours.

2. Divide the soup among 4 wide, shallow soup bowls. Top each serving with 2 or 3 grinds of pepper.

Makes 4 servings

Per serving: 126 calories, 0 g fat, 0 g saturated fat, 2 g protein, 28 g carbohydrates, 2 g fiber

BLACK BEAN
AND TWO-BERRY SOUP

The contrast between the pureed beans, berries, and toasted almonds in this chilled soup is delightful, while its dark colors tell that it is loaded with antioxidants. Make sure the blueberry juice is unsweetened. For the wine, an Argentine Cabernet Sauvignon is good. Use chilled ingredients and the soup can be served immediately.

1	(19-ounce) can black beans, drained	¼	teaspoon ground cinnamon
			Salt and freshly ground pepper
¾	cup unsweetened blueberry juice	¾	cup fresh or partially thawed frozen blueberries
¼	cup dry red wine		
⅓	cup reduced-fat plain yogurt	1	(4-ounce) carton fresh blackberries
2	tablespoons black currant or wild blueberry fruit spread		
		4	tablespoons toasted slivered almonds (see page 74)
2	tablespoons frozen orange juice concentrate		

1. Whirl the beans, blueberry juice, and wine in a food processor until they form a smooth puree. Add the yogurt, fruit spread, orange juice concentrate, and cinnamon. Whirl to blend. Season to taste with salt and pepper. Refrigerate, covered, until chilled, 4 hours or up to 2 days.

2. If refrigerated, let the soup sit at room temperature for 20 minutes. Divide it among 4 wide, shallow soup bowls. Divide the berries among the bowls and sprinkle on the almonds just before serving.

Makes 4 servings

Per serving: 225 calories, 4 g fat, 0 g saturated fat, 9 g protein, 39 g carbohydrates, 8 g fiber

● **ANOTHER WAY**
Serve this versatile soup at brunch or breakfast, as a first course for a light summer meal, or as a refreshing dessert.

● **BEST TECHNIQUE**
Microwave frozen blueberries until no longer icy, about 30 seconds.

● **BEST INGREDIENT**
Some brands of canned beans are softer and puree better than others. Westbrae, Progresso, and Whole Foods' 365 Organic brand are ideal for this recipe.

● **FOOD FACT**
The beans and berries in this soup give it double the grams of fiber per serving than a bowl of oatmeal.

SOUPED-UP CHICKEN BROTH

In the 1990s, a natural foods company asked me to create a canned chicken broth. I aimed to make it almost homemade. It tasted so good, the New York Times declared it the best in a blind tasting. Sadly, it is no longer available, but you can get similar flavor by souping up other commercially made chicken broth with aromatic vegetables.

1	(32-ounce) carton fat-free, reduced-sodium chicken broth	1	small onion, halved
4"	piece celery	1"	piece parsnip or celeriac, optional
2"	piece leek, white part only	1	sprig flat-leaf parsley
1	small carrot, cut into 1" pieces	4	whole peppercorns

In a medium saucepan, combine the broth, celery, leek, carrot, onion, parsnip or celeriac if using, parsley, and peppercorns. Bring to a boil, then reduce the heat and simmer, covered, for 20 minutes. Uncover and let sit 20 minutes. Pass the mixture through a fine strainer into a bowl. Discard the solids. Use immediately or cool to room temperature, then transfer to a tightly covered container and refrigerate for up to 4 days. Or, freeze, tightly covered.

CHAPTER FOUR
SALADS

[**THREE VINAIGRETTES**
Ginger Vinaigrette 140
Pomegranate Walnut Vinaigrette 141
Fresh Herb Vinaigrette 141]

Red Lettuce, Endive, and Red Grapefruit Salad 122, California Salad with Citrus Dressing 124,

Chopped Arugula Salad with Edamame and Avocado 125, Spinach Salad with Maple Mustard Dressing 126,

Parsley and Grape Tomato Salad 127, Marinated Tomato Salad 128, Michel's Kaleslaw 129,

Black Bean Salad with Butternut Squash and Broccoli 130, Roasted Beet and Walnut Salad 132,

Purple Potato Salad with Smoked Salmon 133, Curried Egg Salad with Spinach 134,

Mexican Mole Chicken Salad 135, Turkey Waldorf Salad 136, Chipotle Salmon Salad 138,

Spiced Buttermilk Dressing 139

RED LETTUCE, ENDIVE, AND RED GRAPEFRUIT SALAD

The grapefruit vinaigrette of this jewel salad topped with toasted pine nuts is a refreshing surprise.

● **SECTIONING CITRUS FRUIT**

To free the sections from any citrus, slice off the top and bottom of the fruit. Standing the fruit on its flat bottom on a work surface, work a knife down the side, following the curved shape of the fruit to remove the peel and white pith in strips. Holding the peeled fruit over a bowl, work the knife in along the membrane on both sides of the section, releasing the flesh into the bowl. Squeeze the juice from the membrane into the bowl.

● **ANOTHER WAY**

The vinaigrette is also good with romaine lettuce and baby salad greens.

Add slices of roasted chicken breast to make this a main dish.

1	red grapefruit	4	cups red Boston lettuce torn into bite-size pieces
1	tablespoon Dijon mustard		
½	teaspoon salt	4	cups red leaf lettuce torn into bite-size pieces
	Freshly ground pepper		
¼	cup fruity extra-virgin olive oil	1	small endive, cut crosswise into ½" strips
4	teaspoons pine nuts		

1. Peel and section the grapefruit (see left), reserving ½ cup of the juice and the sections.

2. In a small bowl, whisk the grapefruit juice with the mustard, salt, and 4 or 5 grinds pepper until smooth. Continue whisking while adding the oil in a thin stream, until emulsified. Set aside.

3. Toast the pine nuts in a dry, small skillet over medium heat, stirring constantly, until they look oily then start to color, about 2 minutes. When the nuts are lightly browned in spots, spread them on a plate to cool.

4. In a mixing bowl, combine the Boston, the leaf lettuce, and the endive. Toss with ¼ cup of the dressing. Divide the salad among 4 salad plates. Arrange one-quarter of the grapefruit sections over each serving. Sprinkle on the nuts and serve. Extra dressing keeps 3 days, covered, in the refrigerator.

Makes 4 servings

Per serving: 172 calories, 16 g fat, 2 g saturated fat, 1 g protein, 7 g carbohydrates, 1 g fiber

CALIFORNIA SALAD
WITH CITRUS DRESSING

● **FOOD FACT**

Broccoli sprouts are the most potent source of the many health benefits broccoli offers.

● **ANOTHER WAY**

Adding chickpeas or tuna fish (or both) to this salad makes it a main dish.

California is synonymous with abundant salads and unexpected culinary combinations. That is why I have named this combination of lettuces, shredded carrot, slivered dates, and broccoli sprouts, tossed with a sunny dressing, after the Golden State. It makes good healthy food irresistible.

SALAD

4	cups red leaf lettuce in bite-size pieces
4	cups romaine lettuce in bite-size pieces
1	carrot, coarsely shredded
1	green bell pepper, cut into 8 rings
4	Medjool dates, pitted and thinly sliced lengthwise
½	cup finely chopped sweet onion
½	cup broccoli sprouts
½	cup toasted walnuts (see page 74)

DRESSING

2	tablespoons fresh orange juice
1	tablespoon fresh lemon juice
1	teaspoon salt
	Freshly ground pepper
2	teaspoons extra-virgin olive oil

1. **FOR THE SALAD:** In a bowl, combine the red leaf and romaine lettuces. Divide the greens among 4 wide, shallow salad bowls. Sprinkle each serving with one-quarter of the carrot and top with 2 pepper rings. Then top with the dates, onion, sprouts, and nuts, in that order.

2. **FOR THE DRESSING:** In a small bowl, whisk the orange and lemon juices with the salt until the salt dissolves. Add 3 or 4 grinds pepper. Whisk in the oil.

3. Spoon the dressing over the salad and serve immediately.

Makes 4 servings

Per serving: 233 calories, 13 g fat, 1 g saturated fat, 5 g protein, 30 g carbohydrates, 6 g fiber

CHOPPED ARUGULA SALAD
WITH EDAMAME AND AVOCADO

Inspired by the chopped salads popular around the Eastern Mediterranean, this version combines pungent greens and sweet edamame with creamy avocado and a refreshing mint and basil dressing.

1	tablespoon salt	1	rib celery, cut diagonally into ½" slices
1	cup frozen shelled edamame		
1	small bunch arugula, stemmed and cut crosswise into ½" strips, 2 cups	¼	cup Fresh Herb Vinaigrette (page 141)
2	cups flat escarole, cut crosswise into ½" strips	1	ripe Hass avocado, pitted and sliced (see Best Technique, right)

1. In a medium saucepan, combine 2 cups water and the salt. Bring to a boil. Add the edamame and cook until the beans are tender but still firm, 7 minutes. Drain and spread in a single layer on a plate. Cool them by an open window, near a fan, or by fanning the beans with a sheet of cardboard, until room temperature.

2. In a mixing bowl, use a fork to toss together the arugula, escarole, celery, and edamame. Add the dressing and toss to coat the salad lightly.

3. Fan 4 avocado slices on one side of each of 4 salad plates. Mound the dressed salad in the center. Drizzle 1 teaspoon of the remaining dressing over the avocado. Serve immediately.

Makes 4 servings

Per serving: 220 calories, 18 g fat, 2 g saturated fat, 6 g protein, 11 g carbohydrates, 6 g fiber

● FOOD FACT

A crucifer, arugula provides some of the same nutritional benefits as broccoli and cabbage.

● ANOTHER WAY

For a meatless meal, this can be a main dish.

● BEST TECHNIQUE

To slice a pitted avocado, use a large spoon to ease the flesh from the shell of each avocado half, keeping it in one piece. Place on a work surface, cut side down. Cut each half lengthwise into 8 slices.

SPINACH SALAD
WITH MAPLE MUSTARD DRESSING

● FOOD FACT

Goji berries are loaded
with antioxidants,
including beta carotene
and vitamin C.

● ANOTHER WAY

Adding diced chicken
breast makes this a main
dish.

*Spinach is especially good with a slightly sweet and sharp dressing. As a final
touch, cocoa nibs are sprinkled on in place of croutons. With flavor reminiscent
of black olives, they add a nutty crunch.*

DRESSING

2	tablespoons chopped sweet onion
2	tablespoons apple cider vinegar
1	tablespoon maple syrup
1	tablespoon coarse seed mustard
½	teaspoon salt
¼	teaspoon freshly ground pepper
1	tablespoon canola oil

SALAD

6	cups packed baby spinach
2	tablespoons goji berries or ¼ cup dried cranberries
2	tablespoons raw pumpkin seeds
4	teaspoons cocoa nibs

1. **FOR THE DRESSING:** Whirl the onion, vinegar, maple syrup, mustard,
salt, and pepper in a blender or mini food processor. Whirl until the onion is
pureed. Add the oil and whirl to blend.

2. **FOR THE SALAD:** In a mixing bowl, toss the spinach with the dressing to
coat. Divide the spinach among 4 salad plates. Sprinkle on the goji berries or
cranberries, pumpkin seeds, and cocoa nibs. Serve immediately.

Makes 4 servings

Per serving: 159 calories, 9 g fat, 2 g saturated fat, 3 g protein, 18 g carbohydrates, 5 g fiber

PARSLEY AND GRAPE TOMATO SALAD

Combining all the ingredients used in tabbouleh except the bulgur produces a light, wheat-free side dish perfect for a hot summer day, or anytime you need a colorful side salad. It shows how good parsley tastes when used liberally.

SALAD

4	cups loosely packed flat-leaf parsley, chopped
½	cup loosely packed spearmint leaves, chopped
1	cup diced seeded cucumber
½	pint grape tomatoes, halved

DRESSING

2	tablespoons fresh lemon juice
1	teaspoon salt
⅛	teaspoon ground cumin
	Freshly ground pepper
1	tablespoon extra-virgin olive oil

1. **FOR THE SALAD:** In a bowl, combine the parsley, spearmint, cucumber, and tomatoes. Toss with a fork to mix.

2. **FOR THE DRESSING:** In a small bowl, combine the lemon juice, salt, cumin, and 5 grinds pepper. Whisk until the salt dissolves. Whisk in the oil.

3. Pour the dressing over the salad and mix well with a fork. Set aside for 20 minutes to allow the flavors to meld. This salad keeps, tightly covered in the refrigerator, for 24 hours.

Makes 4 servings

Per serving: 67 calories, 4 g fat, 1 g saturated fat, 2 g protein, 7 g carbohydrates, 3 g fiber

● **FOOD FACT**

Since a tomato's skin is richer in phytonutrients than its flesh, grape and other small tomatoes provide more per serving than larger varieties.

● **ANOTHER WAY**

Add canned tuna to make this a main dish.

MARINATED TOMATO SALAD

● **FOOD FACT**

Chives provide beta-carotene and vitamin K.

● **ANOTHER WAY**

Serve with mozzarella bocconcini to make this a main dish.

The ideal tomatoes for this salad are firm and not quite ripe, making it a great choice for supermarket tomatoes. Beefsteak tomatoes are the best, as their meaty flesh soaks up the tangy marinade.

2	beefsteak tomatoes, 1¼–1½ pounds		Pinch of red-pepper flakes, optional
¼	cup fresh lemon juice	1	tablespoon extra-virgin olive oil
2	teaspoons wildflower honey	1	tablespoon chopped chives
½	teaspoon salt		

1. Cut each tomato into 12 wedges and place in a shallow, wide bowl.

2. In a small bowl, combine the lemon juice, honey, and salt. Whisk until the salt dissolves. Add the pepper flakes, if using. Whisk in the oil.

3. Pour the marinade over the tomatoes, turning them gently with a fork to bathe them in it. Set aside at room temperature for 15 minutes. Turn and baste the tomatoes with the marinade and let sit 15 minutes longer. Drain the tomatoes and arrange on a serving plate. Discard the marinade. Sprinkle on the chives and serve immediately.

Makes 6 servings

Per serving: 42 calories, 25 g fat, 1 g saturated fat, 1 g protein, 5 g carbohydrates, 1 g fiber

MICHEL'S KALESLAW

Michel Nischan, a chef committed to seasonal cooking, uses dark leafy greens for winter salads. This is my simplified version of his delicious slaw made with kale, succulent napa cabbage, and tender savoy cabbage.

SLAW

1	1¼-pound head napa cabbage, halved lengthwise
½	small head savoy cabbage
2	packed cups curly kale, stems removed and torn into 1½" pieces

DRESSING

2	tablespoons honey mustard
½	teaspoon ground coriander
½	teaspoon ground ginger
1	teaspoon salt
2	tablespoons apple cider vinegar
1	tablespoon apple cider
1	teaspoon fresh lemon juice
4	teaspoons canola oil
	Freshly ground pepper

● **FOOD FACT**

Raw cabbage provides more vitamin C than cooked.

● **ANOTHER WAY**

Top with slices of diced preservative-free ham to make this salad a one-dish meal.

1. **FOR THE SLAW:** Starting from the bottom, cut the napa cabbage halves crosswise into ½" strips that are mostly the white, crisp part, making 1½ cups. Reserve the remaining cabbage for another use. Quarter the savoy cabbage and cut into thin strips. In a large bowl, combine the napa cabbage, savoy cabbage, and kale. Toss to mix.

2. **FOR THE DRESSING:** In a small bowl, whisk together the mustard, coriander, ginger, salt, vinegar, cider, and lemon juice, until the salt and mustard dissolve. Add the oil in a thin stream, until the dressing is creamy. Season with pepper to taste.

3. Pour the dressing over the greens. Toss with a fork until the greens start to wilt. Cover the slaw and refrigerate for 1 hour before serving, or up to 3 days. The slaw becomes more tender as it sits.

Makes 4 servings

Per serving: 118 calories, 5 g fat, 1 g saturated fat, 4 g protein, 16 g carbohydrates, 4 g fiber

BLACK BEAN SALAD WITH BUTTERNUT SQUASH AND BROCCOLI

● **ANOTHER WAY**

Transform this side salad into a main dish by adding diced chicken breast or baked marinated tofu.

I improvised this cooked salad one night when I needed a meal quickly. If you use packaged, precut broccoli florets, peeled squash, plus canned beans, this chunky salad is ready in 15 minutes. But when time is available, do start with whole broccoli and squash, which give the dish more flavor when freshly cut.

1	cup butternut squash, cut into ½" cubes	1	(15-ounce) can black beans, drained
1	cup small broccoli florets, cut to ½" with little stem		Ginger Vinaigrette (page 140)
		2	tablespoons raw pumpkin seeds

1. Using a steamer insert in a large, deep saucepan, steam the squash for 3 minutes. Add the broccoli and continue steaming until tender-crisp, 4 minutes. Immediately transfer the squash and broccoli to a colander and rinse under cold running water until cooled. Drain well and place in a mixing bowl.

2. Add the beans, pour in the dressing, and toss with a fork to combine.

3. In a dry skillet over medium heat, toast the pumpkin seeds until they crackle and start to pop, 3 to 4 minutes. Add them to the salad and toss to combine. Let the salad sit 15 minutes before serving.

Makes 4 servings

Per serving: 192 calories, 10 g fat, 1 g saturated fat, 7 g protein, 22 g carbohydrates, 6 g fiber

ROASTED BEET
AND WALNUT SALAD

Roasting beets turns them sugar-sweet and meltingly tender—and it is as easy as baking a potato. Sliced, marinated in Pomegranate Walnut Vinaigrette, and sprinkled with some poblano chile, they make a lovely side salad. If you don't like heat, use goat cheese and omit the chile.

2	beets, with 1" stem and root attached	¼	cup chopped toasted walnuts (see page 74)
	Pomegranate Walnut Vinaigrette (page 141)	½	roasted poblano pepper, chopped, or 4 (½") slices
8	large Boston or butter lettuce leaves		chilled fresh goat cheese

1. Preheat the oven to 400°F.

2. Wrap the beets in a large sheet of foil and place on a rack in the oven. Roast until a sharp knife pierces them easily to the center, 60 to 75 minutes, unwrap, and when the beets are cool enough to handle, peel and cut into ½" slices.

3. Place the beets in a resealable plastic bag. Add the dressing. Seal and massage to coat the beets. Set aside to marinate for 15 minutes or up to 1 hour. Remove the beets and discard the marinade.

4. Line 4 salad plates with the lettuce leaves. Arrange the beets on the lettuce, dividing evenly. Sprinkle on the nuts. Add either a sprinkle of poblano or a slice of goat cheese. Serve immediately.

Makes 4 servings

Per serving: 121 calories, 10 g fat, 1 g saturated fat, 2 g protein, 8 g carbohydrates, 2 g fiber

PURPLE POTATO SALAD
WITH SMOKED SALMON

Forget the bagel. Smoked salmon goes just as well with potatoes, and offers bet-ter nutrition, especially the nutty-tasting purple ones which get their vibrant color from the same antioxidants found in blueberries. The firmer texture and stronger flavor of Smoked Coho or sockeye salmon are ideal in the salad. When entertaining, it is a penny-wise way to share a favorite luxury.

8	small (about 1 pound) purple potatoes	½	cup (1–1½ ounces) chopped Coho smoked salmon
2	tablespoons reduced-fat sour cream	⅓	cup chopped chives
		¼	cup chopped fresh dill
2	tablespoons regular or light buttermilk	¼	cup chopped flat-leaf parsley
			Salt and freshly ground pepper

1. Place the potatoes in a deep saucepan and cover with 2" cold water. Over high heat, boil until the potatoes are easily pierced with a thin knife, 15 to 18 minutes. Drain and set aside until cool enough to handle.

2. Halve the potatoes. Peel half of the pieces. In a mixing bowl, combine the potatoes, sour cream, and buttermilk and mix with a fork until the potatoes are coated. Add the salmon, chives, dill, and parsley and stir gently to mix. Season to taste with salt and pepper. Let the salad sit for 20 minutes so the flavors can meld. Serve the salad the day it is made.

Makes 4 servings

Per serving: 107 calories, 5 g fat, 2 g saturated fat, 11 g protein, 7 g carbohydrates, 3 g fiber

CURRIED EGG SALAD WITH SPINACH

● **ANOTHER WAY**

If you do not want to make Curried Onions on Top, add ¼ cup finely chopped raw sweet onion and ½ teaspoon curry powder along with the mayonnaise.

Add another teaspoon of mayonnaise to the salad and use as a sandwich filling on whole wheat toast or in a warm pita bread.

Blending spinach and curried onions into egg salad adds bold flavors as well as valuable nutrients and antioxidants. Serve this on its own or use it to make the best egg salad sandwich.

4	cups packed flat-leaf spinach leaves	2	teaspoons reduced-fat mayonnaise
4	large hard-cooked eggs, peeled		Salt and freshly ground pepper
¼	cup Curried Onions (page 245)	1	green bell pepper, cut into rings
1	teaspoon fresh lemon juice	1	red bell pepper, cut into rings

1. Rinse the spinach and shake well, leaving some water clinging to the leaves. Cook the spinach in a dry medium skillet over medium-high heat, stirring constantly, until the leaves are soft but still have slight resistance to the bite, about 4 minutes. Spread the spinach on a plate and cool completely. When cool enough to handle, squeeze dry and chop.

2. In a mixing bowl, coarsely chop the eggs. Add the spinach, onions, and lemon juice. Using a fork, mix to combine. Blend in the mayonnaise. Season to taste with salt and pepper.

3. Mound the salad on 3 plates and top with the red and green pepper rings.

Makes 3 servings

Per serving: 144 calories, 8 g fat, 3 g saturated fat, 10 g protein, 9 g carbohydrates, 3 g fiber

MEXICAN MOLE CHICKEN SALAD

I consider this a deconstructed mole because the spice rub on the chicken plus the raisins and almonds in the salad include most of the ingredients in the renowned Mexican sauce. This lusty salad is perfect if your family resists healthy eating.

● **BEST INGREDIENT**

This dish is crammed with 11 Essential Best Foods, including cinnamon, ginger, plus turmeric in the curry powder.

1	tablespoon natural unsweetened cocoa powder	1	Granny Smith apple, halved and thinly sliced lengthwise
2	teaspoons curry powder	1	green bell pepper, cut into 1/4" strips
1	teaspoon sweet or hot Hungarian paprika		
1/2	teaspoon ground coriander	1	small red onion, cut into thin rings
1	teaspoon salt	4	tablespoons raisins
1/4	teaspoon freshly ground pepper	4	tablespoons slivered almonds, toasted (see page 74)
4	(4-ounce) pieces boneless, skinless chicken breast		
8	cups loosely packed baby spinach	1/3	cup Spiced Buttermilk Dressing (page 139)

1. Preheat the oven to 350°F.

2. On a small plate, combine the cocoa, curry powder, paprika, coriander, salt, and pepper. One at a time, dredge the chicken pieces in the seasoning, coating them all over liberally, then place on a baking sheet. Bake the chicken until a thermometer inserted in the center registers 165°F and the juices run clear, about 20 minutes. Set the chicken aside to cool until lukewarm or room temperature.

3. In each of 4 wide, shallow salad bowls, make a bed of the spinach. Add the apple, then the green pepper strips. Cut each chicken breast across the grain into 3/4" diagonal slices and arrange on top of each salad. Add the onion rings, raisins, and almonds. Spoon on the dressing and serve.

Makes 4 servings

Per serving: 264 calories, 6 g fat, 1 g saturated fat, 31 g protein, 24 g carbohydrates, 6 g fiber

TURKEY WALDORF SALAD

At the deli counter, many supermarkets sell roasted turkey sliced from a whole breast. It tastes homemade and avoids the sodium and preservatives used in the commercially made boneless kind.

The original Waldorf salad included only apples, celery, and mayonnaise—the walnuts came later. I like adding turkey and almonds, turning this salad into a colorful, fruited main dish containing valuable omega-3s. Do try the flax seed garnish—its taste is nicely nutty.

DRESSING

2	tablespoons reduced-fat (2%) plain Greek yogurt
1	tablespoon reduced-fat mayonnaise
2	teaspoons fresh lemon juice
	Salt and freshly ground pepper

SALAD

2	cups (8 ounces) diced roasted turkey breast
16	black or red seedless grapes, halved
1	rib celery, chopped
1	Fuji apple, diced
⅓	cup chopped walnuts
1	head Boston lettuce
2	tablespoons sliced almonds
2	tablespoons ground flax seed, optional

1. **FOR THE DRESSING:** In a small bowl, whisk together the yogurt, mayonnaise, and lemon juice. Season to taste with salt and pepper.

2. **FOR THE SALAD:** In a mixing bowl, combine the turkey, grapes, celery, apple, and walnuts. Add the dressing, and using a fork, toss to mix. On each of 4 salad plates, make a bed of the lettuce leaves. Mound the salad on top of the lettuce. Sprinkle on the almonds, and flax seeds if using. Serve immediately.

Makes 4 servings

Per serving: 237 calories, 10 g fat, 2 g saturated fat, 24 g protein, 14 g carbohydrates, 2 g fiber

CHIPOTLE SALMON SALAD

Chipotle chile is just the thing if you like dishes with smokin' heat. For more delicate tastebuds, add just enough chile to provide smoky flavor without the flames. Firm coho salmon holds together and goes well with the assertive flavors in the salad.

¼	cup finely chopped sweet onion	2	tablespoons fresh lime juice
¼	cup finely chopped green bell pepper	¾	pound skinless Coho salmon fillet, poached or baked
¼	cup finely chopped orange bell pepper	3	tablespoons chopped cilantro leaves
¼–½	teaspoon ground chipotle chile pepper		Salt and freshly ground pepper
1	small clove garlic, minced	8	romaine heart lettuce leaves
			Large tortilla chips

1. In a small mixing bowl, combine the onion, green and orange bell peppers, chipotle chile, garlic, and lime juice. In a larger bowl, coarsely flake the salmon with a fork. Add the onion mixture to the fish and, using 2 forks, combine gently so the fish remains chunky. Gently mix in the cilantro. Season to taste with salt and pepper.

2. Cover and let stand at room temperature for 20 minutes, or refrigerate for up to 1 hour, to let the flavors develop.

3. On each of 4 dinner plates, arrange 2 lettuce leaves side by side pointing their tips in opposite directions. Spoon the salad into the leaves. Place some large tortilla chips on either side to accompany the salad. Serve immediately.

Makes 4 servings

Per serving: 172 calories, 6 g fat, 1 g saturated fat, 21 g protein, 8 g carbohydrates, 1 g fiber

SPICED BUTTERMILK DRESSING

This creamy salad topper sparked with cumin and bright lime makes a nice change from bottled ranch dressing. It is so low in fat that you can pour it on liberally. I like it on romaine lettuce, tomatoes, baby spinach, and with Mexican Mole Chicken Salad (page 135).

⅔	cup regular or light buttermilk	½	teaspoon ground cumin
1	tablespoon fresh lime juice	1	teaspoon salt
1	teaspoon canola oil	¼	teaspoon freshly ground pepper
1	clove garlic, minced		

In a measuring cup, combine the buttermilk, lime juice, oil, garlic, cumin, salt, and pepper. Whisk to mix. Set aside for up to 4 hours.

Makes ⅔ cup, about 5 servings

Per serving (2 tablespoons): 29 calories, 2 g fat, 1 g saturated fat, 1 g protein, 1 g carbohydrates, 0 g fiber

● **BEST TECHNIQUE**

A well-dressed salad is coated with dressing, not dripping with it. One tablespoon of vinaigrette per serving usually does this, especially if you place the dressing in the bottom of the salad bowl, add the salad, and toss by gently lifting the leaves and other ingredients up from the bottom and turning them over for 30 to 60 seconds. Serve a dressed salad immediately.

Three Vinaigrettes

These decidedly different salad dressings include far more than the mustard, vinegar, and oil standard in a vinaigrette. Ranging in color from topaz and garnet red to lively green, each also provides particular phyto-benefits. Because their flavors change when allowed to sit for more than a few hours, two of the recipes make just enough for a four-serving meal. If you want more, simply multiply the recipe.

GINGER VINAIGRETTE

Europeans eat their salad after a meal because it aids digestion. Ginger does, too, making it an ideal salad dressing ingredient. Also use this dressing as a sauce to spoon over poached salmon.

2	tablespoons rice vinegar	1	teaspoon brown sugar
1	tablespoon fresh lime juice	½	teaspoon salt
1	teaspoon reduced-sodium soy sauce	¼	teaspoon freshly ground pepper
		2	tablespoons canola oil
1	teaspoon grated fresh ginger	1	tablespoon minced shallot

Place the vinegar, lime juice, soy sauce, ginger, sugar, salt, and pepper in a small jar, cover tightly, and shake until the salt dissolves. Add the oil and shallot. Replace the lid and shake vigorously to combine. This dressing keeps for 24 hours, covered, in the refrigerator. Shake very well before using.

Makes ¼ cup, 4 servings

Per serving (1 tablespoon): 71 calories, 7 g fat, 1 g saturated fat, 0 g protein, 2 g carbohydrates, 0 g fiber

POMEGRANATE WALNUT VINAIGRETTE

This robust dressing goes especially well with spinach salad, roasted beets, and kidney beans.

2	tablespoons pomegranate juice		Freshly ground pepper
1	tablespoon red wine vinegar	1	tablespoon canola oil
½	teaspoon salt	1	teaspoon roasted walnut oil

In a small bowl, whisk together the juice, vinegar, and salt until the salt dissolves. Add 3 to 4 grinds pepper. Whisk in the canola and walnut oils. Use the dressing the day it is made.

Makes ¼ cup, 4 servings

Per serving (1 tablespoon): 46 calories, 5 g fat, 1 g saturated fat, 0 g protein, 1 g carbohydrates, 0 g fiber

FRESH HERB VINAIGRETTE

The vivid flavors and fresh green color of this dressing make you feel as if you are in an herb garden.

¼	cup packed basil leaves	1	tablespoon red wine vinegar
¼	cup packed spearmint leaves	1	teaspoon salt
¼	cup fresh lemon juice	¼	teaspoon freshly ground pepper
2	tablespoons chopped shallots	½	cup extra-virgin olive oil

Whirl the basil, spearmint, lemon juice, shallot, vinegar, salt, and pepper in a mini food processor until pureed. Add the oil and whirl to blend. The dressing keeps 2 days, tightly covered, in the fridge.

Makes ¾ cup, 12 servings

Per serving (1 tablespoon): 88 calories, 9 g fat, 1 g saturated fat, 0 g protein, 1 g carbohydrates, 0 g fiber

CHAPTER FIVE
POULTRY AND MEAT

THREE GROUND TURKEY FAVORITES

Juicy Turkey Burgers 145

Turkey and Spinach Mini–Meat Loaves 146

Turkey Meatball Chili 148

Turkey Cutlets with Cranberry-Pomegranate Salsa 143, Turkey Oreganato 144,

Chicken with Pear and Avocado 150, Peanut Chicken Stir-Fry 152, Lemon Sesame Chicken 154,

Persian Chicken with Sour Cherries 155, Jerk Pork Chops with Warm Pineapple-Grapefruit Salsa 156,

Buttermilk-Brined Pork Chops 158, Pork Tenderloin with Blueberry-Plum Sauce 159,

Herb-Stuffed Flank Steak 160, Cocoa-Crusted Beef Filet with Pomegranate Sauce 162,

Three-Onion Pot Roast 164

TURKEY CUTLETS WITH CRANBERRY-POMEGRANATE SALSA

Transforming a Thanksgiving favorite, uncooked cranberry relish, into a salsa makes it perfect with turkey cutlets. You deserve the goodness in these foods more than once a year: Together, they make a low-fat main course.

SALSA

1   (12-ounce) bag fresh or frozen
        cranberries, picked over
1   medium navel orange,
        ends sliced off, cut into
        16 pieces
⅓   cup sugar, or to taste
5   tablespoons fresh or frozen
        pomegranate seeds

1   serrano chile pepper, seeded and
        minced
     Salt and freshly ground pepper

TURKEY

4   (4-ounce) turkey cutlets
     Salt and freshly ground pepper
2   teaspoons unsalted butter
2   teaspoons olive oil

● **FOOD FACT**

Fresh or frozen, raw cranberries deliver the most vitamin C and other nutrients.

● **BEST TECHNIQUE**

When pomegranates are in season (October through May), freeze the *arils*, what we call seeds, in containers and enjoy this dish and most others using pomegranates any time you wish.

1. **FOR THE SALSA:** Pulse the cranberries and orange in a food processor until finely chopped, about 1 minute, stopping one or twice to scrape down the bowl. Transfer the salsa to a bowl and mix in the sugar. Cover and refrigerate 1 hour. This salsa gets sweeter the longer it sits.

2. Before serving, mix the pomegranate seeds and chile into the salsa. Season to taste with salt and pepper.

3. **FOR THE TURKEY:** Pound the turkey cutlets between 2 sheets of waxed paper to ½" thickness. Season them lightly with salt and pepper.

4. In a large skillet set over medium-high heat, melt the butter with the oil. Add the cutlets and cook, turning several times, until lightly browned on both sides and white in the center, 8 to 10 minutes. Serve, accompanied by the salsa.

Makes 4 servings

Per serving: 287 calories, 5 g fat, 2 g saturated fat, 29 g protein, 34 g carbohydrates, 5 g fiber

TURKEY OREGANATO

● **BEST TECHNIQUE**

Pounding cutlets between 2 sheets of waxed paper with a smooth meat mallet tenderizes them and helps them cook evenly. The light flour coating keeps them juicy.

Chicken piccata inspired this 20-minute dish, where oregano added to the usual lemon and capers amps up its flavor. For me, using turkey transforms the original from a delicate, fancier dish to a satisfying dinner.

4	(4-ounce) turkey cutlets	¼	cup white wine
3	tablespoons flour	1	tablespoon finely chopped fresh
½	teaspoon salt		oregano or 1 teaspoon dried
¼	teaspoon freshly ground pepper	1	tablespoon small capers, rinsed
1–2	tablespoons extra-virgin olive oil		and drained
1	cup fat-free, reduced-sodium chicken broth	1	tablespoon fresh lemon juice

1. Pound the turkey cutlets between 2 sheets of waxed paper to ⅜" thickness.

2. On a plate, combine the flour with the salt and pepper. Dredge each cutlet in the flour, shaking excess so it is just lightly coated.

3. In a large skillet, heat 1 tablespoon oil over medium-high heat. Add 2 cutlets and cook, reducing the heat if necessary, until lightly browned, about 3 minutes. Turn and brown on the other side, 2 minutes. Continue turning the cutlets until they are white in the center, 1 to 2 minutes longer. Transfer to a platter and cover loosely with foil to keep warm. Repeat, adding oil if needed, to cook the remaining cutlets.

4. Add the broth, wine, and oregano to the pan, vigorously scraping the pan bottom with a spatula to loosen the browned bits. Boil until the sauce is reduced to ¼ cup, about 6 minutes. Off the heat, add the capers and the lemon juice. Spoon the pan sauce over the turkey and serve immediately.

Makes 4 servings

Per serving: 192 calories, 4 g fat, 1 g saturated fat, 30 g protein, 6 g carbohydrates, 0 g fiber

Ground Turkey Favorites

If you serve burgers, meat loaf, or meatballs regularly, here are three ways to renew excitement about them. Using ground turkey in place of beef often produces unpleasantly dry results. These recipes help you avoid this. They all come out most succulent using ground turkey that is 90% to 93% lean. And watch the timing carefully to avoid overcooking.

JUICY TURKEY BURGERS

These plump burgers are great served on a toasted bun and topped with the works—onion, tomato, and pickle slices plus ketchup, mustard, and mayonnaise.

1	pound ground turkey breast, 90–93% lean	2½	tablespoons dried blueberries, optional
1	large egg white or 2 tablespoons liquid egg whites	½–1	teaspoon salt
3	tablespoons finely chopped mild onion, such as Spanish or Vidalia	¼	teaspoon freshly ground pepper
		2	tablespoons olive or canola oil

1. In a mixing bowl, combine the turkey, egg white, onion, blueberries (if using), salt, and pepper. Using a fork, mix until thoroughly blended. Moistening your hands so the turkey does not stick to them, form the mixture into five 1" thick patties.

2. In a heavy medium skillet, heat the oil over medium-high heat. Add the burgers, leaving at least 1" between them. Cook until the burgers are browned on the bottom, 5 minutes. Turn and cook until a thermometer inserted sideways into the centers registers 165°F, about 5 minutes. Immediately transfer the burgers to a serving plate or place on hamburger buns and serve while hot.

Makes 5 servings

Per serving: 189 calories, 13 g fat, 3 g saturated fat, 17 g protein, 1 g carbohydrates, 0 g fiber

● **BEST TECHNIQUE**

Adding an egg white keeps these white meat turkey burgers pleasantly moist.

If using the blueberries, push them inside so they will not burn during cooking.

● **FOOD FACT**

Antioxidants in blueberries and dried cherries help counteract effects of charring and other undesirable substances that can form when meat cooks.

TURKEY AND SPINACH MINI–MEAT LOAVES

● **SERVE WITH**

Moroccan Tomato Compote (page 166) or prepared tomato sauce

● **BEST INGREDIENT**

I use Barbara's Bakery Instant Mashed Potatoes which are fluffy and made only of Idaho potatoes in their skin. Natural food stores carry them.

Using instant potato flakes in place of dried bread crumbs keeps these little loaves nicely moist. As single servings, they also bake faster than the usual size.

1	tablespoon extra-virgin olive oil
1	medium red onion, finely chopped
1	clove garlic, finely chopped
1½	pounds lean ground turkey breast, 90–93% lean
1	(10-ounce) package frozen chopped spinach, thawed and squeezed dry
½	cup natural instant mashed potatoes
1	large egg white
1	teaspoon dried oregano
¼	teaspoon ground chipotle chile pepper
1	teaspoon salt
⅛	teaspoon freshly ground pepper
2	large plum tomatoes, cut into thin crosswise slices

1. Preheat the oven to 350° F. Line a jelly-roll pan with foil and set aside.

2. In a medium skillet, heat the olive oil over medium-high heat. Sauté the onion until the onion is soft, 5 minutes.

3. In a mixing bowl, combine the turkey, onion mixture, spinach, potatoes, egg white, oregano, ground chile, salt, and pepper. Mix with a fork until blended. Shape the mixture into six 4" × 2" × 1" loaves and place on the prepared baking pan 2" apart. Cover with foil.

4. Bake for 30 minutes. Uncover, and arrange 3 tomato slices in an overlapping row on top of each loaf. Bake until a thermometer inserted in the center registers 165°F and the meat is no longer pink, 15 minutes longer. Let the loaves sit for 15 minutes. Serve immediately.

Makes 6 servings

Per serving: 237 calories, 12 g fat, 3 g saturated fat, 22 g protein, 8 g carbohydrates, 2 g fiber

TURKEY MEATBALL CHILI

These turkey meatballs in a spicy tomato sauce include everything you get in a bowl of beefy Texas chili, but in a lighter way. Kids particularly love this dish. And getting youngsters to help make the meatballs is a great way to get them into the kitchen. Serve over rice, pasta, or with beans added, if you wish.

1⅓	cups chopped onion, divided	1	medium green bell pepper, chopped
¾	pound ground turkey breast, 90–93% lean	1	clove garlic, finely chopped
⅓	cup quick-cooking oats (not instant)	2	tablespoons chili powder
¼	cup chopped cilantro leaves + ⅓ cup for serving	1	tablespoon chopped fresh oregano
2	tablespoons chopped flat-leaf parsley	1	(28-ounce) can plum tomatoes
1	teaspoon + 1 tablespoon ground cumin, divided	24	cilantro stems, tied in a bundle
½	teaspoon ground cinnamon	1	teaspoon sugar, optional
	Salt and freshly ground pepper	3	cups cooked brown rice, optional
2	tablespoons extra-virgin olive oil	½	cup finely chopped red onion, for garnish

1. Finely chop ⅓ cup of the onion. Transfer to a mixing bowl. Add the turkey, oats, ¼ cup chopped cilantro, parsley, 1 teaspoon cumin, cinnamon, ½ teaspoon salt, and ⅛ teaspoon black pepper. Mix with a fork until well blended. Moistening your hands just enough to keep the turkey from sticking to them, form the mixture into 16 meatballs.

2. In a deep medium skillet, heat the oil over medium-high heat. Add the meatballs and cook, turning them with tongs, until browned on all sides, 6 minutes. Remove the meatballs to a plate.

3. Add the remaining 1 cup onion to the pan and sauté until translucent, 4 minutes. Add the bell pepper and garlic and sauté until the onion is soft,

3 minutes. Add the chili powder, oregano, and remaining 1 tablespoon cumin. Cook, stirring, until fragrant, 1 minute. Add the tomatoes and their liquid. Using a wooden spoon, break up the tomatoes. Add the cilantro bundle and sugar if using. Return the meatballs to the pan. When the liquid starts to boil, reduce the heat and simmer until the meatballs are cooked and tender, 30 minutes. Remove the cilantro stems and discard. Season to taste with salt and pepper.

4. To serve with rice, if desired, divide the rice among 4 wide, shallow bowls. Top each with 4 meatballs and ¾ cup sauce. Pass the red onion and the remaining ⅓ cup cilantro to add as desired.

Makes 4 servings

Per serving: 320 calories, 15 g fat, 3 g saturated fat, 19 g protein, 25 g carbohydrates, 7 g fiber

CHICKEN WITH PEAR AND AVOCADO

● **BEST INGREDIENT**

Use a pear that is almost but not fully ripe.

● **BEST TECHNIQUE**

A pear planker resembles the tool used to slice an apple into wedges. It cores and cuts a pear into neat, thick slices. It is available at www.pearpanache.com.

Avocados are buttery in texture and Bartlett pears have buttery flavor. Pairing them with sautéed chicken and a light, white-wine pan sauce makes a superb dish. Ready in 20 minutes, it turns dinner into an occasion.

4	(4-ounce) boneless, skinless chicken breast halves
1	tablespoon canola oil
	Salt and freshly ground pepper
1	tablespoon unsalted butter
1	leek, white part only, halved lengthwise and thinly sliced crosswise
1	Bartlett or Anjou pear, peeled and cut into $3/8$" slices
$1/4$	cup dry white wine
$1/2$	cup fat-free, reduced-sodium chicken broth
$1/2$	large or 1 small ripe Hass avocado, cut into 12 slices (see Best Technique, page 125)

1. Pound the chicken pieces between 2 sheets of waxed paper to $1/2$" thickness.

2. In a medium skillet, heat the oil over medium-high heat. Season the chicken with salt and pepper. Sauté the chicken until lightly browned on both sides and white in the center, about 6 minutes, turning once. Transfer the chicken to a plate, cover with foil, and set aside.

3. Melt the butter in the pan. Add the leek and sauté until soft, 5 minutes. Add the pear and cook until warmed through, 3 minutes, turning once. Add the leek and pear to the chicken.

4. Deglaze the pan with the wine, using a wooden spoon to scrape up the browned bits, then boil until the wine is almost evaporated, 2 minutes. Add the broth and boil until it is reduced by half, 4 minutes.

5. On each of 4 dinner plates, place a piece of chicken. Top each with 3 avocado slices and spoon one-quarter of the pear and leek on top of each. Drizzle on the hot pan juices. Serve immediately.

Makes 4 servings

Per serving: 285 calories, 13 g fat, 3 g saturated fat, 28 g protein, 12 g carbohydrates, 4 g fiber

PEANUT CHICKEN STIR-FRY

● **FOOD FACT**

Green bell peppers are an excellent source of vitamin C.

● **BEST TECHNIQUE**

Chinese cooks call marinating chicken, shrimp, or meats in raw egg white *velveting* because it keeps the food tender as it cooks and gives it a velvety texture.

The flavors in this Cantonese-style dish arrive in waves, starting with roasted peanuts, followed by pungent ginger, garlic, and scallions, and finishing with the sweetness of red peppers.

CHICKEN

1	large egg white
¾	pound boneless, skinless chicken breasts, cut into ½" pieces
1	teaspoon peanut oil
2	teaspoons cornstarch
½	teaspoon salt

SEASONING SAUCE

2	tablespoons fat-free, reduced-sodium chicken broth
1	tablespoon sherry
1	tablespoon reduced-sodium soy sauce
1	teaspoon sugar
¼	teaspoon freshly ground pepper
¼	teaspoon red-pepper flakes

STIR-FRY

¼	cup peanut oil
¼	cup chopped scallions, green and white parts
1	clove garlic, minced
1	teaspoon minced fresh ginger
1	medium red bell pepper, cut into 1" strips
1	small green bell pepper, cut into 1" strips
⅓	cup unsalted dry roasted peanuts

1. **FOR THE CHICKEN:** In a mixing bowl, whisk the egg white until frothy. Add the chicken, oil, cornstarch, and salt, mixing with a fork until well blended. Cover and refrigerate for 20 minutes.

2. **FOR THE SEASONING SAUCE**: In a small bowl, combine the broth, sherry, soy sauce, sugar, pepper, and pepper flakes. Leave the spoon in the bowl.

3. **FOR THE STIR-FRY**: In a wok over the highest heat possible, heat the oil until it shimmers. Add the marinated chicken, separating the pieces with the wok paddle. When the chicken looks white, 2½ to 3 minutes, remove it with a slotted spoon to a plate and set aside. Pour off all but 1 tablespoon oil from the wok and return it to the heat.

4. Add the scallions, garlic, and ginger, and stir-fry until fragrant, 30 seconds. Add the red and green bell peppers and stir-fry until their color is bright, 1 minute. Add the peanuts and stir-fry until they darken slightly, 30 seconds. Stir and add the seasoning sauce, followed by the chicken and any accumulated juices. Stir-fry until the chicken is white in the center, about 1 minute. Serve immediately.

Makes 4 servings

Per serving: 328 calories, 22 g fat, 4 g saturated fat, 24 g protein, 9 g carbohydrates, 2 g fiber

LEMON SESAME CHICKEN

● FOOD FACT

Mung bean sprouts contain a little protein and fiber but add moist flavor and crunch to dishes.

● TOASTING SEEDS

Place sesame or pumpkin seeds in a dry small skillet set over medium heat. Cook, shaking the pan often, until they start to pop, 3 to 4 minutes. Immediately transfer the seeds to a plate to cool.

At the Benihana restaurants, chefs keep boneless chicken jumping on a griddle, serving it up with dramatic knife work. Using a cast-iron skillet, I make my own, calmer version.

	Juice of ½ lemon		Salt and freshly ground pepper
1	teaspoon toasted sesame oil	2	tablespoons peanut oil
1	pound boneless, skinless chicken breasts, cut into 1" pieces	8	ounces mung bean sprouts
		1	tablespoon toasted sesame seeds

1. In a small bowl, combine the lemon juice and sesame oil with ½ teaspoon salt and set aside. Season the chicken with 1 teaspoon salt and freshly ground black pepper.

2. In a large skillet, preferably cast-iron, heat the peanut oil over medium-high heat. Add the chicken, arranging the pieces in one layer. Cook until the chicken is golden outside and white in the center, about 6 minutes, turning it once. Transfer it to a serving plate.

3. Spread the bean sprouts over the bottom of the pan and cook for 2 minutes. Stir until the sprouts start to brown in places but are still slightly crunchy, 1 minute. Spoon the bean sprouts over the chicken.

4. Pour the lemon juice mixture over the chicken and bean sprouts. Sprinkle on the sesame seeds. Serve immediately.

Makes 4 servings

Per serving: 226 calories, 11 g fat, 2 g saturated fat, 28 g protein, 5 g carbohydrates, 1 g fiber

PERSIAN CHICKEN WITH SOUR CHERRIES

This dish is inspired by a stew from ancient Persia that included tart fruits and cinnamon. Its juices are so good that you will want to serve it from a deep platter that lets you spoon them on generously.

● **BEST TECHNIQUE**

Using chicken breast with ribs still attached keeps the meat more moist.

1	tablespoon extra-virgin olive oil	1	teaspoon ground cinnamon
1	medium (1¼-pound) skinless whole chicken breast with ribs, cut into 4 pieces	½	teaspoon ground ginger
		¼	teaspoon ground nutmeg
		1	teaspoon salt
1	medium onion, chopped	¼	teaspoon freshly ground pepper
1	Granny Smith apple, peeled and diced	¼	cup chopped cilantro leaves
⅓	cup dried sour cherries	2–2½	cups fat-free, reduced-sodium chicken broth

1. In a small Dutch oven, heat the oil over medium-high heat. Add the chicken and cook, turning the pieces until they are browned lightly on all sides, 8 to 10 minutes. Transfer the chicken to a plate.

2. Add the onion to the pot and sauté until lightly browned, 5 minutes. Mix in the apple, cherries, cinnamon, ginger, nutmeg, salt, and pepper.

3. Return the chicken to the pot, arranging it over the fruit mixture. Add the cilantro, and broth to come halfway up the sides of the chicken. When the liquid boils, reduce the heat, cover, and simmer until a thermometer inserted in the thickest part of the chicken registers 160°F and the juices run clear, about 20 minutes, turning the chicken once.

4. Divide the chicken, fruit, and juices among 4 dinner plates and serve.

Makes 4 servings

Per serving: 231 calories, 5 g fat, 1 g saturated fat, 29 g protein, 17 g carbohydrates, 4 g fiber

JERK PORK CHOPS WITH WARM PINEAPPLE-GRAPEFRUIT SALSA

● **FOOD FACTS**

The enzymes in pineapple tenderize meat and aid your digestion.

Golden pineapples contain significantly more vitamin C than other varieties.

A wet jerk paste both seasons lean pork chops and keeps them succulent. The sweet and tart fruit salsa is almost a full side dish that adds other tropical flavors to this vibrant dish. Make it just before grilling the chops.

JERK PASTE AND PORK

¾	cup chopped onion
1	large or 2 small scallions, sliced
1	tablespoon fresh lime juice
1	teaspoon salt
1	teaspoon ground allspice
1	teaspoon freshly ground pepper
½	teaspoon dried thyme
½	teaspoon ground cinnamon
½	teaspoon ground nutmeg
⅛	teaspoon cayenne pepper
4	(6-ounce) boneless center-cut pork chops

SALSA

1	tablespoon canola oil
1	medium red onion, cut into ½" crescents
1	small jalapeño chile pepper, seeded and cut lengthwise into thin strips
1½	cups fresh pineapple chunks cut in ½" pieces
2	tablespoons firmly packed dark brown sugar
1	red grapefruit, peeled and sectioned (see page 122)

1. **FOR THE JERK PASTE:** Whirl the onion, scallions, lime juice, salt, allspice, black pepper, thyme, cinnamon, nutmeg, and cayenne in a blender to a pulpy puree. Pour the jerk paste into a 1-quart resealable plastic bag. Add the pork chops, massaging to coat them with the marinade. Refrigerate for 12 to 24 hours.

2. Preheat a grill to medium-high.

3. **FOR THE SALSA:** Just before grilling the chops, heat the oil in a medium skillet over medium-high heat. Add the red onion and jalapeño and cook, stirring occasionally, until the onion is limp, about 5 minutes. Add the

pineapple and sugar and cook, stirring, until the sugar melts, about 2 minutes. Add the grapefruit and cook until it is warmed through, 2 minutes. Leave the salsa in the pan off the heat and keep warm.

4. Wipe the jerk paste off the chops. Grill the chops, rotating them 90 degrees after 2 minutes, until they are well-marked on one side, about 3 minutes. Turn and repeat on the second side, 3 minutes. Reduce the heat to medium and grill until a thermometer inserted in the centers of the chops registers 160°F and the juices run clear. Set each chop on a dinner plate. Add salsa alongside.

Makes 4 servings

Per serving: 424 calories, 20 g fat, 6 g saturated fat, 33 g protein, 29 g carbohydrates, 4 g fiber

BUTTERMILK-BRINED PORK CHOPS

Including buttermilk in the brine for these chops tenderizes them as well as makes them juicier. Serve them with Apple Ratatouille (page 243) or mashed sweet potatoes and sautéed collard greens for a colorful, complete meal.

● **FOOD FACT**

The lactic acid in buttermilk tenderizes meat and poultry the same way vinegar does in a marinade.

● **WHEN IS IT DONE?: USING A DIGITAL THERMOMETER**

Using an instant-read digital thermometer makes sure foods reach a safe internal temperature and helps avoid overcooking. This is especially important with pork and turkey, which can still look slightly pink when fully cooked. So if you do not own a digital thermometer, please get one.

1	cup regular or light buttermilk	1	teaspoon ground coriander
1	clove garlic, thinly sliced	4	(6-ounce) boneless center-cut
½	tablespoon kosher salt		pork chops
1	tablespoon brown sugar	1	tablespoon canola oil

1. In a 1-quart resealable plastic bag, combine the buttermilk, garlic, kosher salt, sugar, and coriander. Add the pork chops and massage to coat them well. Refrigerate for 4 to 24 hours.

2. Remove the chops from the brine and pat dry with paper towels. Discard the brine. In a medium skillet, heat the oil over medium-high heat. Add the chops and cook, turning once and reducing the heat if necessary to prevent burning, until browned and a thermometer inserted in the centers of the chops registers 160°F and the juices run clear, about 12 minutes. Serve immediately.

Makes 4 servings

Per serving: 260 calories, 11 g fat, 3 g saturated fat, 32 g protein, 5 g carbohydrates, 0 g fiber

PORK TENDERLOIN
WITH BLUEBERRY-PLUM SAUCE

A dark wine sauce, sautéed fruit, and berries spooned over tender pork medallions make this dish elegant yet lean. It comes together in minutes and is a perfect choice when you want to show off a full-bodied red wine.

● **ANOTHER WAY**

If you like venison, it also goes well with this sauce.

1	(¾–1-pound) pork tenderloin	¼	cup Tawny Port wine
	Salt and freshly ground pepper	2	tablespoons black currant or wild
1	tablespoon unsalted butter		blueberry fruit spread or jam
1	small red onion, cut into thin	1	tablespoon balsamic vinegar
	crescents	3	black plums, each halved, pitted,
½	cup thinly sliced shallots		and cut into 12 slices
¾	cup pomegranate juice	1	cup frozen wild blueberries

● **FOOD FACT**

Black plums are a good source of vitamin C, beta-carotene, and anthocyanins.

1. Preheat the broiler. Season the pork with ⅛ teaspoon salt and 4 or 5 grinds of pepper. Broil the meat for 6 minutes. Turn and continue broiling until a thermometer inserted in the center of a chop registers 155°F and the juices run clear, 6 minutes longer. Set the meat on a platter, cover loosely with foil, and let stand for 10 minutes.

2. Meanwhile, in a medium skillet, melt the butter over medium heat. Add the onion and shallots and sauté until they are browned, 8 minutes. Add the pomegranate juice, Port, jam, and vinegar. Boil 5 minutes to reduce the sauce slightly. Add the plums and berries, and cook until the plums are tender but still hold their shape, 4 to 5 minutes. Season to taste with salt and pepper.

3. Cut the meat into 1" medallions and divide among 4 dinner plates. Spoon the sauce around and over the meat.

Makes 4 servings

Per serving: 266 calories, 6 g fat, 3 g saturated fat, 19 g protein, 31 g carbohydrates, 3 g fiber

HERB-STUFFED FLANK STEAK

A red wine marinade and goat cheese filling set this grilled steak apart. Be sure to remove the meat from the marinade after 1 hour or the wine will overpower the other flavors in the dish.

● **BEST TECHNIQUE**

To cook the rolled meat properly requires a grill capable of indirect heat.

MARINADE AND STEAK

¼	cup dry red wine
2	tablespoons fresh lemon juice
1	tablespoon reduced-sodium soy sauce
½	teaspoon freshly ground pepper
2	tablespoons extra-virgin olive oil
1	(1½–1¾-pound) flank steak

STUFFING

4	cloves garlic
½	cup chopped flat-leaf parsley
1	tablespoon chopped fresh thyme
2	teaspoons grated lemon zest
½	teaspoon salt
¼	teaspoon freshly ground pepper
1	tablespoon extra-virgin olive oil
⅓	cup crumbled fresh goat cheese

1. **FOR THE MARINADE:** In a 1-gallon resealable plastic bag, combine the wine, lemon juice, soy sauce, and pepper and shake to dissolve. Add the oil and set aside.

2. Place the meat on a work surface with a short end facing you. Using a long, thin knife, cut the meat horizontally in half so the steak opens like a book. Place the steak in the marinade bag, seal, and refrigerate for 1 hour.

3. Preheat a gas or charcoal grill to medium. For charcoal, mound the briquettes toward one side of the grill.

4. **FOR THE STUFFING:** Place the garlic on a cutting board. With a heavy knife, chop and smear it to a paste. Place the garlic paste in a small bowl. Add the parsley, thyme, lemon zest, salt, pepper, and oil.

5. Remove the steak from the marinade and pat dry. Discard the marinade. Lay the meat on a work surface so what was the seam lies horizontally. Cover the meat with the filling, leaving a 1" border at the top. Sprinkle on the goat cheese. Working from the bottom, roll the steak up like a jelly roll. Thread toothpicks along the edge to seal the roll closed.

6. Grill the meat over direct heat, turning it every 3 minutes to brown it on all sides, 9 minutes in all. If using a gas grill, turn off the center row of burners. For charcoal heat, move the meat to a cooler side of the grill. Cover and grill the meat over indirect heat, starting to check at 8 minutes and removing the steak when a thermometer inserted in the center registers 130°F for medium-rare or 140°F for medium. Let the steak stand for 10 minutes, then cut cross-wise into 12 slices.

Makes 4 servings

Per serving: 346 calories, 18 g fat, 6 g saturated fat, 39 g protein, 3 g carbohydrates, 1 g fiber

COCOA-CRUSTED BEEF FILET
WITH POMEGRANATE SAUCE

The flavors in this dry-rubbed tenderloin served with a ruby sauce are so well-knit that people will want to compliment the chef in your kitchen. You will find, however, that each step in this sophisticated dish is simple.

1	tablespoon Seasoned Cocoa Nib Powder (opposite)	1	tablespoon coarsely chopped flat-leaf parsley
1	(1-pound) beef tenderloin, well trimmed	1	clove garlic, finely chopped
		2	cardamom pods, crushed
1	tablespoon extra-virgin olive oil	1	teaspoon dried thyme
½	cup fat-free, reduced-sodium beef broth	⅓	cup Ruby Port wine
		1½	tablespoon cold unsalted butter, cut into 6 pieces
¼	cup pomegranate juice		
2	tablespoons chopped shallots		Salt and freshly ground pepper

1. Preheat the oven to 400°F. Rub the meat generously all over with the cocoa nib powder. In a medium skillet, heat the oil over medium-high heat. Sear the meat all over, turning every 2 minutes, until browned, 8 minutes in all. Transfer the meat to a shallow baking pan. Set the skillet aside.

2. Roast the meat until a thermometer inserted in the center registers 130°F for medium-rare or 140°F for medium, 18 to 20 minutes. Let it sit at room temperature for 10 minutes to allow the juices to settle. Transfer the meat to a carving board and cover lightly with foil, reserving the juices in the pan.

3. Pour off the fat from the skillet, reserving the dark bits sticking to the pan. Set the pan over medium-high heat. Add the broth, pomegranate juice, shallots, parsley, garlic, cardamom, and thyme, plus any juices from the roasting pan. Scraping with a wooden spoon, gather up all the bits sticking to the pan. Boil until the liquid is reduced by one-third, about 3 minutes. Strain the contents into a bowl, pressing them with the back of a wooden spoon, then discard the solids. Wipe out the skillet.

4. Return the strained liquid to the skillet and set over medium-high heat. Add the Port and boil until the sauce is reduced by one-quarter, 2 to 3 minutes. Off the heat, add 1 or 2 pieces of the butter. Holding the handle of the pan in one hand, swirl the liquid until the butter melts into the sauce. Repeat two times with the remaining butter. Season to taste with salt and pepper. There will be about ⅓ cup sauce.

5. Carve the meat into 4 slices and arrange on a warmed serving platter. Pass the sauce separately.

Makes 4 servings

Per serving: 254 calories, 13 g fat, 5 g saturated fat, 23 g protein, 8 g carbohydrates, 1 g fiber

SEASONED COCOA NIB POWDER

2	tablespoons cocoa nibs	½	teaspoon kosher salt
¼	teaspoon black peppercorns		

In a spice mill or clean coffee grinder, combine the nibs and peppercorns. Whirl into a powder, stopping two or three times to stir the mixture so it does not cake. Add the salt. Seal in a small jar and refrigerate for up to 1 week.

Makes about 3 tablespoons

Per serving (¼ tablespoon): 14 calories, 1 g fat, 0 g saturated fat, 0 g protein, 1 g carbohydrates, 1 g fiber

● **FOOD FACT**

Kosher salt contains less than half the amount of sodium found in regular table salt.

THREE-ONION POT ROAST

● **BEST INGREDIENT**

The first cut is the leanest part of the brisket. Trim it of all visible fat.

● **BEST TECHNIQUE**

Using a pot just large enough to hold the meat and taking careful time while browning it are important to keep the meat moist and give it the most flavor.

● **ANOTHER WAY**

Prepare this pot roast in advance if you like, and cool to room temperature in the pan. Refrigerate the meat and sauce in separate, tightly sealed containers for up to 4 days. Reheat them together in a covered baking dish at 350°F.

Remember when pot roast was brisket smothered in dry onion soup mix and ketchup? My version gives you all their flavors without their excesses of sodium, sugar, and other undesirable ingredients.

1	tablespoon extra-virgin olive oil	1	tablespoon sweet paprika
1	(1½–1¾-pound) first cut beef brisket	2	teaspoons onion powder
		½	teaspoon garlic powder
2	large red onions, thinly sliced	⅛	teaspoon cayenne pepper
1	large Spanish onion, thinly sliced	1	teaspoon salt
6	scallions, chopped, green and white parts	¼	teaspoon freshly ground pepper
		½	cup hot water

1. Preheat the oven to 350°F.

2. In a Dutch oven just large enough to hold the meat, heat the oil over medium-high heat. Brown the meat well all over, 20 minutes, turning as needed. Set the meat aside and pour out all but 2 tablespoons of the fat.

3. Add half the onions and scallions to the pan. Set the meat on top and cover it with the remaining onions and scallions. Sprinkle on the paprika, onion and garlic powders, cayenne, salt, and pepper.

4. Add the water. Cover the pan and place in the oven. Bake until the meat can be pulled apart with a fork, about 2 hours.

5. On a cutting board, cut the meat across the grain into ½" slices. Place the sliced meat in a roasting pan and cover with the onions and pan juices. Cover with foil, return to the oven, and bake until the meat is tender, 30 to 45 minutes. Serve the meat, passing the sauce in a bowl.

Makes 6 to 8 servings

Per serving (for 8 servings): 217 calories, 7 g fat, 2 g saturated fat, 26 g protein, 12 g carbohydrates, 2 g fiber

CHAPTER SIX
FISH AND SEAFOOD

Roasted Salmon with Moroccan Tomato Compote 166, *Teriyaki Salmon Steaks* 168,

Potato-Crusted Salmon 169, *Perfect Poached Salmon with Two Sauces* 170, *Curry Cream Sauce* 170,

Dried Tomato–Mint Salsa 171, *Spice-Rubbed Salmon Kebabs with Tzatziki Sauce* 172,

Citrus Salmon Cakes 174, *Grilled Salmon with Coconut Chutney* 175, *Salmon Tacos with Avocado Cream* 176,

Roasted Salmon, Grape Tomatoes, and Leeks with Sparkling Wine Sauce 178,

Grilled Red Snapper with Avocado-Mango Salsa 180, *Trout with Meyer Lemon Gremolata* 182,

Four-Pepper Shrimp 183, *Thai Shrimp Curry with Broccoli, Carrots, and Green Peas* 184,

Tuna Muffuletta 186

ROASTED SALMON WITH MOROCCAN TOMATO COMPOTE

● **BEST TECHNIQUES**

To make ginger juice: Finely grate ginger using a rasp, ginger grater, or finest holes of regular grater. Over a small bowl, squeeze the pulp to extract the juice. A few bits of pulp in the juice will not matter.

To ripen the tomatoes, allow to sit at room temperature until they turn dark red.

● **ANOTHER WAY**

For a buffet, roast a whole side of king salmon and serve the sauce on the side.

Moroccan Tomato Compote is also good with halibut, as a dipping sauce for calamari, and meat loaf.

After devouring the ginger-accented tomato sauce served at Joe's Restaurant in Venice, California, I asked to meet the chef. Happily, Joe Miller generously shared his recipe. For best flavor, he uses spearmint and meaty, Early Girl tomatoes. Good alternatives, when they are not available, are dark red Campari or very ripe plum tomatoes.

COMPOTE

2	pounds ripe Early Girl, Campari, or plum tomatoes, halved and seeded
3	cloves garlic, crushed
12	sprigs fresh thyme or 1 teaspoon dried thyme
3"	sprig rosemary
2	tablespoons extra-virgin olive oil
½	teaspoon fresh ginger juice (see Best Technique, left)
	Salt and freshly ground pepper

SALMON

1	tablespoon extra-virgin olive oil
1	pound king or sockeye salmon fillet, cut into 4 pieces
¼	cup chopped spearmint leaves

1. **FOR THE COMPOTE:** Preheat the oven to 400°F. Line a jelly-roll pan with foil. Place the tomatoes, garlic, and thyme in the pan. Pull the needles from the rosemary and add them. Coat the tomatoes with the oil and, using your hands, arrange in a single layer, cut side down. Cover with foil. Roast until the tomatoes are soft, 45 minutes. Remove from the oven. Increase the oven temperature to 425°F.

2. When the tomatoes are cool enough to handle, lift off their skins and discard, along with the thyme branches. Using a slotted spoon, transfer the tomato flesh, garlic, and rosemary to a food processor. Reserve the juices in the pan. Whirl the tomatoes and herbs to a pulpy puree. Spoon in some of the reserved pan juices, if needed, to make the compote just thick enough to plop. Whirl in the ginger juice. Season to taste with salt and pepper. There will be 1 to 1½ cups sauce, depending on the kind of tomatoes used.

3. **FOR THE SALMON**: In a medium ovenproof skillet, heat the oil over medium-high heat. Arrange the salmon fillets in the pan, skin side up, and cook until browned, 3 minutes. Using a wide spatula, turn the salmon. Transfer the pan to the oven and roast until the salmon is slightly translucent at the center of its thickest part, 4 to 5 minutes. Carefully remove the hot pan from the oven.

4. Mix the mint into the sauce just before serving. Serve the fish, accompanied by the warm compote in a sauceboat.

Makes 4 servings

Per serving: 349 calories, 24 g fat, 4 g saturated fat, 25 g protein, 9 g carbohydrates, 3 g fiber

TERIYAKI SALMON STEAKS

Teriyaki sauce complements the flavor of all kinds of salmon while giving it an attractive glaze. Homemade teriyaki sauce tastes far better than bottled and takes just 2 minutes to make.

⅓	cup mirin, or ¼ cup dry sake and 1 tablespoon sugar	4	(5–6-ounce) king salmon steaks Salt and freshly ground pepper
¼	cup reduced-sodium soy sauce	1	teaspoon canola oil
1	tablespoon sugar		
½	teaspoon grated fresh ginger, or ¼ teaspoon ground		

1. In a small bowl, combine the mirin or sake and sugar, soy sauce, sugar, and ginger. Stir to blend and set aside.

2. Season the salmon on one side with salt and pepper. In a large skillet, heat the oil over medium-high heat. Add the salmon, seasoned side up, and cook until browned and crisp on the bottom, about 3 minutes. Using a wide spatula, turn and brown the salmon on the second side, 2 to 3 minutes. Transfer to a plate. Pour all the fat from the pan, then rinse out and dry.

3. Return the pan to the heat. Pour in the teriyaki mixture. When it boils, stir just to dissolve the sugar. Add the salmon in one layer. When the liquid simmers, reduce the heat and cook until the fish is slightly translucent in the center, 2 minutes. If it needs to cook longer, turn it. When done, transfer the salmon to a serving plate.

4. Increase the heat to high and boil the liquid until it resembles dark maple syrup, about 1 minute. Spoon the sauce over the fish to glaze it. Serve immediately.

Makes 4 servings

Per serving: 347 calories, 18 g fat, 3 g saturated fat, 30 g protein, 12 g carbohydrates, 0 g fiber

POTATO-CRUSTED SALMON

Coating fish fillets with dry potato flakes gives them a crisp, golden covering. Only potato flakes used in products such as Barbara's Instant Mashed Potatoes or Shiloh Farms potato flakes work, never granulated potato buds, which do not get crunchy.

● **ANOTHER WAY**

For children reluctant to eat fish, cut fillets into 1" strips before coating and serve as fish sticks. These smaller pieces will cook more quickly.

4	(4–6-ounce) skinless king or sockeye salmon fillets Salt and freshly ground pepper	¼	cup natural dehydrated potato flakes or instant mashed potatoes
		2	teaspoons extra-virgin olive oil

1. Season the salmon with a pinch of salt and 2 or 3 grinds pepper on each side. Spread the potato flakes in an even layer on a salad plate.

2. In a medium skillet, heat the oil over medium-high heat. One piece at a time, coat the salmon in the potato flakes, pressing to help them adhere. Immediately place the salmon in the pan. Cook, using tongs to turn the pieces every 2 minutes, until the salmon is crusty and golden brown on all sides and just opaque in the center, 6 to 8 minutes.

Makes 4 servings

Per serving: 244 calories, 16 g fat, 2 g saturated fat, 23 g protein, 3 g carbohydrates, 0 g fiber

PERFECT POACHED SALMON WITH TWO SAUCES

● **BEST TECHNIQUE**

Chicken broth in the poaching liquid subtly enhances the flavor of the fish and helps keep it moist.

Poached salmon conjures up visions of meals prepared by a chef. But you can make it to moist perfection, too. For a festive buffet, offer both sauces.

1	carrot, cut into 1" pieces	1	bay leaf
1	rib celery, cut into 1" pieces	3	cups fat-free, reduced-sodium
1	leek, white part and pale green		chicken broth
	part, cut into 1" pieces	1	cup cold water
1	small onion, quartered		Juice of 1 lemon
4	sprigs flat-leaf parsley	1	(1-pound) skinless king salmon
3	sprigs fresh thyme		fillet, preferably wild

1. In a deep skillet, combine the carrot, celery, leek, onion, parsley, thyme, bay leaf, broth, and 1 cup water. Bring to a boil over medium-high heat, cover, reduce the heat, and simmer 10 minutes. Add the lemon juice.

2. Place the salmon in the poaching liquid. Return the liquid to a gentle simmer and cook, uncovered, until the salmon is just translucent at the center of the thickest part, allowing 8 minutes for each inch of thickness. Using a wide pancake turner, transfer the salmon to a plate to cool completely.

Makes 4 servings

Per serving (without sauce): 221 calories, 13 g fat, 2 g saturated fat, 24 g protein, 1 g carbohydrates, 0 g fiber

 # CURRY CREAM SAUCE

● **BEST INGREDIENT**

Look for a sulfite-free coconut milk, preferably organic, such as from Thai Kitchen.

Coconut milk gives this gently spicy sauce richness and body.

1	cup light coconut milk, divided	1	tablespoon reduced-fat plain
¼	cup finely chopped onion		yogurt
1	tablespoon curry powder	1	teaspoon fresh lime juice
1	tablespoon flour		Salt and freshly ground pepper
¼	cup apple juice		

1. In a small saucepan, heat ¼ cup of the coconut milk over medium heat. Add the onion and cook until it is translucent, 3 minutes. Mix in the curry powder and flour and cook, stirring constantly, until fragrant, 30 seconds.

2. Add the apple juice and cook, stirring, until the onion is soft, 5 minutes. Add the remaining coconut milk and cook, stirring, until the sauce coats the back of a spoon, 3 minutes. Off the heat, stir in the yogurt and lime juice. Season to taste with salt and pepper.

Makes 1½ cups, 6 servings

Per serving (4 tablespoons): 74 calories, 4 g fat, 3 g saturated fat, 2 g protein, 8 g carbohydrates, 1 g fiber

DRIED TOMATO–MINT SALSA

This sharp-flavored blend of capers, parsley, mint, and garlic goes well with king salmon, which has the highest fat content of all salmon.

½	cup coarsely chopped sun-dried tomatoes	2	teaspoons capers, rinsed and drained
1	cup fresh flat-leaf parsley	1	tablespoon fresh lemon juice
¾	cup spearmint leaves	3	tablespoons extra-virgin olive oil
1	clove garlic, chopped		Freshly ground pepper

Whirl the sun-dried tomatoes, parsley, mint, garlic, capers, and lemon juice in a mini food processor until finely chopped. With the motor running, drizzle in the oil. Season to taste with pepper. Let sit 20 minutes to allow the flavors to meld.

Makes ¾ cup, 4 servings

Per serving (3 tablespoons): 127 calories, 11 g fat, 2 g saturated fat, 2 g protein, 7 g carbohydrates, 3 g fiber

● **ANOTHER WAY**
Add 2 tablespoons walnuts to the salsa and toss with pasta or rice, or blend in ½ cup crumbled feta and serve on grilled bread as bruschetta.

SPICE-RUBBED SALMON KEBABS WITH TZATZIKI SAUCE

● **BEST TECHNIQUES**

Metal skewers conduct heat that helps food cook inside.

Threading foods loosely on skewers helps it cook through.

If using bamboo skewers, soak them in cold water for 30 minutes.

Salmon makes good kebabs, holding together well on the grill and cooking quickly enough to stay moist. The garlicky yogurt and cucumber sauce accompanying these skewers is refreshing contrasted with the warm fish.

SAUCE		KEBABS	
2	Kirby cucumbers, peeled and thinly sliced	1	tablespoon coriander seed
¾	cup (a 6- or 7-ounce container) reduced-fat (2%) Greek yogurt or reduced-fat plain yogurt	1	tablespoon fennel seed
		1	pound king or coho salmon fillet, skinned and cut into 8 cubes
1	large clove garlic, finely chopped	12	large cherry tomatoes
2	teaspoons fresh lemon juice	1	green bell pepper, cut into 1½" squares
1	teaspoon red wine vinegar	1	large red onion, cut into ¾" wedges
	Salt and freshly ground pepper	4	8" skewers

1. Preheat a grill or broiler.

2. **FOR THE SAUCE:** Combine the cucumber, yogurt, garlic, lemon juice, and vinegar in a bowl. Season to taste with salt and pepper. Set aside at room temperature for 30 minutes.

3. **FOR THE KEBABS:** In a dry, heavy skillet, roast the coriander and fennel seeds over medium-high heat until fragrant, 60 to 90 seconds, shaking the pan constantly. On a plate, cool the spices completely. In a spice mill or clean coffee grinder, whirl the roasted spices to a powder. Add ½ teaspoon salt and ¼ teaspoon freshly ground pepper. This spice rub keeps in a container in the refrigerator for up to 5 days.

4. Place the spices on a plate. Pat the salmon with a paper towel and dredge in the rub, pressing to help it to adhere. For each skewer, thread on a tomato, a pepper square, and a salmon cube. Add 3 outer layers from an onion wedge,

another tomato, more onion, another salmon cube, a pepper square, and tomato.

5. Coat the kebabs lightly with cooking spray. Grill or broil for 8 minutes, or until the salmon is translucent just in the center; it will continue cooking to opaque when the kebabs are served. Pass the sauce separately.

Makes 4 servings

Per serving: 298 calories, 15 g fat, 3 g saturated fat, 28 g protein, 14 g carbohydrates, 4 g fiber

CITRUS SALMON CAKES

Egg white is the only binding in these salmon cakes, keeping them low in carbs and wheat-free. Wild fish works best because it is leaner than farm-raised. Coho salmon's flavor complements the fresh herbs in these fish cakes especially well.

1	pound fresh or frozen wild salmon, preferably coho, cut into 1" chunks	¼	cup chopped dill leaves
		2	teaspoons fresh lime juice
		½	teaspoon lemon pepper
1	large egg white	1	teaspoon salt
½	cup finely chopped scallions, green parts only	½	teaspoon freshly ground pepper
		1	tablespoon extra-virgin olive oil

1. If using frozen fish, defrost it in the refrigerator to keep it firm. Pulse the fish 3 or 4 times in a food processor to chop it coarsely. Add the egg white, scallions, dill, lime juice, lemon pepper, salt, and pepper. Pulse 10 to 12 times, or until the ingredients are just blended. Do not whirl to a smooth paste; the fish should look nubbly. Form the mixture into four 2½" patties. If desired, wrap the patties individually in plastic wrap and refrigerate for up to 8 hours.

2. In a heavy medium skillet, heat the oil over medium-high heat. Add the salmon cakes and cook until lightly browned, about 3 minutes. Turn and cook until browned on the second side and opaque in the center, about 3 minutes. Serve immediately.

Makes 4 servings

Per serving: 207 calories, 10 g fat, 2 g saturated fat, 26 g protein, 1 g carbohydrates, 1 g fiber

GRILLED SALMON
WITH COCONUT CHUTNEY

Coconut, ginger, cilantro, and a sizzle of Indian spices contrast well with the richness of salmon.

¼	cup reduced-fat unsweetened dried coconut	1 or 2	serrano chile peppers
1	tablespoon boiling water		Salt and freshly ground pepper
¼	cup spearmint leaves	2	teaspoons canola oil, plus more for brushing
¼	cup cilantro leaves	½	teaspoon black mustard seeds
¼	cup reduced-fat plain yogurt	¼	teaspoon cumin seeds
1"	piece fresh ginger, chopped	4	(4–6-ounce) salmon fillets or small steaks
1	tablespoon finely chopped onion		

● **BEST INGREDIENT**

Natural food stores sell unsweetened reduced-fat dried coconut made without sulfites. It contains 40 percent less fat than regular dried coconut.

● **ANOTHER WAY**

If you are not a fan of chiles, use just a touch or omit them and enjoy all the other flavors in the cool, pale green chutney.

1. In a small bowl, combine the coconut and boiling water. Set aside until the coconut absorbs the water and is fluffy, 15 minutes.

2. Combine the coconut with the mint, cilantro, yogurt, ginger, onion, chile pepper, 1 teaspoon salt, and ¼ teaspoon pepper in a mini food processor. Add 2 tablespoons water. Whirl until the herbs are finely chopped. Set aside.

3. In a small heavy skillet, heat the oil over medium heat. Add the mustard and cumin seeds. They should sizzle. Fry until the mustard seeds are popping and the cumin colors lightly, 1 minute. Add to the coconut mixture and whirl to blend. Set aside for up to 1 hour.

4. Preheat the grill to medium-high. Coat the salmon lightly with oil on both sides and season with salt and pepper. Grill the salmon over the hottest part of the grill for 4 minutes. Turn and cook until just translucent in the center at the thickest part, 3 to 5 minutes. Transfer the fish to 4 plates. Pass the chutney in a bowl.

Makes 4 servings

Per serving: 365 calories, 23 g fat, 5 g saturated fat, 35 g protein, 3 g carbohydrates, 1 g fiber

SALMON TACOS
WITH AVOCADO CREAM

Nothing like fast-food fish tacos, two of these overstuffed beauties make a healthy main dish that includes whole-grain tortillas. Although served on a plate, this messy combination is best eaten with your hands.

AVOCADO CREAM

⅓   cup Spiced Buttermilk Dressing
      (page 139)
¼   ripe avocado, peeled and cubed

SALSA

2   ripe large tomatoes, seeded and
      chopped
½   red onion, finely chopped
1 or 2   serrano chile peppers, seeded
      and finely chopped
      Juice of 1 lime
      Salt and freshly ground pepper

TACOS

8   (6" diameter) corn tortillas
1   tablespoon canola oil
1   pound coho or king salmon fillet,
      skinned and cut into 8 pieces
2½   cups (½ small head) finely
      shredded green cabbage
½   cup cilantro leaves

1. Preheat the oven to 350°F.

2. **FOR THE AVOCADO CREAM:** Whirl the buttermilk dressing with the avocado in a blender or mini food processor, until smooth. Set aside.

3. **FOR THE SALSA:** In a mixing bowl, combine the tomatoes, onion, chile pepper, and lime juice. Season to taste with salt and pepper. Set aside.

4. **FOR THE TACOS:** Wrap the tortillas in foil and warm in the oven until moist and soft, 8 minutes. Set aside.

5. In a heavy skillet, heat the oil over medium-high heat. Add the salmon and cook, turning with tongs every 2 minutes, until golden on all sides and slightly translucent in the center at the thickest part, 8 minutes in all.

6. Place 2 tortillas on each of 4 dinner plates. Arrange ½ cup cabbage in the center of each tortilla, top with 2 tablespoons of the salsa, a piece of salmon, a dollop of avocado cream, and some cilantro. Serve immediately.

Makes 4 servings

Per serving: 386 calories, 15 g fat, 3 g saturated fat, 30 g protein, 35 g carbohydrates, 7 g fiber

Here's the Catch

Atlantic salmon is a species. Always farmed, it is sold fresh, smoked and sometimes canned. Pacific wild salmon includes five species. They run from May through September, with different ones predominating at different times, so check with your fishmonger for availability.

- **King or Chinook:** Biggest, fattest and richest in omega-3s, with pink, moist flesh.
- **Sockeye, red, or blueback:** Smaller fish with redder, firmer flesh. Available canned and smoked as well as fresh.
- **Coho or silver:** Medium-size fish with dry, firm, pink-orange flesh.
- **Pink:** Most abundant species and second only to king in omega-3 content. Has soft flesh and mild flavor. Used mostly for canning.
- **Chum or Keta:** Has little omega-3 content. Used mainly in food service.

ROASTED SALMON, GRAPE TOMATOES, AND LEEKS WITH SPARKLING WINE SAUCE

● **BEST TECHNIQUE**

Normally loaded with butter, this version of *beurre blanc*, the classic French sauce, contains only 1 tablespoon, just enough to give the sauce body and blissful flavor.

Prosecco, an Italian sparking wine rarely used in cooking, is essential to this dish's sauce, which is my unique version of a French classic. Guests can use the rest of the bottle of wine to toast the cook.

1	pint grape tomatoes	½	cup Prosecco sparkling white wine
2	leeks, white parts only, cut into ¼" rounds	1	tablespoon minced shallot
1	tablespoon extra-virgin olive oil, divided	½	cup fat-free, reduced-sodium chicken broth
1	teaspoon dried thyme	1	tablespoon cold unsalted butter, cut into small pieces
	Salt and freshly ground pepper		
4	(6-ounce) salmon fillets, skin removed		

1. Preheat the oven to 400°F.

2. In a baking pan with shallow sides, combine the tomatoes and leeks. Add 1 tablespoon of the oil, the thyme, ½ teaspoon salt, and 4 or 5 grinds pepper. Toss with your hands to coat the vegetables. Roast until the tomatoes are wrinkled and the leeks soft but not mushy, 15 minutes. Remove from the oven and set aside. Increase the oven temperature to 425°F.

3. In a medium ovenproof skillet, heat the remaining oil over medium-high heat. Arrange the salmon in the pan, skinned side up, and cook until browned, 3 minutes. Using a wide spatula, turn the salmon. Transfer the pan to the oven and roast until the salmon is just translucent in the center where it is thickest, 4 to 5 minutes. Carefully remove the pan from the oven, as it is very hot. Place it on the back of the stove.

4. In a small, nonreactive saucepan, combine the wine and shallot and set over medium-high heat. Boil until the wine is reduced to 2 tablespoons, about 4 minutes. Pour in the broth and boil until there is ¼ cup liquid. Off the heat, while whisking vigorously, drop in the cold butter a few pieces at a time, blending them in before adding more. Season to taste with salt and pepper.

5. Place a salmon fillet in the center of each of 4 dinner plates. Spoon roasted tomatoes and leeks on either side and spoon the sauce over the fish. Serve immediately.

Makes 4 servings

Per serving: 369 calories, 17 g fat, 4 g saturated fat, 36 g protein, 11 g carbohydrates, 2 g fiber

GRILLED RED SNAPPER
WITH AVOCADO-MANGO SALSA

● **BEST TECHNIQUE**

Lining the grill or pan with foil means minimal clean up.

Everyone loves the tropical flavors in this dish. Perfect for company or a family dinner, few dishes this attractive also come together so easily.

SALSA

1	ripe medium avocado, diced
¾	cup finely chopped mango
¼	cup finely chopped red onion
1	jalapeño chile pepper, seeded and finely chopped
1	tablespoon fresh lime juice
2	tablespoons chopped cilantro leaves
1	teaspoon dried Mexican oregano
	Salt and freshly ground pepper

RED SNAPPER

4	(6–8-ounce) red snapper fillets
1	tablespoon extra-virgin olive oil

1. Preheat a grill or broiler to medium-hot.

2. **FOR THE SALSA:** In a mixing bowl, combine the avocado, mango, onion, jalapeño, and lime juice. Stir with a fork. Add the cilantro and oregano and stir again. Season to taste with salt and pepper. Set aside for 20 minutes to allow the flavors of the salsa to meld.

3. **FOR THE RED SNAPPER:** Brush the fillets lightly with the oil and season lightly with salt and pepper. Grill the fish, skin side down, until it is opaque in the center at the thickest part and flakes easily, about 5 minutes. Or place the fillets on a shallow pan and broil until they are opaque in the center and flake easily, about 6 minutes. Serve immediately, accompanied by the salsa.

Makes 4 servings

Per serving: 319 calories, 12 g fat, 2 g saturated fat, 36 g protein, 11 g carbohydrates, 4 g fiber

TROUT WITH MEYER LEMON GREMOLATA

● **FOOD FACT**

Trout is a fair source of omega-3s.

Earthy shiitake mushrooms and aromatic Meyer lemon are good companions in this unconventional gremolata topping. Lightly cooked, it adds an easy elegance to the broiled fish.

1	tablespoon extra-virgin olive oil	¾	cup finely chopped shiitake mushrooms
1	large carrot, cut into ¼" dice, ½ cup		
1	large rib celery, cut into ¼" dice, ½ cup	1	Meyer lemon
			Salt and freshly ground pepper
1	leek, white part only, finely chopped	4	(6-ounce) trout fillets

1. Preheat the broiler to high.

2. **FOR THE GREMOLATA:** In a medium skillet, heat the oil over medium-high heat. Add the carrot and celery and cook, stirring often, for 2 minutes. Mix in the leek and mushrooms and cook until the mushrooms release their liquid, 4 minutes. Continue cooking, stirring often, until the celery and carrot are tender but still al dente, and the pan is almost dry, about 4 minutes. Transfer the vegetables to a bowl. Grate 1 teaspoon zest and squeeze 2 tablespoons juice from the lemon. Stir both into the vegetables. Season to taste with salt and pepper. Set aside. The gremolata can be made up to 1 hour ahead.

3. **FOR THE TROUT:** Line a baking sheet with foil and coat it with cooking spray. Arrange the trout fillets skin side down on the pan in one layer. Season lightly with salt and pepper. Broil until the fish is slightly charred around the edges and firm and opaque at the thickest part, 5 to 6 minutes. Immediately transfer the trout to four dinner plates. Spoon one-quarter of the Gremolata over each fillet. Serve immediately.

Makes 4 servings

Per serving: 377 calories, 19 g fat, 3 g saturated fat, 37 g protein, 15 g carbohydrates, 2 g fiber

FOUR-PEPPER SHRIMP

Sweet red and green bell peppers, paprika, a touch of cayenne, and sherry give this simple sauté Spanish flavor. It is an ideal one-dish dinner served over cooked brown rice.

● **FOOD FACT**

Oil helps your body absorb the beta-carotene and lycopene in red bell peppers, paprika, and tomatoes.

3	tablespoons extra-virgin olive oil	1	cup tomato sauce
1	medium onion, finely chopped	1	tablespoon sherry
1	clove garlic, minced	1	pound large (21–30 count)
1	tablespoon sweet paprika, preferably Spanish		shrimp, peeled and deveined
½	teaspoon ground cumin	4	cups cooked long-grain brown rice
	Pinch of cayenne pepper	½	roasted green bell pepper, finely
1	roasted red bell pepper, finely chopped (see page 117)		chopped (optional)

1. In a large skillet, heat the oil over medium-high heat. Sauté the onion and cook, stirring often, for 2 minutes. Add the garlic and sauté until the onion is translucent, 3 minutes. Add the paprika, cumin, and cayenne and cook, stirring constantly, until fragrant, 1 minute. Add the red pepper, tomato sauce, and sherry. Cook until the sauce starts to simmer, 3 minutes.

2. Reduce the heat to medium. Add the shrimp and cook, turning two or three times, until opaque in the center, 6 to 8 minutes. Serve over the rice, sprinkling on the green peppers if using.

Makes 4 servings

Per serving: 455 calories, 14 g fat, 2 g saturated fat, 27 g protein, 54 g carbohydrates, 6 g fiber

THAI SHRIMP CURRY WITH BROCCOLI, CARROTS, AND GREEN PEAS

● **ANOTHER WAY**

In place of baby carrots, use a regular one, cut diagonally into ½" slices.

Thai cooks use coconut milk generously in curries like this one, where it knits together chile heat and pungent spices. I use light coconut milk to lower the fat while keeping its explosion of tropical flavor in balance. This recipe omits fish sauce, allowing those who dislike it or are allergic to it to enjoy the stir-fry. A wide, shallow frying pan where food can move works as well as a wok for stir-frying.

2	scallions, sliced, white and green parts	½	teaspoon salt
1	tablespoon minced garlic	¼	teaspoon freshly ground pepper
1	teaspoon grated fresh ginger	2	tablespoons peanut oil, divided
1–2	teaspoons green Thai chili paste	¾	pound medium (31–40 count) shrimp, peeled
½	cup light unsweetened coconut milk, divided	1	red onion, cut into ½" crescents
¼	cup fat-free, reduced-sodium chicken broth	2	cups 1" broccoli florets
		6	baby carrots, halved lengthwise
½	teaspoon sugar	½	cup frozen baby green peas

1. In a small bowl, combine the scallions, garlic, ginger, and chili paste with 2 tablespoons of the coconut milk. Whisk to dissolve the paste and set aside. In a measuring cup, combine the remaining coconut milk with the broth, sugar, salt and pepper.

2. In a wok, heat 1 tablespoon of the oil over high heat. Add the shrimp and stir-fry until bright pink, 2 minutes. Using a slotted spoon, remove them to a plate.

3. Add the remaining 1 tablespoon oil to the wok. Stir-fry the onion for 1 minute, and add to the shrimp. Stir-fry the broccoli, carrots, and peas for

1 minute. Add the chili paste mixture and cook for 30 seconds. Return the shrimp and onion to the pan. Add the coconut milk mixture and stir-fry until the shrimp are opaque, 2 minutes. Serve immediately.

Makes 4 servings

Per serving: 220 calories, 11 g fat, 3 g saturated fat, 19 g protein, 12 g carbohydrates, 3 g fiber

TUNA MUFFULETTA

● **BEST INGREDIENT**

Both sweet and spicy
tasting, a peppadew looks
like a cross between a
small red pepper and a
tomato. Pickled peppadews
are widely available in
supermarkets.

Using canned tuna in place of the cured meats used in this sandwich made famous by Central Grocery in New Orleans, turns it into a lighter, smarter choice. Along with its obligatory olive salad, I also include roasted red peppers. Since the prepared versions of the olive salad sold by Web sites contain preservatives, I prefer making my own.

OLIVE SALAD

6	pitted Sicilian-style green olives, chopped
4	pitted kalamata olives, chopped
3	pickled peppadew, red peppers, chopped
1	small rib celery, chopped
1	tablespoon drained small capers

MUFFULETTA

⅓	cup red wine vinegar
2	tablespoons extra-virgin olive oil, divided
2	cloves garlic, sliced
	Salt and freshly ground pepper
1	roasted red pepper, cut into thin strips (see page 117)
1	(8") round Italian white bread, halved horizontally
1	cup baby spinach leaves
4	thin slices Provolone cheese
1	(6-ounce) can water-packed albacore tuna, drained
1	teaspoon dried oregano

1. **FOR THE SALAD:** In a mixing bowl, combine the chopped Sicilian and kalamata olives, peppadews, celery, and capers. This salad keeps, tightly covered in the refrigerator, for 5 days.

2. **FOR THE MUFFULETTA:** In a plastic or other nonreactive container, combine the vinegar, 1 tablespoon of the oil, the garlic, ¼ teaspoon salt, and 3 or 4 grinds of pepper. Mix in the roasted pepper. Cover and refrigerate overnight or up to 3 days.

3. Spoon 2 tablespoons of the vinegar marinade over the bottom of the bread. Cover the bread with the spinach, then the cheese.

4. In a bowl, mash the tuna, oregano, and remaining oil. Season to taste with salt and pepper. Spread the tuna over the cheese. Spoon the olive salad over the tuna.

5. Scoop most of the bread from the top half of the loaf. Pack the hollow with the marinated peppers. Spoon on 3 tablespoons of the marinade. Close the sandwich. Wrap in plastic wrap and refrigerate for 12 to 24 hours. A whole muffuletta will keep for up to 3 days in the refrigerator, tightly wrapped.

Makes 6 servings

Per serving: 349 calories, 13 g fat, 4.6 g saturated fat, 18 g protein, 43 g carbohydrates, 4 g fiber

CHAPTER SEVEN
PASTA, WHOLE GRAINS, AND RICE

THREE CHEESE PANINI

Grilled Cheddar and Tomato Panini 189

Goat Cheese, Sun-Dried Tomato, and Arugula Panini 190

Melted Swiss, Smoked Turkey, and Apple Panini 191

WBBJ Sandwich 192, *Greek Pizzettes* 193, *Red Quinoa with Corn and Pecans* 194, *Popped Quinoa Pilaf* 196,

Pomegranate Tabbouleh 197, *Crisp Buckwheat Polenta with Mushroom Topping* 198, *Peanut Fried Rice* 200,

Black Rice with Blackberries 201, *Fusilli with Broccoli Bolognese* 202, *Five-Way Chili Spaghetti* 204,

Macaroni and Cheese with Broccoli 206, *Singapore Noodles* 207, *Spinach Lasagna with Creamy Tomato Sauce* 208,

Baked Rigatoni with Butternut Squash and Turkey Sausage 210, *Polenta Lasagna with Red Wine Lentils* 212

Three Cheese Panini

A proper grilled cheese sandwich is crisp outside and oozing with melted creamy cheese inside. Adding to their perfection, each of these three Italian-accented versions uses a whole grain bread that complements its filling. These panini help you add two servings of whole grain goodness to your day.

GRILLED CHEDDAR AND TOMATO PANINI

Sharp aged Cheddar and a thick slice of juicy tomato, always good partners, are even better warmed between slices of buttered whole wheat sandwich bread. Using 50 percent reduced-fat cheese helps to compensate for the butter's calories.

2	teaspoons unsalted butter, softened	2	ounces reduced-fat sharp Cheddar cheese, thinly sliced
1	teaspoon finely chopped flat-leaf parsley	1	thick slice beefsteak tomato
2	slices whole wheat sandwich bread		

1. In a small bowl, combine the butter and parsley. Mash together using the back of a spoon. Spread one side of each bread slice with the butter. Place the bread buttered side down on a plate.

2. Arrange the cheese to cover one slice of bread. Top with the tomato and the second slice of bread, buttered side up.

3. Grill in a hot panini press or other two-sided grill until the bread is browned and crisp and the cheese melted, about 3 minutes. Serve immediately.

Makes 1

Per panini: 310 calories, 14 g fat, 7 g saturated fat, 20 g protein, 30 g carbohydrates, 4 g fiber

GOAT CHEESE, SUN-DRIED TOMATO, AND ARUGULA PANINI

● **GRILLING PANINI**

If you do not have a panini press or two-sided grill, make these sandwiches on a griddle or in a heavy skillet. Weight the sandwich by placing a smaller pan on top of it, and turn the sandwich to brown both sides. Do not use a stove-top grill pan, whose ridges will burn the bread.

This creamy cheese and tomato combination is most Mediterranean. It calls for artisanal bread with a sturdy center and rustic crust, either sliced from the long loaf we call Italian bread or bold-tasting sourdough rye. Grilling brings out the flavors of the cheese, tomatoes, and pungent greens in the sandwich.

1½ ounces fresh goat cheese	Arugula leaves
2 slices rustic whole wheat Italian bread or sourdough rye bread	Basil leaves
Salt and freshly ground pepper	1 teaspoon extra-virgin olive oil
3 or 4 marinated sun-dried tomato halves, well drained	

1. Spread half the cheese on one side of each slice of bread. Season with salt and pepper. Arrange the tomatoes on one slice. Cover the other slice of bread with the arugula, tearing the leaves to fit as needed. Lay the basil over the arugula. To close the sandwich, put the two slices together with the greens facing the tomatoes.

2. Brush the outside of the sandwich with the oil.

3. Grill on a hot panini press or other two-sided grill until the bread has grill marks and the sandwich is warmed through but not hot, about 2 minutes.

Makes 1

Per panini: 423 calories, 21.6 g fat, 7 g saturated fat, 17 g protein, 39 g carbohydrates, 5 g fiber

MELTED SWISS, SMOKED TURKEY, AND APPLE PANINI

Two kinds of mustard accentuate the sharp, smoky, and sweet flavors in this sandwich. The bread should be a full-bodied multigrain sandwich loaf, perhaps Alvarado Street Bakery's sprouted multigrain.

1	tablespoon unsalted butter	2	slices Jarlsberg Lite cheese
½	teaspoon Dijon mustard	1	slice plain or smoked turkey breast
2	slices sprouted grain or multigrain bread	6	(¼"-thick) slices Golden Delicious or Granny Smith apple
1½	teaspoons sweet and hot or honey mustard		

1. In a small bowl, stir the butter and Dijon mustard together until well combined. Spread half the mixture on one side of each bread slice. Place the bread, buttered side down, on a plate.

2. Spread half the sweet and hot mustard on each slice of bread and top with a slice of cheese. Fold the turkey and arrange it over the cheese on one of the slices. Cover the turkey with the apple slices. To close the sandwich, put the two bread slices together, cheese sides facing.

3. Grill in a hot panini press or other two-sided grill until the bread is browned and crisp and the cheese melted, about 3 minutes. Serve immediately.

Makes 1

Per panini: 522 calories, 20 g fat, 11 g saturated fat, 37 g protein, 45 g carbohydrates, 3 g fiber

WBBJ SANDWICH

● **BEST INGREDIENT**
French walnut oil is more flavorful than US brands. When buying domestic brands using a roasted oil compensates for this flavor difference.

Walnut butter and blueberry jam provide different antioxidants than peanut butter and jelly. Grown-ups love this super-healthy combination almost as well.

2	tablespoons blueberry fruit spread	2	tablespoons Walnut Butter
2	slices Italian whole wheat bread or good quality white sandwich bread		(see below)

Spread half of the fruit spread on each slice of bread. Spread the walnut butter on one slice. Close the sandwich, cut diagonally into thirds or into four triangles, and serve.

Makes 1

Per sandwich: 434 calories, 22 g fat, 2 g saturated fat, 12 g protein, 61 g carbohydrates, 6 g fiber

WALNUT BUTTER

Freshly made walnut better is creamy and full-flavored. You will not find it at the market because walnuts are so costly but can whirl it up yourself in about 10 minutes.

1	cup walnuts, toasted (see page 74)	2	teaspoons walnut oil, preferably roasted
½	teaspoon salt	1	teaspoon canola oil

By hand, chop the nuts coarsely, discarding any dried skin and dust. Add the salt. Pulse the nuts in a mini food processor to chop them finely. With the motor running, drizzle in the oils. Whirl until the nuts are ground into butter, stopping to scrape down the sides two or three times.

Makes ½ cup

GREEK PIZZETTES

Piling a Greek salad on a round flatbread topped with melted feta gives you a warm sandwich and a crisp salad at the same time. It is best when the tangy dressing from the salad soaks into the bread.

2	(8"-diameter) whole wheat Mediterranean-style flatbreads or pocketless pitas	1	large pepperoncini pepper, seeded and torn into 8 pieces
½	cup crumbled reduced-fat feta	1	thin slice large red onion
1	cup chopped romaine lettuce	1	tablespoon red wine vinegar
1	small Kirby cucumber, thinly sliced	1	small clove garlic, minced
4 or 6	anchovy fillets, optional	¼	teaspoon salt
½	cup cherry tomatoes, halved		Freshly ground pepper
		2	teaspoons extra-virgin olive oil
		½	teaspoon dried oregano

● **BEST INGREDIENT**

Use only pocketless pita bread. The kind you can split dries out under the broiler and falls apart when soaked with the dressing.

● **ANOTHER WAY**

For a party, set all the salad ingredients and the dressing out in individual bowls to let people assemble their own pizzette on warm breads you bring from the kitchen or grill.

1. Preheat the broiler. Place the flatbreads or pitas on a baking sheet and sprinkle half the feta over each. Broil 3 inches from the heat until the cheese melts, 1 to 2 minutes. If necessary, do this one at a time.

2. Top each flatbread or pita with half of the lettuce, cucumber slices, anchovies, if using, tomatoes, and pepperoncini pieces, in that order. Separate the onion into rings and scatter them on top.

3. In a small bowl, combine the vinegar, garlic, salt, and 3 or 4 grinds of pepper. Whisk in the oil. Drizzle the dressing over the pizzettes. Sprinkle on the oregano. Serve immediately.

Makes 2

Per pizzette: 337 calories, 11 g fat, 3 g saturated fat, 16 g protein, 49 g carbohydrates, 9 g fiber

RED QUINOA WITH CORN AND PECANS

● BEST INGREDIENT

Red quinoa has a milder, more nutty flavor than the familiar pale beige kind. Natural food markets and many conventional supermarkets carry it.

Melding four native American ingredients, including turkey in the bacon, this side dish has the earth-red and golden colors of the Southwest. It can anchor a meatless meal or serve as a great grain side dish.

3	teaspoons canola oil, divided	½	cup fat-free, reduced-sodium chicken broth
1	strip turkey bacon, finely chopped	1½	teaspoons apple cider vinegar
1	small red onion, finely chopped		Salt and freshly ground pepper
2	cups cooked red quinoa	⅓	cup chopped pecans
¾	cup frozen yellow corn kernels		

1. In a medium saucepan, heat 2 teaspoons of the oil over medium high heat. Add the bacon and cook, stirring, until it colors, 2 minutes. Remove with a slotted spoon and set aside.

2. Add the remaining 1 teaspoon oil to the pot. Mix in the onion and cook, stirring often, until it is golden, 4 minutes. Add the quinoa, corn, broth, and cooked bacon. Cook, stirring, until the pilaf is heated through, 3 minutes. Off the heat, mix in the vinegar and season to taste with salt and pepper. Transfer to a serving bowl and sprinkle on the pecans.

Makes 4 servings

Per serving: 462 calories, 17 g fat, 2 g saturated fat, 14 g protein, 68 g carbohydrates, 7 g fiber

POPPED QUINOA PILAF

● **BEST INGREDIENT**

Supermarkets as well as natural food stores have carrot juice in the refrigerator case alongside the fruit juices and drinks.

● **SERVE WITH**

Baked halibut or Persian Chicken with Sour Cherries (page 155)

For this dish, the first step is toasting the quinoa until most of the grains jump and crackle. The result is a remarkably light pilaf. Its burnished color and pumpkin-like flavor come from carrot juice, while bay leaf and cinnamon add warm undertones.

½	cup carrot juice	1	bay leaf
¾	cup quinoa	1	(3") cinnamon stick
1	tablespoon extra-virgin olive oil	½	teaspoon salt

1. In a large measuring cup, combine the carrot juice with 1½ cups water. Set aside.

2. Rinse the quinoa in a fine strainer, drain well, and transfer to a small Dutch oven or heavy, deep saucepan. Cook over medium-high heat, stirring constantly with a wooden spatula or spoon until the grains stick to the bottom of the pot and then start to move freely and smell toasty, about 5 minutes. Stop stirring but shake the pot frequently so the grain does not burn. When the quinoa is popping steadily, move the pot off the heat and pour in the carrot juice mixture, standing back as it will splatter. Immediately return the pot to the heat and reduce the heat so the mixture simmers.

3. Add the oil, bay leaf, cinnamon stick, and salt. Cover and cook until the quinoa is tender and little white rings are floating with the grain, about 25 minutes. Off the heat, let the quinoa sit, covered, for 10 minutes.

4. Remove the bay leaf and cinnamon stick. Using a fork, fluff the quinoa. Adjust the seasoning to taste.

Makes 4 servings

Per serving: 160 calories, 5 g fat, 1 g saturated fat, 4 g protein, 24 g carbohydrates, 2 g fiber

POMEGRANATE TABBOULEH

Whole buckwheat, also called kasha, makes a lighter tabbouleh than bulgur wheat. Toasted walnuts, oregano, and a touch of red-pepper flakes give it warm flavors perfect when the air has a winter chill. Pomegranate molasses used in place of lemon juice gives it a tart-sweet taste and deep, rich color.

1½	cups cooked whole buckwheat	1	tablespoon pomegranate molasses
½	cup finely chopped sweet onion		
½	cup toasted walnuts (see page 74), chopped	⅛–¼	teaspoon red-pepper flakes, preferably Turkish Marash
⅓	cup chopped flat-leaf parsley		Salt and freshly ground pepper
¼	cup fresh oregano, chopped	1	tablespoon roasted walnut oil
2	tablespoons tomato paste		

In a mixing bowl, combine the buckwheat, onion, nuts, parsley, and oregano. Using a fork, mix gently until well combined. Add the tomato paste, molasses, and red-pepper flakes and mix again. Season to taste with salt and pepper. Drizzle on the oil and toss gently until the dish looks moist. Let sit for 20 minutes to allow the flavors to meld. This grain salad keeps for 3 days, tightly covered in the refrigerator.

Makes 4 servings

Per serving: 225 calories, 14 g fat, 1 g saturated fat, 1 g protein, 24 g carbohydrates, 4 g fiber

● **BEST TECHNIQUE**

This dish shows how salt balances other flavors, including the tartness of the pomegranate molasses and heat of red pepper.

● **BEST INGREDIENT**

Mildly hot, naturally sun-dried Turkish Marash peppers have a slight sweetness. Look for Turkish Marash pepper flakes in ethnic food stores or online at www.zingermans.com.

CRISP BUCKWHEAT POLENTA WITH MUSHROOM TOPPING

● BUYING & STORING GRAINS

• Grains should be well-cleaned and have a slightly earthy aroma.

• Avoid a powdery or dusty look, or rancid odor.

• Store in airtight container in a dry, dark place or in the refrigerator or freezer.

● ANOTHER WAY

Crisp Buckwheat Polenta is also good for breakfast.

Hot buckwheat can be served as a savory side dish or a soft breakfast porridge. When it cools, you can cut it into slabs and pan-fry until crisp and golden outside and creamy inside, just like corn polenta. The mushrooms on top are inspired by the Russian and Jewish ways of serving kasha, which is roasted buckwheat, with a mushroom sauce.

¾	cup medium cracked buckwheat	1	tablespoon extra-virgin olive oil
½	teaspoon salt		Mushroom Topping (opposite)

1. In a medium saucepan, combine 2½ cups cold water, buckwheat, and salt. Place over medium heat and bring to a boil. Reduce the heat and simmer, stirring often, until the buckwheat absorbs the liquid, about 5 minutes. As the mixture pulls away from the sides of the pot, forming a soft ball resembling mashed potatoes, keep stirring, using the same cutting and turning motion as for blending whipped egg whites, until the polenta is velvety and soft, 5 minutes. Remove the pot from the heat.

2. Rinse an 8" square baking dish with cold water. Shake it out, but do not dry the dish. Spread the polenta using a rubber spatula to make it an even 1" layer in the dish. Cool the polenta to room temperature. Cover with plastic wrap and refrigerate for up to 3 days.

3. Cut the cold polenta into 6 pieces. In a medium skillet, heat the oil over medium-high heat. Add the polenta. Cook until brown and crisp on the bottom, 5 minutes. Turn and cook until crisp on the second side. Place on salad or dinner plates and spoon on the mushroom topping.

Makes 6 servings

Per serving: 210 calories, 8 g fat, 1 g saturated fat, 7 g protein, 28 g carbohydrates, 3 g fiber

MUSHROOM TOPPING

Italians call this trifolati, or "truffle-style," because this way of cooking mush-rooms gives them an earthy, intense flavor reminiscent of truffles.

1	tablespoon extra-virgin olive oil	2	tablespoons dry white wine
1	tablespoon finely chopped shallot	1	tablespoon chopped flat-leaf parsley
1	clove garlic, minced		Salt and freshly ground pepper
16	ounces white mushrooms, stems removed and cut into 6 or 8 wedges		

In a medium skillet, heat the oil over medium-high heat. Add the shallot, garlic, and ¼ teaspoon salt. Sauté until the shallot softens, 1 minute. Add the mushrooms and sauté until they release their liquid, 4 minutes. Add the wine, increase the heat, and cook, stirring occasionally, until all the moisture has evaporated and the mushrooms color slightly, 5 minutes. Off the heat, mix in the parsley and season to taste with salt and pepper.

Makes 4 servings

Per serving: 6 calories, 4 g fat, 1 g saturated fat, 4 g protein, 5 g carbohydrates, 1 g fiber

PEANUT FRIED RICE

● **BEST TECHNIQUE**

Rice must be ice-cold or it will stick to the pan and fall apart when fried. I suggest using chilled leftovers from takeout or freezing extra when making rice for another dish.

If your stove cranks out enough heat, you may be able to get the smoky flavor that Chinese cooks call "the breath of the wok" into this blend of aromatic rice, sweet red peppers, scallions, and nuts.

2	tablespoons peanut oil	1	teaspoon grated fresh ginger
⅓	cup peanuts, raw or unsalted dry roasted	3	cups cooked brown basmati rice, refrigerated or frozen
1	onion, chopped	½	cup chopped scallions, green and white parts
1	red bell pepper, cut into ½" dice		
¼	pound shiitake mushrooms, stems removed, coarsely chopped, ¾–1 cup	1	tablespoon reduced-sodium soy sauce
		¼	teaspoon freshly ground pepper
2	cloves garlic, finely chopped	1	teaspoon grated lime zest

1. Set a slotted spoon and plate covered with a double layer of paper towels by the stove. Heat a dry wok over the highest heat possible. Drizzle in the oil. While shaking the wok, add the peanuts and keep them moving as they color. When the peanuts are golden, 30 to 60 seconds, use the slotted spoon to transfer them to the paper-lined plate to drain. Pour off all but 1 tablespoon of the oil.

2. Over highest heat, stir-fry the onion until golden, 2 minutes. Add the red pepper, mushrooms, garlic, and ginger and stir-fry 1 minute. Add the rice, breaking it up with a paddle and stir-fry, alternating pressing the rice against the side of the wok and tossing it. When it looks fluffy, add the peanuts, scallions, soy sauce, and pepper. Stir-fry until the scallions are bright green, 1 minute. Immediately transfer the rice to a serving bowl, sprinkle on the lime zest, and serve.

Makes 4 servings

Per serving: 255 calories, 15 g fat, 2 g saturated fat, 8 g protein, 53 g carbohydrates, 6 g fiber

BLACK RICE WITH BLACKBERRIES

Black on black produces more than a chic look when it pairs fresh blackberries with black rice, a medium-size whole grain with a chewy texture. Add jalapeño and chipotle and you have an antioxidant-crammed dish that rocks with flavor.

¾ cup Forbidden Rice or other black rice

1 tablespoon canola oil

1 large shallot, chopped

1 large jalapeño chile pepper, seeded and finely chopped

⅛ teaspoon chipotle chile powder

1 cup fresh blackberries

½ teaspoon salt

Freshly ground pepper

2 tablespoons sliced almonds

1. Cook the rice according to package directions. Set aside in the pot.

2. In a small skillet, heat the oil over medium-high heat. Add the shallot and jalapeño and cook, stirring often, until the shallot is soft, 5 minutes. Mix in the chipotle powder and cook, stirring, until fragrant, 30 seconds. Spoon the mixture over the warm rice. Add the berries, salt, and 3 or 4 grinds pepper. Using a fork, gently toss to combine. Adjust the salt and pepper to taste. Spoon the rice into a serving bowl, sprinkle on the almonds, and serve immediately.

Makes 4 servings

Per serving: 147 calories, 6 g fat, 0 g saturated fat, 3 g protein, 22 g carbohydrates, 2 g fiber

FUSILLI WITH BROCCOLI BOLOGNESE

● **BEST INGREDIENT**

Authentic Parmigiano-Reggiano cheese imported from Parma has a complex flavor that makes it stand out from all other Parmesan cheeses. Always aged at least 12 months, it is handmade using techniques that have barely changed for centuries. Every wheel is stamped so it can be traced to the dairy where it was made.

Bolognese is the luxurious northern Italian pasta sauce made with beef, cream, butter, wine, and tomatoes. Here, lean ground turkey, milk, butter used modestly, and mushrooms give you the layers of flavor for which this sauce is famous, plus a bonus of broccoli. Fusilli's curves and grooves are perfect for catching the goodness of this dense sauce, which also deserves the accompaniment of authentic, freshly grated Parmigiano-Reggiano cheese.

1	small carrot, cut into ½" slices	½	cup dry white wine
1	medium rib celery, cut into ½" slices	½	cup milk or unsweetened soy milk
½	medium onion, coarsely chopped	2	tablespoons tomato paste
3	mushrooms, stemmed and halved or quartered	1	(28-ounce) can diced tomatoes
1	tablespoon unsalted butter	⅛	teaspoon freshly grated nutmeg
2	tablespoons extra-virgin olive oil	1	pound whole wheat or semolina fusilli
1¼	cups broccoli florets, with minimal stems		Salt and freshly ground pepper
¾	pound ground turkey, 90–93% lean		Freshly grated Parmigiano-Reggiano

1. Pulse the carrot, celery, onion, and mushrooms in a food processor until finely chopped.

2. Melt the butter with the oil in a deep skillet. Add the broccoli and the chopped vegetables and sauté until the mushrooms release their liquid and it evaporates, about 6 minutes. Mix in the turkey and cook until no longer pink, 4 minutes, breaking the meat up with a wooden spoon.

3. Add the wine and cook until it is almost evaporated, 8 minutes. Add the milk, reduce the heat, and simmer until it is almost evaporated, 4 minutes. Mix in the tomato paste, canned tomatoes with their juice, and the nutmeg.

Reduce the heat to medium-low and simmer until the tomatoes are soft but about half of the pieces still hold their shape, 30 minutes. The sauce will be moist and chunky.

4. Meanwhile, in a large pot of boiling water, cook the pasta according to package directions. Drain in a colander, then turn the pasta into a warmed serving bowl, add the sauce, and toss to combine. Pass a bowl of freshly grated Parmigiana–Reggiano cheese at the table.

Makes 6 servings

Per serving: 517 calories, 17 g fat, 4 g saturated fat, 23 g protein, 69 g carbohydrates, 10 g fiber

FIVE-WAY CHILI SPAGHETTI

The milder taste of whole grain farro pasta from Italy makes it a good intermediate step between regular semolina pasta and stronger tasting whole wheat pastas. Besides Italian food stores and fancier supermarkets, you can order it online at www.markethallfoods.com.

For the chocolate, I like Lindt Excellence Ecuador 75% Cocoa Dark Extra Fine Chocolate or Dagoba New Moon 74% Organic Chocolate, which are strong but not acidic tasting.

The chili served in Cincinnati chili parlors is dark and spicy from cinnamon and chocolate. Ordering a "five-way" gets you chili served over spaghetti, topped with kidney beans, grated Cheddar, and chopped onion.

1	tablespoon canola oil	1	ounce dark chocolate (70–85% cocoa), chopped
1	pound ground beef, 90% lean		
1¼	cups chopped onion, divided	1	cup fat-free, reduced-sodium beef broth, divided
1	small green bell pepper, chopped		
2	cloves garlic, finely chopped		Salt and freshly ground pepper
2	tablespoons chili powder	¾	pound whole wheat spaghetti
1½	teaspoons dried basil	1	cup canned kidney beans, rinsed and drained
1½	teaspoons dried oregano		
1	teaspoon ground cumin	½	cup shredded reduced-fat Cheddar cheese
1	(28-ounce) can whole tomatoes in tomato sauce		

1. In a large Dutch oven, heat the oil over medium-high heat. Add the beef, 1 cup of the onion, the green pepper, and garlic. Cook, breaking up the beef until it is no longer pink, 6 minutes. Add the chili powder, basil, oregano, and cumin. Stir to mix and cook 1 minute longer.

2. Add the tomatoes, chocolate, and ½ cup of the broth. Bring to a boil, reduce the heat, and simmer 20 minutes. Add the remaining broth and cook until the chili is dark and thick, 20 to 25 minutes. Season to taste.

3. Meanwhile, in a large pot of boiling water, cook the pasta. In the microwave, warm the kidney beans. Finely chop the remaining onion.

4. Drain the pasta and divide it among 4 dinner plates. Top each serving with ½ cup chili, ¼ cup beans, 2 tablespoons cheese, and 1 tablespoon onion. Serve immediately. Cover and refrigerate the remaining chili for up to 4 days.

Makes 4 servings

Per serving: 741 calories, 22 g fat, 8 g saturated fat, 47 g protein, 96 g carbohydrates, 19 g fiber

MACARONI AND CHEESE
WITH BROCCOLI

● **BEST INGREDIENT**

This recipe is a good way to use leftover cooked broccoli.

● **ANOTHER WAY**

Add whole grains by using half whole wheat and half semolina pasta. First boil the whole wheat macaroni for 2 minutes, then add the semolina pasta and cook until both are tender.

Southerners classify mac 'n' cheese as a vegetable. Broccoli in my version makes this more than fanciful thinking. It is as creamy as baked versions and ready even faster.

2	cups small broccoli florets	1	cup (4 ounces) shredded sharp white Cheddar cheese
½	pound elbow macaroni		
1¾	cups reduced-fat (1%) milk	½	cup (2 ounces) shredded Asiago cheese
2	tablespoons unsalted butter		
2	tablespoons all-purpose flour		Salt and freshly ground pepper
1	cup (3 ounces) shredded Jack or Gouda cheese		

1. In a large pot of boiling water, cook the broccoli for 3 minutes. Using a slotted spoon, transfer the broccoli to a colander and run cold water over it until cool. Drain, then whirl the broccoli in a salad spinner to dry well. Set aside.

2. Add the pasta and cook according to package directions. Drain in a colander.

3. While the pasta cooks, warm the milk and set aside. In a medium saucepan, melt the butter over medium heat. Whisk in the flour and cook, whisking constantly as the mixture bubbles and turns fluffy, 2 minutes. While whisking, slowly add the warm milk. Cook, stirring, until the sauce is smooth and coats a spoon, 5 minutes. Off the heat, mix in the three cheeses until they melt. Season to taste with salt and pepper. Add the pasta and broccoli, mixing well. Serve immediately.

Makes 4 servings

Per serving: 563 calories, 29 g fat, 17 g saturated fat, 27 g protein, 53 g carbohydrates, 4 g fiber

SINGAPORE NOODLES

In Chinese cooking, Singapore signals curry flavor in a dish. For the perfect, mildly spicy flavor, the Caribbean curry powder sold in the ethnic section at supermarkets is ideal.

¼	pound thin rice noodles	1	teaspoon minced fresh ginger
1	tablespoon mild curry powder	½	pound small shrimp (41-50
1	teaspoon sugar		count), peeled and deveined
1	teaspoon salt	1	small red bell pepper, cut into
½	cup fat-free, reduced-sodium		thin vertical strips
	chicken broth	1	medium red onion, cut into thin
1	tablespoon plus 2 teaspoons		crescents
	peanut oil	6	snow peas, cut lengthwise into
4	scallions, green part only, cut into		thin strips
	1" strips	2	large eggs, well-beaten

1. In a large bowl, cover the noodles with boiling water. Soak for 20 minutes, drain, and set aside.

2. In a small bowl, combine the curry powder, sugar, salt and broth, and set aside.

3. Heat a wok over high heat. Add 1 tablespoon of the oil. Stir-fry the scallions and ginger until fragrant, 30 seconds. Add the shrimp and stir-fry until they turn pink, 2 minutes. Turn the contents of the wok into a bowl.

4. Return the wok to the heat. Add 1 teaspoon of the oil. Stir-fry the red pepper, onion, and snow peas until they are bright and crisp-tender, 2 minutes. Add to the shrimp.

5. Wipe out the wok and return it to the heat. Add the remaining 1 teaspoon oil. Add the eggs and rotate the pan to make a thin pancake. Add the noodles. Stir and chop until the eggs are mixed with the noodles. Add the curry mixture, the cooked shrimp, and vegetables to the pan. Stir-fry until the shrimp are cooked through, 3 minutes. Serve immediately.

Per serving: 291 calories, 10 g fat, 2 g saturated fat, 19 g protein, 35 g carbohydrates, 4 g fiber

SPINACH LASAGNA
WITH CREAMY TOMATO SAUCE

● BEST INGREDIENT

Healthy and good-tasting organic prepared foods include Amy's canned soups, Trader Joe's or Cascadian Farm frozen organic spinach, and Muir Glen's organic canned tomatoes.

Although it uses canned tomato soup, frozen spinach, and instant lasagna noodles, this meatless casserole wins raves and takes only 20 minutes to prepare. The secret is choosing good quality convenience products. I prefer those that are natural, so they are made without preservatives and excess sodium.

1	(14-ounce) package soft silken tofu, drained and pureed	1	teaspoon salt
		¼	teaspoon freshly ground pepper
1	(10-ounce) package frozen spinach, thawed and squeezed dry	1	tablespoon extra-virgin olive oil
		1	clove garlic, minced
1	cup (4 ounces) diced part-skim mozzarella cheese	1	(14-ounce) can diced tomatoes
		1	(14½-ounce) can cream of tomato soup
2	teaspoons fresh lemon juice	6	sheets instant lasagna noodles
3	or 4 drops hot pepper sauce	½	cup grated Parmesan cheese

1. Preheat the oven to 350°F. Coat a 13" × 9" × 2" baking dish with cooking spray and set aside.

2. In a mixing bowl, combine the tofu, spinach, mozzarella, lemon juice, hot pepper sauce, salt, and pepper, using a fork.

3. In a medium saucepan, heat the oil over medium-high heat. Add the garlic and cook until it is fragrant, 30 seconds. Add the tomatoes with their juice and cook, stirring occasionally, until they are half broken down, 4 minutes. Add the soup and bring the sauce to a simmer. Reduce the heat and simmer 3 minutes.

4. Spread 1 cup of the hot sauce over the bottom of the prepared baking dish. Arrange 3 sheets of the pasta on the bottom of the dish, leaving space around

each one. Spread the spinach mixture evenly over the pasta. Top with the 3 remaining sheets of pasta. Cover with the remaining sauce. Sprinkle on the Parmesan cheese. Cover with foil.

5. Bake until the pasta is soft, the cheese melted, and the filling heated through, 30 minutes. Let sit for 10 minutes, covered, before serving.

Makes 6 servings

Per serving: 273 calories, 12 g fat, 5 g saturated fat, 17 g protein, 25 g carbohydrates, 4 g fiber

BAKED RIGATONI
WITH BUTTERNUT SQUASH
AND TURKEY SAUSAGE

● **BEST INGREDIENT**
Use large, thinner-walled rigatoni, like De Cecco, not the smaller, thicker kind made by Ronzoni and other manufacturers.

This meaty casserole is inspired by Sicilian pasta al forno. Made with fontina cheese and cream, it also contains seven Essential Best Foods. It is an ideal winter dish.

1	tablespoon extra-virgin olive oil	2	cups tomato sauce	
1	onion, chopped	1	cup vegetable broth	
2	cloves garlic, chopped	⅓	cup heavy cream	
½	cup dry white wine		Salt and freshly ground pepper	
¾	pound sweet Italian turkey sausage meat	1	pound large rigatoni	
½	teaspoon ground cinnamon	2	cups (4 ounces) shredded fontina cheese	
1	pound ¾" diced butternut squash, 4 cups	¼	cup grated Parmesan cheese	

1. Preheat the oven to 450°F. Coat a 13" × 9" × 2" baking dish with cooking spray and set aside.

2. In a large Dutch oven, heat the oil over medium-high heat. Add the onion and sauté for 2 minutes. Stir in the garlic and sauté until the onion is golden, 3 minutes. Pour in the wine and cook until it has evaporated and the onion is browned, 8 minutes. Add the sausage and cook, using a wooden spoon to break up chunks, until it is no longer pink. Add the cinnamon.

3. Add the squash, tomato sauce, broth, and cream. Cook, stirring occasionally, until the liquid boils. Reduce the heat and simmer, covered and stirring occasionally, until the squash is tender, 15 minutes. Season to taste with salt and pepper. Set aside.

4. Meanwhile, in a large pot of boiling water, cook the pasta according to package directions until tender but not soft. Drain well.

5. Add the pasta to the sauce and stir. Add 1 cup of the fontina cheese and mix well. Spread the pasta in the prepared baking dish, flattening it on top. There should be plenty of liquid in the sauce. Top with the remaining 1 cup fontina and then the Parmesan cheese.

6. Bake until the cheese melts and bubbles, 15 minutes. Let sit 5 minutes before serving.

Makes 8 servings

Per serving: 501 calories, 19 g fat, 9 g saturated fat, 25 g protein, 54 g carbohydrates, 3 g fiber

POLENTA LASAGNA
WITH RED WINE LENTILS

This lasagna alternates layers of Red Wine Lentils, precooked polenta, and ricotta blended with goat cheese. It is so satisfying that people seldom realize it is meatless. Once the lentils are made, this dish comes together speedily.

1	(16–18-ounce) tube prepared polenta	2	ounces fresh goat cheese
	Red Wine Lentils (page 222)	⅓	cup grated pecorino cheese, divided
1	(16-ounce) container part-skim ricotta cheese		Salt and freshly ground pepper

1. Preheat the oven to 375°F. Coat an 8" square baking dish with cooking spray and set aside.

2. Cut the polenta in half crosswise. Place each half cut side down and cut it vertically into 6 slices. Arrange half of the slices to cover the bottom of the prepared baking dish. There will be some spaces. Cover the polenta with half of the lentils.

3. In a mixing bowl, combine the ricotta and goat cheeses until well blended. Mix in 3 tablespoons of the pecorino cheese. Season the mixture to taste with salt and pepper. Spread half the mixture over the lentils. Repeat, using the remaining polenta, lentils, and cheese mixture. Sprinkle with the remaining pecorino on top. Cover with foil.

4. Bake for 40 minutes. Remove the foil and bake until the cheese bubbles, 10 minutes longer.

Makes 6 servings

Per serving: 374 calories, 13 g fat, 6 g saturated fat, 22 g protein, 39 g carbohydrates, 7 g fiber

CHAPTER EIGHT

EGGS, BEANS, AND SOY

A TRIO OF SCRAMBLED EGGS

Scrambled Egg Hash 216

Scrambled Eggs with Pasta and Cherry Tomatoes 217

Cajun Eggs and Greens 218

Asparagus with Egg Milanese 214, *Kale Frittata* 220, *Kidney Beans with Potatoes and Dill*

Red Wine Lentils 222, *Ginger Lentils* 223, *Chocolate Baked Beans* 224, *Baked Beans on Toast*

Golden Cauliflower and Tofu Curry 226, *Black and White Hoppin' John*

ASPARAGUS WITH EGG MILANESE

● BEST INGREDIENT

In springtime, make this dish twice, first with supermarket ingredients and then using asparagus and truly fresh eggs from a farmers' market. Compare the taste and you will appreciate the simple splendor of locally raised foods in their season.

● BEST TECHNIQUE

Using a rasp to grate hard cheeses produces easily twice the volume, letting you enjoy their flavor using half the amount.

Together, the four ingredients in this dish show what makes Italian food great. In it, the egg's yolk becomes the golden sauce for lightly cooked asparagus, and both are enhanced by grated Parmesan cheese and a touch of browned butter that brings nutty flavor as the finishing touch.

1	pound medium asparagus, trimmed	4	large eggs
			Salt and freshly ground pepper
3	teaspoons unsalted butter, divided	8	teaspoons freshly grated Parmesan cheese

1. Pour ⅓ cup water into a large skillet and bring to a boil over medium-high heat. Add the asparagus. Cover and cook for 4 minutes. Immediately transfer the asparagus to a large bowl of ice water and cool completely. Drain and pat dry on paper towels. This can be done up to 1 hour ahead. Dry the pan.

2. In the same skillet over medium heat, melt 1 teaspoon of the butter. Add the asparagus and cook, turning them with tongs, until coated with the butter and just heated through, about 1 minute. Divide the asparagus among 4 dinner plates.

3. Over medium heat, melt the remaining 2 teaspoons butter in the same pan. Break the eggs into the pan, spacing them well apart, and season with salt and pepper. Cook until the eggs are as you like them. Set an egg over the asparagus on each plate and sprinkle on the grated cheese. Serve immediately.

Makes 4 servings

Per serving: 140 calories, 9 g fat, 4 g saturated fat, 10 g protein, 5 g carbohydrates, 2 g fiber

A Trio of Scrambled Eggs

Any time of day, scrambled eggs are the best comfort food. Each of these versions is substantial enough to make a sustaining breakfast, filling brunch, or satisfying supper.

 ## SCRAMBLED EGG HASH

● **BEST TECHNIQUE**

To draw out the most fat, start bacon in a cold pan and cook it slowly over medium heat, turning the strips 3 or 4 times.

On Sundays, my father always made peppers and eggs accompanied by crisp bacon and hash brown potatoes. I transformed this into a one-pan dish using preservative-free bacon and frozen hash browns.

4	large eggs	1	small onion, chopped
4	large egg whites or ½ cup liquid egg whites	½	medium green bell pepper, chopped
½	teaspoon salt	2	cups preservative-free frozen hash brown potatoes
	Freshly ground pepper		
4	strips preservative-free bacon	¼	cup chopped flat-leaf parsley, optional
3	tablespoons canola oil, divided		

1. In a bowl, whisk together the eggs, egg whites, salt, and 3 or 4 grinds pepper.

2. In a medium skillet, cook the bacon over medium-low heat until crisp. Drain on paper toweling, crumble, and set aside. Wipe out the pan.

3. Heat 1 tablespoon of the oil in the pan over medium-high heat. Add the onion and pepper and sauté until the onion is translucent, 4 minutes. Add 1 tablespoon oil, then the potatoes. Using a wooden spatula, turn and break up the potatoes, scraping up what sticks to the pan, until they are soft and some are browned, 5 minutes. Add the remaining oil and the eggs, bacon, and parsley, if using. As the eggs set, lift and turn the contents of the pan in chunks, scraping the bottom of the pan occasionally, until the eggs are done as you like them. Serve immediately.

Makes 4 servings

Per serving: 312 calories, 19 g fat, 3 g saturated fat, 15 g protein, 22 g carbohydrates, 2 g fiber

SCRAMBLED EGGS WITH PASTA AND CHERRY TOMATOES

When you face a stressful day, fortify yourself with this dish, which I discovered at a West Hollywood, California, eatery. Its combination of pasta and eggs often tempts children who are fussy eaters.

6	large basil leaves	2	teaspoons unsalted butter
2	large eggs	1	cup cooked elbow macaroni
1	large egg white	6	cherry tomatoes, halved
¼	teaspoon salt	2	tablespoons shredded Parmesan
	Freshly ground pepper		cheese

1. Stack the basil leaves and roll lengthwise into a fat roll. Holding the roll with one hand, use a sharp knife to slice crosswise into fine shreds. Set aside.

2. In a bowl, whisk together the eggs, egg white, salt, and 3 or 4 grinds pepper.

3. In a medium skillet, melt the butter over medium heat. Add the egg mixture. As soon as the eggs set on the bottom, add the pasta. Scramble until the eggs are almost done as you like, then mix in the tomatoes. Divide the eggs between two plates. Sprinkle on the cheese and basil. Serve immediately.

Makes 2 servings

Per serving: 248 calories, 11 g fat, 5 g saturated fat, 14 g protein, 24 g carbohydrates, 2 g fiber

CAJUN EGGS AND GREENS

● BEST INGREDIENT

Replacing andouille sausage with hot-smoked salmon and spices gives these eggs flavor, but with even less cholesterol and saturated fat.

● ANOTHER WAY

For flavorful, lean collards, cut fresh stemmed leaves crosswise into thin strips and cook them in an equal mixture of chicken broth and water until they are as tender as you like, 30 to 60 minutes. Add liquid as needed to keep the greens half submerged until almost done, then let most of it boil off.

If you love soul food, try these eggs scrambled with collard greens, hot smoked salmon, and Cajun spices.

2	cups cooked collard greens	¼	cup finely chopped preservative-
4	teaspoons canola oil, divided		free andouille sausage or
1	onion, chopped		hot-smoked salmon
	Cajun Spice (opposite)		
4	large eggs		

1. Squeeze the greens dry and chop them finely. Set aside.

2. Heat 2 teaspoons of the oil in a medium skillet over medium-high heat. Add the onion and sauté for 2 minutes. Add the Cajun Spice and cook until the onion is soft, 2 to 3 minutes. Add the greens and stir until they are heated through, 1 minute.

3. In a bowl, whisk the eggs until well beaten. Add the remaining oil to the pan. Pour in the eggs. When they start to set, reduce the heat to medium and scramble until the eggs are done as you like. Sprinkle the salmon over the eggs. Serve immediately.

Makes 4 servings

Per serving: 151 calories, 10 g fat, 2 g saturated fat, 9 g protein, 7 g carbohydrates, 3 g fiber

CAJUN SPICE

½ teaspoon paprika

¼ teaspoon freshly ground pepper

¼ teaspoon garlic powder

¼ teaspoon dried oregano

¼ teaspoon dried thyme

¼ teaspoon salt

Pinch of cayenne pepper, or to taste

In a small bowl, combine all ingredients. Use immediately, or store in a tightly sealed container in the refrigerator for up to 5 days.

KALE FRITTATA

● **ANOTHER WAY**

The braised kale on its own is a superb side dish.

Braised kale and Gruyère cheese make this a heartier choice than the usual frittata. Finishing it under the broiler will eliminate any jitters you may have about flipping a frittata.

5	large eggs	½	bunch green curly kale, stemmed and chopped, 5–6 cups
3	large whites		
½	teaspoon salt	2	teaspoons chopped oregano leaves or ½ teaspoon dried
	Freshly ground pepper		
2	tablespoons extra-virgin olive oil, divided	¾	cup (1½ ounces) shredded Gruyère cheese
1	large shallot, finely chopped		

1. Preheat the broiler.

2. In a bowl, whisk together the eggs, egg whites, salt, and 5 or 6 grinds black pepper.

3. In an ovenproof medium skillet, heat 1 tablespoon of the oil over medium-high heat. Add the shallot and sauté 1 minute. Add the kale and mix until it collapses, 2 minutes. Add ⅓ cup water, cover, and cook until the kale is tender but not soft, 5 minutes. Uncover and cook off any liquid.

4. Push the kale to one side of the pan. Add the remaining oil. Pour in the eggs. With a spatula, spread the kale evenly over the eggs. As the eggs set, lift the edges of the frittata while tilting the pan. Occasionally, pull aside the eggs in the center of the pan to let liquid flow to the bottom. When the eggs are almost set in the center, 2 minutes longer, sprinkle on the oregano, then the cheese.

5. Broil the frittata until the cheese bubbles, 1 to 2 minutes. Let the frittata sit 5 minutes, then cut it into wedges. Serve hot or warm.

Makes 6 servings

Per serving: 179 calories, 13 g fat, 5 g saturated fat, 12 g protein, 3 g carbohydrates, 1 g fiber

KIDNEY BEANS
WITH POTATOES AND DILL

Both Greek and Turkish restaurants serve this quintessentially Mediterranean dish as a first course. I also include it in meze, by offering it along with Rosemary-Marinated Olives (page 78) and Garlic Greens (page 242).

1	tablespoon extra-virgin olive oil	¾	cup fat-free, reduced-sodium chicken broth
¼	cup finely chopped onion		
1	small carrot, cut into ½" slices	2	tablespoons tomato paste
1	small or medium leek, white part only, cut into ½" slices	1	teaspoon sugar
			Juice of ½ lemon
1	red-skinned potato, peeled and cut into ¾" cubes		Salt and freshly ground pepper
1	(15-ounce) can kidney beans, drained	2	tablespoons chopped fresh dill

● **BEST TECHNIQUE**

Cooking dried beans from scratch allows you to control the amount of sodium in finished dishes. It gives them much better flavor as well. When using canned beans, natural brands such as Eden, Westbrae, and Whole Foods 365 Organic contain less sodium than other choices.

1. In a medium skillet, heat the oil over medium-high heat. Add the onion and cook, stirring occasionally, until translucent, 3 minutes. Add the carrot and leek and cook until the onion is soft, 2 minutes.

2. Add the potato, beans, broth, tomato paste, sugar, and lemon juice, stirring to mix them with the vegetables. Reduce the heat, cover, and simmer until the leek is al dente, about 10 minutes.

3. Uncover and cook until the liquid in the pan is reduced by two-thirds and looks syrupy. Season to taste with salt and pepper. Transfer the mixture to a wide, shallow serving bowl and cool to room temperature. Garnish with the dill and serve.

Makes 4 servings

Per serving: 151 calories, 4 g fat, 1 g saturated fat, 6 g protein, 24 g carbohydrates, 6 g fiber

RED WINE LENTILS

Along with the wine, tomatoes and cinnamon flavor these moist lentils. They are a good way to convert anyone hesitant about eating this versatile legume.

● **FOOD FACT**

Lentils provide about the same amount of fiber as beans, but seem to cause less digestive distress for most people.

● **ANOTHER WAY**

Make a double batch and use half to make Polenta Lasagna with Red Wine Lentils (page 212) another night.

1	tablespoon extra-virgin olive oil	1	tablespoon tomato paste
1	small carrot, finely chopped	½	teaspoon dried basil
1	onion, finely chopped	½	teaspoon ground cinnamon
1	large clove garlic, minced	1	bay leaf
1	cup French green lentils	1	(14-ounce) can plum tomatoes,
2–3	cups vegetable broth		drained
½	cup dry red wine		Salt and freshly ground pepper

1. In a small Dutch oven or large saucepan, heat the oil over medium-high heat. Add the carrot and onion and sauté until the onion is translucent, 4 minutes. Mix in the garlic and sauté until it is fragrant, 1 minute.

2. Add the lentils and 2 cups broth. When the liquid boils, reduce the heat, cover, and simmer until the lentils are al dente, about 30 minutes.

3. Add the wine, tomato paste, basil, cinnamon, and bay leaf. A handful at a time, crush the tomatoes through your fist into the pot. Cook, adding more stock ½ cup at a time as needed, until the lentils are soft, about 50 minutes. Remove and discard the bay leaf. Season to taste with salt and pepper.

Makes 4 servings

Per serving: 276 calories, 5 g fat, 1 g saturated fat, 12 g protein, 42 g carbohydrates, 10 g fiber

GINGER LENTILS

Chefs often serve these dark green French lentils underneath baked salmon, halibut, or cod and you could easily follow suit. Also enjoy their creamy texture and earthy flavor in a salad.

1	tablespoon extra-virgin olive oil	1	cup French green lentils
1	carrot, cut into ¼" dice	1	bay leaf
1	onion, cut into ¼" dice	1	(14¼-ounce) can vegetable broth
1	large clove garlic, finely chopped	1¼	cups water
1–2	teaspoons grated fresh ginger		Salt and freshly ground pepper

● **ANOTHER WAY**

If the lentils will accompany fish, use less ginger; add more when they will be a side dish or used in a salad.

1. In a medium saucepan, heat the oil over medium-high heat. Add the carrot, onion, and garlic and sauté until the onion is translucent, 4 minutes. Mix in the ginger and cook, stirring occasionally, until the mixture is moist and golden, 2 minutes.

2. Add the lentils, bay leaf, broth, and water. When the liquid boils, reduce the heat, cover, and simmer until the lentils are tender, about 45 minutes. Season to taste with salt and pepper. Remove and discard the bay leaf. Serve hot, warm, or at room temperature. Covered in the refrigerator, the cooked lentils keep for up to 4 days.

Makes 4 servings

Per serving: 213 calories, 5 g fat, 1 g saturated fat, 11 g protein, 34 g carbohydrates, 8 g fiber

CHOCOLATE BAKED BEANS

● **QUICKER BEANS**

To save time try the quick-soak method: Place the beans in a deep pot and add water to cover by 2". Cook, covered, over medium heat until the water just boils. Remove from the heat and let the covered pot sit for 1 hour. Drain the beans and finish cooking according to your recipe.

● **ANOTHER WAY**

In place of Scharffen Berger Mocha Dark Chocolate, use 1 ounce dark chocolate (70 to 85%) plus 2 tablespoons brewed espresso coffee.

Use a small Dutch oven in place of a bean pot.

Making these dark and pungent beans takes patience—but their ginger, chocolate, and coffee flavors are worth the time required. I love them topped with a poached egg or used for Baked Beans on Toast (opposite).

1	pound navy beans, soaked for 8 hours, or quick-soaked (see Quicker Beans, left)	½	teaspoon pumpkin pie spice
		2	cups hot water, plus more as needed
½	cup tomato sauce	1	small onion
¼	cup unsulfured molasses	2	whole cloves
2	tablespoons wildflower honey	1	ounce Scharffen Berger Mocha Dark Chocolate, chopped
2	teaspoons English mustard powder	1	tablespoon maple syrup
1½	teaspoons ground ginger		Salt and freshly ground pepper

1. Preheat the oven to 350°F. Drain the beans and set aside.

2. In a medium bean pot, combine the tomato sauce, molasses, honey, mustard, ginger, and pumpkin pie spice. Bring to a boil. Add the beans and hot water. Halve the onion vertically, stopping just above the root tip to keep the halves attached. Turn the onion 90° and repeat. Stick in the cloves and add the onion to the beans. Cover the pot.

3. Bake the beans for 1 hour. Reduce the heat to 275°F. Bake for 2 hours, adding 1 cup warm water if needed to keep the beans submerged. Check every hour; bake until the beans are *al dente*, adding water ½ cup at a time, as needed.

4. Stir in the chocolate and maple syrup. Bake 1 to 2 hours, until the beans are very tender, still adding water by the ½ cup to keep the beans submerged. Remove and discard the onion.

Makes 8 servings

Per serving: 271 calories, 2 g fat, 1 g saturated fat, 12 g protein, 54 g carbohydrates, 9 g fiber

BAKED BEANS ON TOAST

In Britain, this is a student's sustenance or a workingman's high tea, what we call supper. Actually, it is smart comfort food. Skip the toast, if you prefer, and serve the beans with an egg and strip of bacon.

● **BEST INGREDIENT**
Choose a whole grain bread that is light and soft so it soaks up the bean juices.

2	teaspoons canola oil		2	slices multigrain or oatmeal bread
¼	cup finely chopped onion			
1	cup Chocolate Baked Beans (opposite) or 1 (15-ounce) can vegetarian baked beans		2	teaspoons unsalted butter
			2	eggs, fried or poached, or 2 strips preservative-free bacon, cooked (optional)
2	tablespoons ketchup			
1	teaspoon brown mustard			

1. In a medium saucepan, heat the oil over medium-high heat. Add the onion and cook, stirring, until translucent, 4 minutes. Add the beans, ketchup, and mustard. Cover and cook until the beans are heated through.

2. Meanwhile, toast the bread. Spread half the butter on each slice and set the bread on two dinner plates. Mound the hot beans on top of the toast, letting them spill over the sides. If serving with eggs, set one on top of each portion. If serving with bacon, set it alongside and serve.

Makes 2 servings

Per serving: 315 calories, 11 g fat, 3 g saturated fat, 11 g protein, 47 g carbohydrates, 9 g fiber

GOLDEN CAULIFLOWER AND TOFU CURRY

Pan-frying makes tofu crisp outside and creamy inside. Added to a vegetable curry, it creates a colorful main dish to serve over brown rice or steamed couscous. Leftovers are ideal for a portable lunch since this dish tastes good at room temperature or reheated.

● BEST INGREDIENT

Pressed tofu is chewy and more enjoyable in stir-fries or when grilled than tofu used straight from the package.

● BEST TECHNIQUES

PRESSING TOFU

• Halve the cake of tofu horizontally. Set the 2 slabs side by side on a double layer of paper towels. Cover them with more towels.

• Set a heavy skillet or small acrylic cutting board on top of the tofu. Add canned tomatoes or other weights and let the tofu sit for 20 minutes.

• Cube or slice the pressed tofu.

• Pressed tofu keeps, covered in cold water in the refrigerator, for up to 3 days.

PAN-CRISPING TOFU

• Coat a heavy, large skillet with cooking spray.

• Add cubed pressed tofu in 1 layer.

• Cook, turning the cubes with tongs, until golden and crisp on 4 sides, 2 minutes per side.

• Store covered in the refrigerator for up to 2 days.

1	tablespoon canola oil	2	cups eggplant cut into 1" cubes
1	red onion, cut into ½" crescents	1	red bell pepper, cut into 1" dice
1	clove garlic, finely chopped	1	orange-fleshed sweet potato,
2	tablespoons curry powder		peeled and cut into ½" slices
½	teaspoon ground cinnamon	1	small zucchini, cut into ½" slices
1½	cups unfiltered apple juice	½	cup raisins
2	cups 1" cauliflower florets		Salt and freshly ground pepper
1	carrot, cut into ½" slices		
14–16	ounces firm tofu, pressed, cut into 1" cubes, and pan-crisped (see Best Techniques, left)		

1. In a large Dutch oven, heat the oil over medium-high heat. Add the onion and sauté 2 minutes. Add the garlic and sauté 1 minute. Mix in the curry powder and cinnamon and cook until fragrant, 30 to 60 seconds.

2. Add the apple juice, cauliflower, and carrot. When the liquid boils, reduce the heat to a simmer, cover, and cook 10 minutes.

3. Add the tofu, eggplant, red pepper, sweet potato, zucchini, and raisins. Cover and simmer until the vegetables are tender but still hold their shape, 20 to 25 minutes. Season to taste with salt and pepper.

Makes 4 to 6 servings

Per serving (for 6 servings): 312 calories, 10 g fat, 2 g saturated fat, 16 g protein, 46 g carbohydrates, 8 g fiber

BLACK AND WHITE HOPPIN' JOHN

● BUYING & STORING LEGUMES

• Select canned beans with low sodium content

• Buy dried legumes where turnover is high to avoid old, dry stock

• Look for dried beans with lustrous skin

• Select whole legumes, except for peeled lentils

• Avoid debris and insect evidence

• Store in cool, dry, dark place for up to 12 months

Traditionally, this Southern dish is eaten on New Year's Day to attract prosperity. This meatless version blends black-eyed peas with light, long-grain brown rice and black soybeans, which are loaded with protein and taste nicely nutty. Using canned beans and leftover rice, the dish is ready in 15 minutes.

1	(15-ounce) can black-eyed peas, rinsed and drained	1	tablespoon thyme leaves, chopped, or 1 teaspoon dried
1	cup cooked long-grain brown rice	1	tablespoon extra-virgin olive oil
1	cup cooked canned black soybeans, rinsed and drained		Juice of 1 lemon
½	cup vegetable broth	1	small clove garlic, minced, optional
½	cup finely chopped red onion	3–4	dashes hot pepper sauce
1	rib celery, finely chopped		Salt and freshly ground pepper

1. In a medium saucepan, combine the black-eyed peas, rice, soybeans, and broth. Cover and cook over medium heat, stirring once or twice, until warmed through.

2. Off the heat, add the onion, celery, thyme, oil, lemon juice, garlic if using, and hot sauce. Using a fork, mix well. Season to taste with salt and black pepper. Serve warm or at room temperature, as a salad.

Makes 4 servings

Per serving: 197 calories, 6 g fat, 1 g saturated fat, 9 g protein, 28 g carbohydrates, 6 g fiber

CHAPTER NINE

VEGETABLES AND SIDE DISHES

[ONIONS IN THREE FLAVORS

Curried Onions 245

Chili Onions 246

Mediterranean Herb Onions 247]

Pomegranate-Glazed Baby Carrots 230, *Corn with Cilantro and Chives* 231,

Green and Yellow Squash Ribbons 232, *Steak-Cut Broccoli* 234,

Roasted Broccoli, Green Beans, and Grape Tomatoes 235, *Indian Roasted Cauliflower* 236,

Red Curried Cauliflower 237, *Lemon Kale with Capers* 238, *Brussels Sprouts and Kale* 239, *Garlic Greens* 240,

Baked Spinach and Feta 241, *Mushroom Kebabs* 242, *Apple Ratatouille* 243,

Red Cabbage with Sour Cherries 244, *Ginger Mashed Sweet Potatoes* 248,

Marshmallow Sweet Potatoes for Grown-Ups 249, *Upside-Down Pineapple Sweet Potatoes* 250,

Orange-Glazed Japanese Squash 252, *Tuscan Potatoes with Bitter Greens* 254, *Deviled Red Potatoes* 255,

Ginger Cranberry Relish 256, *Cranberries and Pearl Onions* 257, *Kumquat-Apple Chutney* 258

POMEGRANATE-GLAZED CARROTS

● **ANOTHER WAY**

For a sharper, more pungent version, use ½ cup pomegranate juice and omit the orange juice.

With just four ingredients, this recipe is perfect for beginning cooks. It also delivers flavors complex enough to please sophisticated diners. Leftovers are good at room temperature.

1	tablespoon unsalted butter	¼	cup pomegranate juice
3	cups baby carrots		Salt and freshly ground pepper
¼	cup fresh orange juice		

1. In a medium skillet, melt the butter over medium heat. Add the carrots and sauté until they are bright orange, 2 minutes.

2. Pour in the orange and pomegranate juices. Season to taste with salt and pepper. Simmer, stirring occasionally, until the carrots are tender-crisp and glazed, 12 minutes.

Makes 4 servings

Per serving: 81 calories, 3 g fat, 1.8 g saturated fat, 1 g protein, 13 g carbohydrates, 2 g fiber

CORN WITH CILANTRO AND CHIVES

Locally grown summer corn needs no embellishment, but the ears of fresh corn sold in supermarkets all year long benefit from this flavor lift.

3	ears fresh corn	¼	cup snipped chives
1	tablespoon unsalted butter		Salt and freshly ground
½	cup tightly packed cilantro leaves, chopped		pepper

● **FOOD FACT**

Cilantro and chives contain beta-carotene and corn provides eye-protecting lutein.

1. Fill a deep, medium skillet with water to a depth of ¾", cover, and bring to a boil over high heat. Add the corn, cover, and steam until tender-crisp, 3 to 4 minutes. Transfer the corn to a plate. When cool enough to handle, stand each ear in the center of a work surface and slice off the kernels.

2. In a medium skillet, melt the butter over medium heat. Mix in the corn and stir until the kernels are heated through. Off the heat, mix in the cilantro and chives. Season to taste with salt and pepper. Serve hot, warm, or at room temperature.

Makes 4 servings

Per serving: 94 calories, 5 g fat, 2 g saturated fat, 3 g protein, 12 g carbohydrates, 2 g fiber

GREEN AND YELLOW SQUASH RIBBONS

Although much loved, summer squash has only modest nutritional value. To add antioxidant benefits here, I shower it with fresh herbs that also bring aromatic flavor.

2	large (9-ounce) zucchini	2	teaspoons basil cut in fine ribbons
2	large (6-ounce) yellow squash		
1	tablespoon extra-virgin olive oil	2	teaspoons finely chopped oregano leaves
2	teaspoons minced shallot		
	Salt and freshly ground pepper		

1. To make long, thin ribbons, halve each squash lengthwise. Using a teaspoon, scoop out the seeds. Cut off the neck and rounded blossom end, then slice the squash lengthwise into ¼" strips. Discard the outermost ones that are mainly skin.

2. In a medium skillet, heat the oil over medium heat. Add the shallot and cook until soft, 1 minute. Add the squash and sprinkle with ½ teaspoon salt. Cook, stirring occasionally, until the squash looks moist, 3 minutes. Increase the heat to medium-high and cook, stirring constantly, until tender, 8 minutes. The pieces should bend easily but still be tender-crisp.

3. Using tongs, remove the squash to a warm serving plate. Spoon the shallots from the pan over the squash and season with salt and pepper to taste. Sprinkle on the basil and oregano and serve immediately.

Makes 4 servings

Per serving: 73 calories, 4 g fat, 1 g saturated fat, 3 g protein, 9 g carbohydrates, 3 g fiber

STEAK-CUT BROCCOLI

● **ANOTHER WAY**

Also serve this side dish
lukewarm as part of an
antipasto.

● **FOOD FACT**

Broccoli stems are rich in
fiber while the florets stand
out for phytochemicals,
including indoles and
sulforaphane.

Slicing broccoli lengthwise into thick slabs that resemble steak-cut potatoes, then browning them with garlic is a fresh way to keep this must-eat vegetable interesting. This is done all in the same pan.

¾	pound broccoli, stalk bottoms trimmed	2–3	large cloves garlic, thinly sliced lengthwise
2	tablespoons extra-virgin olive oil		Salt and freshly ground pepper

1. One at a time, stand the broccoli stalks on end and cut each one vertically into ½" slices. This is done all in the same pan.

2. Pour water into a large skillet to a depth of ¾" and bring to a boil. Add the broccoli in one layer, reduce the heat to medium-high, and cook until the broccoli is tender-crisp, 3 minutes. Drain in a colander. Wipe the pan dry.

3. Return the pan to medium-high heat. Add the oil and garlic and cook until it starts to color. Turn the slices and cook until golden, then remove them using a slotted spoon and drain on a paper towel or discard.

4. Return the broccoli to the pan, in one layer, crowding as needed. Cook until it starts to brown in places, about 3 minutes. Remove the broccoli to a serving platter. Season to taste with salt and pepper. Sprinkle on the reserved garlic, if using, and serve hot or at room temperature.

Makes 4 servings

Per serving: 94 calories, 7 g fat, 1 g saturated fat, 3 g protein, 6 g carbohydrates, 2 g fiber

ROASTED BROCCOLI, GREEN BEANS, AND GRAPE TOMATOES

Roasting turns grape tomatoes candy-sweet and improves the taste of green beans, too. When you start, the pile of vegetables looks like a lot, but roasting shrinks them considerably. Young children particularly like the bright colors of this dish and being able to eat it with their fingers.

● **BEST TECHNIQUE**
Keeping the garlic on top of the vegetables prevents it from burning.

6	ounces green beans, ends trimmed	1	tablespoon extra-virgin olive oil
4	cups broccoli florets cut in 1" pieces	1	teaspoon salt
		¼	teaspoon freshly ground pepper
1	pint (2 cups) grape tomatoes	3	cloves garlic, thinly sliced

1. Preheat the oven to 400°F.

2. On a baking sheet, combine the beans, broccoli, tomatoes, and oil, using your hands to coat the vegetables with the oil. Sprinkle on the salt and pepper and toss again. Sprinkle on the garlic and rub to coat with oil.

3. Roast for 15 minutes. Stir and return to the oven. Roast until the vegetables are tender, 10 minutes longer. Serve warm or at room temperature.

Makes 4 servings

Per serving: 80 calories, 4 g fat, 1 g saturated fat, 3 g protein, 10 g carbohydrates, 5 g fiber

INDIAN ROASTED CAULIFLOWER

Roasting brings out unsuspected sweetness and makes cauliflower tender with a pleasing firmness. Cutting the cauliflower into small florets with very little stem is important. I like to do this tedious work in front of the TV or while listening to my favorite public radio program.

● **BEST TECHNIQUE**

A light-colored baking sheet, preferably air-insulated, helps roasting vegetables brown without burning.

● **FOOD FACT**

Cauliflower contains almost as much folate and vitamin C as broccoli and even more potassium.

4	teaspoons extra-virgin olive oil, divided	1	teaspoon salt
¼	teaspoon ground turmeric		Freshly ground pepper
1	medium (2-pound) cauliflower, cut into ¾" florets		

1. Preheat the oven to 400°F.

2. Drizzle 1 tablespoon of the oil onto a baking sheet. Sprinkle on the turmeric. Spread the cauliflower on the pan in one layer. Drizzle with the remaining oil. Add the salt and several grinds of pepper. Mix with your hands to coat the florets.

3. Roast for 20 minutes. Stir the cauliflower, roast 5 minutes, and stir again. Continue roasting until the cauliflower is almost soft and some tips are dark brown, about 5 minutes longer. Cool the cauliflower on the pan. Serve warm or at room temperature.

Makes 4 servings

Per serving: 100 calories, 5 g fat, 1 g saturated fat, 5 g protein, 12 g carbohydrates, 6 g fiber

RED CURRIED CAULIFLOWER

Inspired by the Manchurian Cauliflower served by Indian chef Suvir Saran at Dévi, his New York City restaurant, I season this dish with both Asian chili paste and Heinz chili sauce. The chili paste adds heat. The red chili sauce, with a sharper tomato flavor than ketchup, is what Americans like to serve with shrimp cocktail. To appreciate all the flavors in this dish, serve it warm, not hot.

● SERVE WITH

Any mild-tasting white fish, including halibut or sole.

1	medium (2-pound) cauliflower, cut into large florets	½	teaspoon grated fresh ginger
2	teaspoons peanut oil	2	tablespoons chili sauce or ketchup
¼	cup finely chopped onion	1	teaspoon Asian fish sauce
1	clove garlic, finely chopped	½–1	teaspoon red Thai chili paste
¼	cup light coconut milk		

1. In a large pot of boiling water, cook the cauliflower until crisp-tender, 5 minutes. Drain in a colander, then plunge into a bowl of ice water until cooled. Drain very well. This can be done 1 day ahead.

2. In a medium skillet, heat the oil over medium-high heat. Add the onion and sauté until golden, 6 minutes. Add the garlic and cook until the onion is lightly browned, about 1 minute. Add the coconut milk. When it boils, reduce the heat to medium. Stir in the ginger, chili sauce or ketchup, fish sauce, and chili paste.

3. Add the cauliflower and sauté until heated through, 2 to 3 minutes. Let the cauliflower sit briefly to serve warm, not hot.

Makes 4 servings

Per serving: 123 calories, 5 g fat, 2 g saturated fat, 5 g protein, 18 g carbohydrates, 6 g fiber

LEMON KALE WITH CAPERS

● **BEST INGREDIENTS**

Consider using an organic lemon since you eat the peel.

Salt-preserved capers from Sicily have the best flavor. To remove excess salt, soak them in cool water while preparing the kale.

● **BEST TECHNIQUE**

To remove the tough stem:
Kale: Hold a leaf in 1 hand, closed like a book and stem up. With your other hand, pull the stem away and down.

Collards: With the leaf on a flat surface, stem toward you, cut down either side next to the stem, making an inverted "V"

Tart lemon and pungent capers bring out the sweet side of steamed kale. Preparing the kale for steaming doesn't take much time, making this a good way to serve dark greens when you want dinner quickly.

1	bunch curly green kale, stems removed and chopped	1	tablespoon extra-virgin olive oil
½	lemon, preferably organic, cut into 5 thin slices, then quartered	1	tablespoon small capers, rinsed and drained

Place a steamer insert in a large, deep saucepan. Add water to the bottom of the pot, cover, and set over high heat. When the water boils, spread one-third of the kale in the steamer. Sprinkle 6 of the lemon pieces over the kale. Repeat, layering the kale and lemon 2 times more. Place any extra lemon on top. Cover tightly and steam until the kale and lemon are tender, about 10 minutes. Transfer the kale and lemon to a serving bowl. Drizzle on the oil. Sprinkle on the capers. Serve immediately.

Makes 4 servings

Per serving: 90 calories, 4 g fat, 1 g saturated fat, 4 g protein, 12 g carbohydrates, 3 g fiber

BRUSSELS SPROUTS AND KALE

Braising these two crucifers with ginger and garlic turns this duo of often-hated vegetables into a dish that inspires requests for seconds.

2	tablespoons extra-virgin olive oil
¾	pound Brussels sprouts, quartered lengthwise
2	large cloves garlic, sliced
1	(1") piece ginger, cut crosswise into 4 slices
1½	pounds kale, stemmed and chopped, about 6 cups
1½	cups fat-free, reduced-sodium chicken broth, divided
1	tablespoon white balsamic vinegar
	Salt and freshly ground pepper

● **BEST INGREDIENT**
White balsamic vinegar, made with white wine vinegar, tastes milder and less sweet than the traditional dark kind.

1. In a large skillet, heat the oil over medium-high heat. Add the sprouts and cook, stirring, until they start to color, 2 minutes. Add the garlic and ginger and cook, stirring constantly, 1 minute.

2. Add the kale and cook, stirring, until it wilts, 3 minutes. Add 1 cup of the broth and cook, stirring occasionally, until the pan is almost dry, about 7 minutes. Add the remaining ½ cup broth and the vinegar. Cook until the vegetables are tender and the liquid has evaporated, about 11 minutes longer. Season with salt and pepper to taste.

Makes 4 servings

Per serving: 160 calories, 8 g fat, 1 g saturated fat, 7 g protein, 19 g carbohydrates, 5 g fiber

GARLIC GREENS

● BEST TECHNIQUE

To prepare leafy greens most deliciously:

• Use scissors to quickly cut the leaves into strips.

• Cook in salted water to bring out sweetness.

• Using water to finish the cooking emphasizes the taste of garlic and the greens; using broth softens these flavors.

Europeans enjoy eating dark leafy greens. This recipe shows how they make them taste good. Do not skip the lemon. Its acid makes all the difference to the flavor of the dish.

4	cups coarsely chopped broccoli raab	1	tablespoon + 2 teaspoons extra-virgin olive oil
4	cups coarsely chopped curly green kale	2–4	large cloves garlic, each cut lengthwise into 4 slices
4	cups coarsely chopped collard greens	½	cup vegetable broth or water
		½	lemon, cut into 4 wedges

1. Add the greens to a large pot of boiling water. When the water returns to a boil, cook for 5 to 8 minutes, depending on whether you want them just tender or very soft. Drain the greens in a colander, then run cold water over them, turning them with tongs, until cooled through. Using a potato ricer, a handful at a time, squeeze as much water as possible from the greens. There will be about 2 cups. The greens can be prepared up to 1 day ahead up to this point and refrigerated in a plastic bag.

2. In a medium skillet, heat 1 tablespoon oil over medium-high heat. Add the garlic slices and cook until pale gold, then remove using a slotted spoon and drain on paper towels or discard.

3. Mix the greens into the oil. Add the broth or water and cook, stirring occasionally, until most of the liquid has evaporated and the greens are nearly dry and as tender as you like them, 8 to 12 minutes. Transfer the greens to a serving bowl. Add the lemon and the reserved garlic, if using. Drizzle on the remaining oil. Serve hot, warm, or at room temperature.

Makes 4 servings

Per serving: 120 calories, 8 g fat, 1 g saturated fat, 5 g protein, 11 g carbohydrates, 4 g fiber

BAKED SPINACH AND FETA

These little soufflés resemble the filling in Greek spinach pie. Baked in muffin cups, they give you the great combination of vegetables and cheese without the calories, carbs, or work of phyllo.

2	tablespoons extra-virgin olive oil, divided	½	cup (2 ounces) crumbled feta cheese
½	small onion, finely chopped	¼	cup grated Parmesan cheese
¼	cup finely chopped leek, white part only	2	large eggs, lightly beaten
1	(10-ounce) package frozen chopped spinach, thawed and squeezed almost dry	½	teaspoon salt
		½	teaspoon freshly ground pepper

1. Place a rack in the center of the oven. Preheat the oven to 350°F. Set 4 foil or paper muffin tin liners on a baking sheet, coat with cooking spray, and set aside.

2. In a medium skillet, heat 1 tablespoon of the oil over medium-high heat. Add the onion and leek and sauté until the onion starts to brown at the edges, about 4 minutes. Mix in the spinach. Add the remaining oil and cook, stirring often, until the spinach is tender, about 5 minutes. Transfer the mixture to a mixing bowl and cool for 5 minutes.

3. Add the feta, Parmesan, eggs, salt, and pepper to the spinach mixture. Mix with a fork until well combined. Spoon the mixture into the prepared muffin cups, filling them to the top.

4. Bake 20 minutes, or until rounded on top like a muffin, lightly browned, and firm when pressed lightly in the center. Serve immediately, in the paper cup or unmolded.

Makes 4 servings

Per serving: 202 calories, 15 g fat, 5 g saturated fat, 10 g protein, 6 g carbohydrates, 1 g fiber

MUSHROOM KEBABS

● BEST TECHNIQUE

Use onion layers that are as wide as the mushrooms, saving the rest of the onion for another use.

Grilling mushrooms concentrates their flavor and makes them more firmly meaty. Use the marinade generously to keep the mushrooms moist while cooking.

12	white or cremini mushrooms
1	large red onion, cut into 1" wedges
12	cherry tomatoes
1	clove garlic

½	teaspoon salt
2	tablespoons extra-virgin olive oil
½	teaspoon chopped fresh thyme leaves, or ½ teaspoon dried

1. Soak four 8"-long bamboo skewers in water for 30 minutes. Preheat a gas or charcoal grill to medium heat.

2. Cut off the stems of the mushrooms even with the bottom of the cap. To assemble each skewer, thread on a mushroom, cap side facing the bottom of the skewer, 2 onion layers, curved side down, and a tomato. Add another mushroom, cap side up, 2 onion layers, curved side down, and a tomato. Repeat, alternating the mushrooms, cap side facing down and up, and ending with a tomato.

3. Coarsely chop the garlic. Sprinkle on the salt. Chop the garlic finely then turn the knife on one side and use it to smear the garlic and salt together until they make a moist paste. Scrape up the garlic and place in a small bowl. Add the oil and thyme, mixing to combine the marinade. Brush the kebabs liberally with the mixture. Grill the kebabs immediately, or cover with foil, and refrigerate up to 3 hours.

4. Grill the kebabs, turning them frequently and basting 3 or 4 times with marinade from the plate, until the mushrooms are charred on several sides and moist in the center, 6 to 8 minutes. Serve hot or lukewarm.

Makes 4 servings

Per serving: 98 calories, 7 g fat, 1 g saturated fat, 2 g protein, 7 g carbohydrates, 1 g fiber

APPLE RATATOUILLE

Apples and tomatoes are surprisingly good together, perhaps because they are botanical cousins. I particularly like this as a side dish with pork chops.

● **FOOD FACT**

Most of an eggplant's phytonutrient value is in its skin, which is purple due to antioxidant anthocyanins.

3	tablespoons extra-virgin olive oil, divided	1	medium zucchini, halved lengthwise and cut crosswise into ¾" slices
1	medium onion, chopped		
2	cloves garlic, chopped	1	small Honeycrisp or Jonagold apple, peeled and cut into ¾" cubes
½	small (1-pound) eggplant, cut into ¾" cubes		
1	medium green bell pepper, diced	½	cup tomato sauce
			Salt and freshly ground pepper

1. In a medium skillet, heat 1 tablespoon of the oil over medium-high heat. Add the onion and sauté for 3 minutes. Add the garlic and cook until the onion is soft, 3 minutes. With a slotted spoon, transfer to a bowl. Add 2 tablespoons of the oil to the pan. Cook the eggplant, turning the cubes, until they are lightly browned on all sides, about 5 minutes. Add them to the onions. Add the remaining oil to the pan. Add the green pepper, zucchini, and apple. Cook, stirring occasionally, until the peppers and zucchini have softened, about 5 minutes.

2. Return the onion and eggplant to the pan. Add the tomato sauce and stir to combine. Reduce the heat to medium, cover, and simmer until the vegetables are soft but still hold their shape, about 6 minutes. Season to taste with salt and pepper. If not using immediately, cool the ratatouille to room temperature and refrigerate, covered, for up to 4 days.

Makes 4 servings

Per serving: 173 calories, 11 g fat, 2 g saturated fat, 3 g protein, 19 g carbohydrates, 7 g fiber

RED CABBAGE
WITH SOUR CHERRIES

Tart cherries, tomato, and honey create a balance of sharp and sweet flavors in this dish. The acid in the fruit helps keep it bright red. Using honey also keeps the cabbage slightly al dente.

2	tablespoons unsalted butter	1	tablespoon tomato paste
7	cups finely shredded red cabbage	⅓	cup dried sour cherries
1	cup vertically thin-sliced red onion	1	(4") stick cinnamon
½	teaspoon salt	2	whole cloves
1½	cups sour cherry, pomegranate, or cranberry juice	¼	teaspoon ground cardamom, optional
2	tablespoons lavender or wildflower honey		Freshly ground pepper

1. In a small Dutch oven or deep medium skillet, melt the butter over medium heat. Add the cabbage, onion, and salt, and sauté until wilted, 5 minutes. Cover tightly, reduce the heat to medium-low, and cook until the cabbage is very moist, 8 minutes.

2. Add the juice, honey, and tomato paste, stirring until the honey dissolves. Add the cherries, cinnamon, clove, and cardamom if using. Season with pepper. When the liquid boils, reduce the heat to a simmer, cover, and cook until the cabbage is very soft, about 1 hour. Remove the cinnamon stick and cloves before serving.

Makes 4 servings

Per serving: 223 calories, 6 g fat, 4 g saturated fat, 3 g protein, 43 g carbohydrates, 6 g fiber

Onions in Three Flavors

I love onions so much that when sautéing them, I steal some from the pan. This made me think about ways to get everyone eating more of this potent health protector and led to making these little flavor bombs. Use them to replace croutons in soups and on salads. Mix them into burgers, meatballs, or meat loaf. Stir them into cooked rice and other grains, sprinkle onto steamed vegetables, and scramble them with eggs. These onions keep well for up to 4 days, tightly covered in the refrigerator.

CURRIED ONIONS

For curry lovers, these golden onions add your favorite flavor to scrambled eggs, baked potatoes, spinach salad, and more.

● **BEST INGREDIENT**
Curry powder is a good way to bring turmeric's potent antioxidant powers to all kinds of dishes.

2	tablespoons light coconut milk	½	teaspoon curry powder
1	onion, cut into ⅜" dice		Salt and freshly ground pepper

In a small skillet, heat the coconut milk over medium-high heat until it bubbles at the edges, 30 seconds. Mix in the onion, curry powder, and ¼ teaspoon salt. Sauté until the onion is translucent and crisp-tender, 4 minutes. Adjust the seasoning with salt and pepper to taste. Cool to room temperature.

Makes ½ cup, 4 servings

Per serving (2 tablespoons): 18 calories, 1 g fat, 1 g saturated fat, 1 g protein, 3 g carbohydrates, 1 g fiber

CHILI ONIONS

Perfect on burgers, these deep, dark, and mildly spiced bits also perk up canned beans, cooked rice, and mashed sweet potatoes.

1	tablespoon canola oil	¼	teaspoon ground cumin
1	onion, cut into ⅜" dice		Salt
½	teaspoon chili powder		

In a small skillet over medium-high heat, heat the oil. Mix in the onion, chili powder, cumin, and ¼ teaspoon salt. Sauté until the onion is translucent and crisp-tender, 4 minutes. Adjust the seasoning with salt to taste. Cool to room temperature.

Makes ½ cup, 4 servings

Per serving (2 tablespoons): 43 calories, 4 g fat, 0 g saturated fat, 1 g protein, 3 g carbohydrates, 1 g fiber

MEDITERRANEAN ONIONS

These herb-flavored onions give a sunny flavor-lift to supermarket tomatoes. Also add them to frozen green peas, mix them into deviled eggs or cottage cheese, or sprinkle on cooked spinach.

1	tablespoon extra-virgin olive oil	¼	teaspoon dried oregano
1	onion, cut into ⅜" dice	¼	teaspoon dried thyme
¼	teaspoon dried basil		Salt and freshly ground pepper

In a small skillet over medium-high heat, heat the oil. Mix in the onion, basil, oregano, thyme, ¼ teaspoon salt, and ⅛ teaspoon pepper. Sauté until the onion is translucent and crisp-tender, 4 minutes. Adjust the seasoning with salt and pepper to taste. Cool to room temperature.

Makes ½ cup, 4 servings

Per serving (2 tablespoons): 44 calories, 4 g fat, 1 g saturated fat, 1 g protein, 3 g carbohydrates, 1 g fiber

GINGER MASHED SWEET POTATOES

● **BEST TECHNIQUE**

Oiling the skin of a sweet potato before baking seals it, keeping in moisture as the potato bakes. This makes the flesh creamy, heightens the flavor, and makes the potato cook faster, too.

Baked sweet potatoes are so creamy that just stirring them vigorously with a fork turns them into perfect mashed potatoes. Whipping in coconut milk adds a rich tropical touch.

1½	pounds orange-fleshed sweet potatoes	½	teaspoon grated fresh ginger
2	tablespoons light coconut milk		Salt and freshly ground pepper

1. Preheat the oven to 400°F.

2. Rub each sweet potato with a few drops of oil or a touch of cooking spray. Place the potatoes on the oven rack and bake until they are soft when squeezed, 40 to 60 minutes. Remove the potatoes and set aside until they are cool enough to handle.

3. Peel the potatoes and place the flesh in a mixing bowl. Add the coconut milk and ginger. Using a fork, mash the potatoes until they are almost smooth; or if they are fibrous, whirl them in a food processor with the other ingredients. Season to taste with salt and pepper.

Makes 4 servings

Per serving: 125 calories, 1 g fat, 1 g saturated fat, 3 g protein, 28 g carbohydrates, 4 g fiber

MARSHMALLOW SWEET POTATOES FOR GROWN-UPS

At Sabbath dinner one Friday at a neighbor's, I fell in love with this minimally sweet version of yams baked under a crust of kosher marshmallows. Hardened by baking, the topping was less cloying than usual because the sugar in the marshmallows had caramelized.

● **BEST INGREDIENT**
Kosher marshmallows, made with gelatin from fish bones, are firmer than other kinds.

1½	pounds orange-fleshed sweet potatoes	1	teaspoon salt	
2	tablespoons light unsweetened coconut milk	2	teaspoons grated orange zest	
¼	teaspoon ancho or jalapeño chile powder	24	kosher marshmallows	

1. Preheat the oven to 400°F. Coat an 8" square baking dish with cooking spray or oil.

2. Rub each sweet potato with a few drops of oil or a touch of cooking spray. Place the potatoes on the oven rack and bake until they are soft when squeezed, 40 to 60 minutes. Remove the sweet potatoes and set aside until cool enough to handle.

3. Peel the potatoes and place the flesh in a mixing bowl. Add the coconut milk, chile powder, salt, and zest. Mash until the potatoes are creamy, or if they are fibrous, whirl them in a food processor with the other ingredients.

4. Spread the potatoes in the prepared baking dish, smoothing them evenly. Top with the marshmallows, spacing them about ½" apart.

5. Bake until the marshmallows are lightly browned and quite dry, about 30 minutes. Let the dish sit at room temperature for 15 minutes before serving. The marshmallows will harden outside and remain soft inside.

Makes 6 servings

Per serving: 156 calories, 1 g fat, 0 g saturated fat, 3 g protein, 37 g carbohydrates, 3 g fiber

UPSIDE-DOWN PINEAPPLE SWEET POTATOES

Too good to serve only on Thanksgiving, these mashed sweet potatoes have starred in our family gatherings since my godmother's mother first served them in 1958. Once unmolded, the dish keeps and reheats well, making it a good contribution to casserole suppers.

2½	pounds orange-fleshed sweet potatoes	2	large eggs, beaten
4	tablespoons (½ stick) unsalted butter	½	teaspoon ground cinnamon
½	cup lightly packed brown sugar	½	teaspoon baking powder
7	slices canned pineapple, drained and dried	1	teaspoon salt
			Freshly ground pepper

1. Preheat the oven to 350°F. Coat a 9" round cake pan with cooking spray and set aside.

2. Rub the sweet potatoes with a few drops of oil or a touch of cooking spray. Place the potatoes on the oven rack and bake until they are soft when squeezed, 40 to 60 minutes. Remove the sweet potatoes and set aside until cool enough to handle.

3. Meanwhile, in a small saucepan over medium heat, melt the butter with the brown sugar. Pour the mixture into the prepared pan, tilting to coat the bottom evenly. Arrange six pineapple slices in a ring around the edge and one in the center of the pan.

4. Peel the potatoes and place the flesh in a mixing bowl. Mash roughly with a fork. Add the eggs, cinnamon, baking powder, salt, and 5 or 6 grinds pepper, and whisk until well blended. Spoon the mixture into the baking pan, spreading it evenly over the pineapple and smoothing the top. Rap the pan sharply on the countertop three or four times to knock out air bubbles.

5. Bake until the top looks dry and feels springy to the touch, 40 minutes. A knife inserted in the center should come out clean. Cool in the pan on a rack for 10 minutes. Run a knife around the side of the pan. Invert a serving plate over the pan and, holding the pan and the plate firmly with oven mitts, flip them so the potatoes drop on to the plate, pineapple side up. Lift off the pan. Serve warm.

Makes 8 servings

Per serving: 272 calories, 7 g fat, 4 g saturated fat, 4 g protein, 50 g carbohydrates, 5 g fiber

ORANGE-GLAZED JAPANESE SQUASH

● **BEST INGREDIENTS**

Consider using an organic squash since you eat the peel.

Mirin is a sweet rice wine available in natural food stores, Japanese markets, and the Asian or natural foods section of large supermarkets. Alternatively, use 1½ tablespoons sake and 1½ teaspoons sugar.

In Japan, cooked vegetables are often served at room temperature or chilled. Elizabeth Andoh, a fellow cookbook writer in Tokyo, showed me this way to cook hard-shelled kabocha squash without peeling it, a great time-saver and nutritionally a good idea. Orange juice gives the squash an autumnal glow.

2	cups fat-free, reduced-sodium chicken broth	1	small (1½-pound) kabocha squash
1	cup chopped leek tops, dark green part only, rinsed and cut into 1" pieces	1	orange
		3	tablespoons mirin (see Best Ingredients, left)
1	small onion, chopped	2	teaspoons soy sauce

1. In a small saucepan, combine the broth, leek, and onion and cook over medium heat until a ring of bubbles forms around the edge of the pot. Reduce the heat and simmer for 10 minutes. Strain, discarding the solids. There should be 1½ cups broth.

2. While the broth simmers, halve the squash vertically. Cut each half into 6 wedges. Use a spoon to scoop away the seeds and soft flesh. Set the squash aside.

3. Grate 2 teaspoons zest from the orange, and juice the orange. Pour 1 cup of the broth into a medium skillet, reserving the remaining broth for another use. Add the orange juice and mirin. Bring the liquid to a boil over medium-high heat. Add the squash, standing the wedges up like melon slices. Set a cover on the pot, allowing the points of the squash to hold it above the rim. Reduce the heat to medium and simmer 4 minutes.

4. Add the soy sauce. Using tongs, gently lay the squash wedges down on their sides, forming a ring with the pieces nestled to keep the squash in one layer. Cover and cook for 2 minutes. Turn the squash end over end, cover, and cook

until a toothpick slips easily through the squash from the skin side, 2 minutes longer.

5. Transfer the squash to a plate, laying the pointed ends in to form a pin-wheel. Reduce the pan juices until they are syrupy and spoon them over the squash. Sprinkle on the zest. Serve at room temperature or cover, refrigerate, and serve chilled.

Makes 4 servings

Per serving: 106 calories, 0 g fat, 0 g saturated fat, 3 g protein, 22 g carbohydrates, 2 g fiber

Winter Squash

Along with familiar acorn and butternut squash, try:

- **Buttercup:** Dark green with a grey-green "cap." Divinely delicious.
- **Calabaza:** Sold cut into wedges. Has pumpkin-like, carrot-tasting flesh.
- **Delicata:** Ridged cylinder of cream striped with dark green. Nicely sweet.
- **Dumpling:** Ridged ball of cream with green or orange with an indented top. Good for stuffing.
- **Kabocha:** Drum-shaped, with dark green rough skin and substantial, potato-like flesh.
- **Red Kuri or Orange Hokkaido:** Chubby, round teardrop with vivid orange skin and slightly sweet flesh.

TUSCAN POTATOES
WITH BITTER GREENS

● **FOOD FACT**

Serving potatoes with their skin adds nutrition as well as flavor to dishes. It also saves time.

● **ANOTHER WAY**

Use whole tiny potatoes from the farmers' market, steaming them until tender, 15 minutes.

Italians make this dish with broccoli raab, dandelion greens, or an assortment of other wild field greens, combining them with a roughly even amount of browned potatoes. Do not skip the lemon—it lifts the flavors of this Mediterranean comfort food from good to brilliant.

1	bunch broccoli raab, 1¼–1½ pounds, tough stems removed	3	garlic cloves, thinly sliced
3	medium yellow-fleshed potatoes, about ¾ pound	¼	teaspoon red-pepper flakes, optional
			Salt and freshly ground pepper
3	tablespoons extra-virgin olive oil	½	lemon, cut into 4 wedges

1. In a large pot of boiling water, cook the raab until tender, 7 minutes. Remove to a colander with a slotted spoon. Add the potatoes to the pot and cook until a sharp knife pierces them easily, about 15 minutes. Drain and set aside.

2. Meanwhile, cool the raab under cold running water. Squeeze out as much moisture as possible. Chop the raab and set aside. When the potatoes are cool enough to handle, peel and cut them into ½" pieces and set aside.

3. In a medium skillet, heat the oil over medium-high heat. Add the garlic and raab. Mix in the potatoes and the pepper flakes, if using. Season with salt and pepper to taste. Cook, without stirring, until the potatoes are lightly browned, 2 to 3 minutes. Gently turn the vegetables and spread them in an even layer, scraping up and including browned bits from the bottom of the pan. Cook until the potatoes and greens are browned lightly on the bottom, 2 minutes. With a spatula, transfer the mixture to a serving plate. Serve immediately, accompanied by the lemon wedges.

Makes 4 servings

Per serving: 200 calories, 11 g fat, 2 g saturated fat, 7 g protein, 20 g carbohydrates, 5 g fiber

DEVILED RED POTATOES

These chunky potatoes, served in their skins, are browned and crusty outside, soft and creamy inside. Generous amounts of onion, peppers, and paprika give this dish health benefits rarely found in comfort food.

● **ANOTHER WAY**

If you like, toss in some cayenne pepper for heat and the added benefits of chile pepper.

1	pound small red-skinned potatoes	½	small red bell pepper, finely chopped, about ½ cup
1½	teaspoons extra-virgin olive oil	1	teaspoon sweet or hot Hungarian paprika
1	onion, finely chopped	1	teaspoon salt
½	small green bell pepper, finely chopped, about ½ cup		Freshly ground pepper

1. Place the potatoes in a deep saucepan and cover with cold water by 1½". Set the pot over high heat. When the water boils, reduce the heat and boil gently until a knife pierces the potatoes easily, 12 to 15 minutes. Drain and halve or quarter the potatoes, depending on their size.

2. In a heavy medium skillet, heat the oil over medium-high heat. Add the onion and sauté for 3 minutes. Add the green and red peppers and cook 2 minutes. Mix in the paprika and salt. Push the onion and peppers to one side of the pan.

3. Add the potatoes to the pan, cut side down, arranging them in one layer. Cook until they are crusty and dark brown, 5 minutes. Turn halved potatoes on their skin side and quartered potatoes to brown the second cut side. Spread the onions and peppers over the potatoes. Cook until the potatoes are browned on the bottom, 3 to 4 minutes longer. Season with pepper to taste. Serve hot.

Makes 4 servings

Per serving: 123 calories, 2 g fat, 0 g saturated fat, 3 g protein, 23 g carbohydrates, 2 g fiber

GINGER CRANBERRY RELISH

● **FOOD FACT**

Eating cranberries raw
provides the most antioxidants because heat affects
them adversely.

This is my favorite way to make the raw cranberry and orange condiment most of us associate with Thanksgiving. It uses far less sugar than traditional versions. If you find it tart, wait an hour before making an adjustment because the relish gets sweeter as it sits.

1½	cups fresh or frozen cranberries	2–3	tablespoons ginger marmalade
½	large or ¾ medium naval orange,		or preserves
	cut into 12 pieces	2	tablespoons sugar

Pulse the cranberries, orange pieces, and ginger marmalade in the bowl of a food processor until finely chopped, about 15 times, stopping to scrape down the sides of the bowl several times and leaving some larger chunks of orange peel. Transfer the mixture to a container. Mix in the sugar. Cover and refrigerate for 1 hour to overnight before serving. This relish keeps in the refrigerator for 3 to 4 days, becoming sweeter, redder, and juicier.

Makes 1½ cups, 12 servings

Per serving (2 tablespoons): 26 calories, 0 g fat, 0 g saturated fat, 0 g protein, 7 g carbohydrates, 1 g fiber

CRANBERRIES AND PEARL ONIONS

Whether you call this a sauce or a condiment, served alongside roast chicken, turkey, beef tenderloin, or pork, its intensely spiced red wine flavors make the meal memorable. Based on a recipe by Chef Michel Nischan, it will make you glad to have a generous amount.

2	tablespoons canola oil	1	cup apple cider
1	(10-ounce) package red pearl	½	cup orange juice
	onions, peeled	½	cup dry red wine
1	teaspoon sugar	¼	cup wildflower honey, or to taste
	Salt and freshly ground pepper	2	(3") sticks cinnamon
2	cups fresh or frozen cranberries	1	whole star anise, optional

● **BEST TECHNIQUE**

To make quick work of peeling pearl onions, toss them into boiling water for 1 minute. Drain and use small sharp knife to cut off the root end. Squeeze the other end to pop the onion out of its skin and tough first layer.

● **BEST INGREDIENT**

Frozen white pearl onions can replace fresh red ones. Boil the frozen onions for 2 minutes, drain, and squeeze them out of their tough outer layer.

1. In a heavy medium stainless steel or other nonreactive skillet, heat the oil over medium-high heat. Add the onions, stirring to coat them with the oil. Sprinkle on the sugar, ¼ teaspoon salt, and 4 grinds pepper. Sauté until the onions are lightly golden all over and more deeply browned in places, 3 minutes. Reduce the heat and cook, shaking the pan frequently, until the onions have softened, 6 to 8 minutes. Using a slotted spoon, transfer the onions to a large, nonreactive saucepan.

2. Add the cranberries, cider, juice, wine, honey, cinnamon, and star anise if using. Cook over medium heat until the liquid boils. Reduce the heat and simmer until the cranberries pop and soften, about 25 minutes. Off the heat, season with salt and pepper to taste. Ladle into a sauceboat and serve lukewarm. This sauce keeps, tightly covered in the refrigerator, for 1 week. Reheat in a nonreactive saucepan over medium heat.

Makes about 3¾ cups, 15 servings

Per serving (¼ cup): 70 calories, 2 g fat, 0 g saturated fat, 1 g protein, 12 g carbohydrates, 1 g fiber

KUMQUAT-APPLE CHUTNEY

This golden, chunky chutney tastes like ginger marmalade with extra heat. It is an easy way to experience the satisfaction of making your own condiments. A small jar makes a thoughtful hostess gift. Double the recipe if you wish.

15	kumquats, halved, seeded, and cut into 8 pieces	⅓	cup fruit-sweetened orange marmalade
2	Granny Smith apples, peeled, cored, and finely chopped	⅓	cup apple cider vinegar
1	small red onion, finely chopped	¼	cup chopped preserved ginger
¾	cup packed brown sugar	1	fresh red chile pepper, thinly sliced
½	cup golden raisins		

1. In a small Dutch oven or large, heavy stainless steel or other nonreactive saucepan, combine the kumquats, apples, onion, brown sugar, raisins, marmalade, vinegar, ginger, and pepper. Add ½ cup water. Cover and cook over medium-high heat until the liquid boils. Reduce the heat and simmer for 15 minutes to draw out the moisture in the ingredients.

2. Uncover and simmer until the apples are tender, about 30 minutes. The chutney will be chunky and deep golden brown. Spoon into 4 sterilized 4-ounce glass canning jars and cover tightly, or scoop into a heatproof container and cover. Cool to room temperature, then refrigerate for 24 hours before serving. This chutney keeps in the refrigerator for 3 weeks.

Makes 2½ cups, 10 servings

Per serving (¼ cup): 176 calories, 1 g fat, 0 g saturated fat, 1 g protein, 44 g carbohydrates, 3 g fiber

CHAPTER TEN
DESSERTS

[
FRUIT SALADS FOR ALL SEASONS

Spring—Spring Fruit Salad with Mint Syrup 269

Summer—Tropical Fruit Salad with White Tea Syrup 271

Autumn—Autumn Fruit Salad in Cider 272

Winter—Berries and Red Grapes in Spiced Red Wine 273
]

Chocolate Soup with Brownie Dippers 260, Chocolate-Covered Pears with Espresso Sauce 263,

Red Grapefruit with Pumpkin Seed Praline 265, Honey-Baked Peaches with Raspberry Sauce 267,

Blood Orange and Cranberry Parfait 274, Blackberry Shortcakes with Ginger Cream 275,

Black Bean Brownies 277, Spiced Fig Bars 279, Sicilian Almond Cookies 280, Green Tea Shortbread 281,

Pumpkin-Date Tea Cakes 282, Chocolate Cupcakes with Cinnamon Frosting 283, Blueberry Banana Bread 285,

Walnut Chocolate Strudels with Cinnamon Honey Syrup 286, Seriously Lemon Meringue Pie 288,

Southern Sweet Potato Pie 291, My Mom's One-Crust Apple Pie 292, Pear and Sweet Potato Crumble 294,

Chocolate Gingerbread with Lemon Yogurt Frosting 296,

Lemon Yogurt Cheesecake with Sour Cherry Sauce 298, Chocolate Cranberry Torte 300,

Peanut Butter Truffles 307, Nutty Popcorn Bundt Ring 304, Avocado Lemon Sherbet 305,

Ginger Pomegranate Granita 306, Frozen Blueberry Yogurt Pops 308

CHOCOLATE SOUP WITH BROWNIE DIPPERS

● **BEST INGREDIENT**

Dark milk chocolate, such as Scharffen Berger 41% Cacao Milk or Valrhona Jivara Lactee, gives this dessert creamy richness with a hint of caramel flavor.

If you love brownies, or steal spoonfuls from the pot when making chocolate pudding, this dessert will be bliss. It uses dark milk chocolate, which is sweet enough that no added sugar is needed. Should you have Chocolate Soup left-over, it is decadently good over oatmeal.

2 cups whole milk	1 tablespoon hazelnut liqueur or dark rum, or 1 teaspoon vanilla extract
2 tablespoons cornstarch	
Pinch of salt	
4 ounces dark milk chocolate, chopped	4 Brownie Dippers (page 262)

1. In a small saucepan, heat the milk over medium heat until it starts to steam, 2 to 3 minutes. Or heat in a microwaveable measuring cup on medium power.

2. Place the cornstarch and salt in a deep, medium saucepan. Add ¼ cup of the hot milk and whisk until the mixture is smooth. Pour in the remaining milk. Set the pot over medium heat and cook, whisking until the milk mixture boils, taking care not to let it boil over, 1 to 2 minutes.

3. Off the heat, add the chocolate and liqueur, rum, or vanilla. Whisk until the chocolate melts and blends with the milk mixture. Allow to sit for 10 minutes to cool slightly.

4. To serve, divide the soup among 4 dessert bowls. Set each on a plate with a brownie dipper and serve.

Makes 4 servings

Per serving: 413 calories, 23 g fat, 12 g saturated fat, 6 g protein, 46 g carbohydrates, 1 g fiber

(continued)

BROWNIE DIPPERS

As intensely chocolate as brownies and crisp as biscotti, these long, thin bars are ideal for dipping into Chocolate Soup. Also dunk them into a cup of freshly brewed coffee or a glass of milk.

1¼	cups unbleached all-purpose flour	⅔	cup packed light brown sugar
½	cup Dutch-process cocoa powder	½	cup granulated sugar
1	teaspoon baking soda	2	large eggs
	Pinch of salt	1	teaspoon vanilla extract
¾	cup (1½ sticks) unsalted butter, softened slightly	2	tablespoons sliced almonds
		2	ounces dark chocolate (70% cocoa), chopped, optional

1. Place a rack in the center of the oven. Preheat the oven to 350°F. Coat a 15½" × 10½" jellyroll pan with cooking spray and set aside.

2. Into a mixing bowl, sift the flour, cocoa, baking soda, and salt. In another mixing bowl, using an electric hand mixer on medium speed, cream the butter, brown sugar, and granulated sugar until fluffy, 2 minutes. Add the eggs, one at a time, and the vanilla, beating well. Mix in the dry ingredients.

3. Spread the batter in an even layer in the prepared pan. Sprinkle on the almonds. Bake 20 minutes, or until the dough in the center of the pan feels firm. Set the pan on a baking rack and cool completely.

4. Using a serrated knife, in the pan, cut the sheet of dippers in half lengthwise, then crosswise, making 5 × 1½" bars. If using, melt the chocolate in a small bowl in the microwave. Arrange the dippers on a rack over a baking sheet. Using a fork, drizzle the melted chocolate over the dippers.

Makes 20

Per dipper: 161 calories, 11 g fat, 5 g saturated fat, 2 g protein, 19 g carbohydrates, 1 g fiber

CHOCOLATE-COVERED PEARS WITH ESPRESSO SAUCE

This conversation-stopping dessert is actually simple to make since poaching pears is as easy as boiling an egg. Melting the chocolate with a touch of butter helps it flow evenly over the fruit. If the coating comes out a bit uneven, everyone will be delighted anyway.

● **ANOTHER WAY**

An alternative to the espresso sauce is Raspberry Sauce (page 268).

1	lemon	4	ounces dark chocolate
6	cups cold water		(70% cocoa), chopped
2	cups sugar, divided	2	teaspoons unsalted butter
1	(4") stick cinnamon	2	tablespoons brewed espresso
2	cloves		coffee
4	ripe Bartlett pears, with stems		

1. From the lemon, cut 2 strips of zest, each 2" × 1". Juice the lemon, keeping the squeezed halves.

2. In a saucepan deep enough to hold the pears standing up, combine the lemon juice, lemon zest, water, 1½ cups sugar, cinnamon, and cloves. Over medium heat, bring the mixture to a boil and boil 5 minutes. Remove from the heat.

3. Meanwhile, using a vegetable peeler, peel the pears, leaving the stems on. With a small melon baller, working from the bottoms, scoop out the cores. Rub the pears all over with a lemon half to prevent discoloring. If necessary to make the pears stand firmly, cut thin slices off the bottoms.

4. Add the pears to the syrup, which should come up to their stems. If necessary, add cold water. Return the pot to medium heat and bring to a simmer. Cook the pears until a thin knife easily penetrates at the thickest point, 15 minutes. Using a slotted spoon, carefully remove the pears and set on a plate to cool to room temperature. Reserve the cooking syrup.

(continued)

5. Using paper towels, pat the pears very dry. In a microwaveable bowl, heat the chocolate and butter together in 10 to 15 second bursts until they are melted. Remove and stir until smooth.

6. To coat the pears, set them on a greased wire rack set over a plate. Spoon the melted chocolate over each pear to coat. Let them set in a cool place until the chocolate sets, forming a shell, 2 to 3 hours.

7. For the sauce, strain 1 cup of the cooking syrup into a small saucepan and add the remaining ½ cup sugar. (Strain the remaining syrup and reserve to use to sweeten lemonade or iced tea.) Bring to a boil over medium-high heat. Reduce the heat to medium and boil until the syrup is reduced by half. Off the heat, add the coffee. Set aside to cool.

8. Carefully, using your fingers and a fork, lift the pears from the rack and set each in the center of a dessert plate. Spoon 2 tablespoons of the sauce around each serving.

Makes 4 servings

Per serving: 452 calories, 14 g fat, 7 g saturated fat, 3 g protein, 91 g carbohydrates, 7 g fiber

RED GRAPEFRUIT
WITH PUMPKIN SEED PRALINE

I call this a Cinderella dessert because of the way praline transforms sugar and pumpkin seeds into a sparkling brittle to top the grapefruit.

2	red grapefruit	4	tablespoons Pumpkin Seed Praline (below)

1. Peel and section the grapefruits (see page 122), squeezing any juice into a separate bowl from the sectioned fruit. One at a time, slice off the top and bottom. Drink or reserve the juice for another use.

2. Fan one-quarter of the grapefruit sections on each of 4 dessert plates, shaking off any excess juice when lifting them from the bowl. Sprinkle 1 tablespoon of the praline over the fruit. Serve immediately, before the juice in the fruit dissolves the caramelized sugar.

Makes 4 servings

Per serving: 117 calories, 3 g fat, 1 g saturated fat, 2 g protein, 22 g carbohydrates, 2 g fiber

● **BEST TECHNIQUE**

Making praline is as easy as boiling water. Just watch it carefully and handle the hot sugar with care.

Moisture in the air can dissolve praline, so make it on a dry day and store in an airtight container. If it hardens into a lump, wrap in waxed paper, and pound to a powder.

PUMPKIN SEED PRALINE

You can also use this crunchy sweetening on fruits, yogurt, and hot cereal.

½	cup sugar	¼	cup raw pumpkin seeds

1. Cover a cookie sheet with baking parchment and set aside. Coat a heat-proof spatula with oil.

2. Place the sugar in a heavy small saucepan. Add ¼ cup water and tilt the pan to evenly moisten the sugar. Over medium-high heat, cook until the sugar is golden brown, rotating the pan occasionally so the caramel colors

(continued)

evenly. Using a pastry brush generously wet with cold water, keep brushing down the sides of the pot to dissolve any sugar crystals or drops of syrup. This is important to prevent the praline from becoming grainy. Off the heat, immediately mix in the pumpkin seeds until they separate, then pour the caramel onto the prepared baking sheet. Using the greased spatula, shape it into a rough 8" × 6" rectangle. Cool completely.

3. Wrap the praline in waxed paper and using a meat mallet, smash it into small chunks and powdery bits.

Makes about ½ cup, 8 servings

Per serving (1 tablespoon): 80 calories, 3 g fat, 1 g saturated fat, 1 g protein, 13 g carbohydrates, 0 g fiber

HONEY-BAKED PEACHES
WITH RASPBERRY SAUCE

This simple dessert is sublime when made with tree-ripe local peaches, the kind so juicy you must use them at once. The rest of the year, less-extraordinary fruit is still delicious made this way.

● **ANOTHER WAY**

Add a small scoop of vanilla yogurt or a dollop of vanilla ice cream, or sprinkle with some chopped preserved ginger.

2	large peaches, halved and pitted	Raspberry Sauce (page 268)
½	cup blueberry, raspberry, or wildflower honey	Pumpkin Seed Praline (page 265), optional
¼	cup fresh orange juice or orange liqueur	

1. Preheat the oven to 350°F. Coat a baking dish that holds the peach halves in one layer with cooking spray.

2. Arrange the peaches, cut side up, in the baking dish. In a small microwaveable bowl, dissolve the honey in the orange juice or liqueur. Microwave on high for about 10 seconds to speed up the process. Spoon the mixture over the peaches. Bake until glazed and easily pierced with a knife but still holding their shape, about 30 minutes. Set aside to cool in the pan to lukewarm.

3. Spoon 2 tablespoons of the raspberry sauce in a ring around the edge of 4 plates. Set a peach half in the center of each plate. Drizzle on more sauce. If using, sprinkle 1 tablespoon praline over each peach half. Serve immediately.

Makes 4 servings

Per serving: 189 calories, 0 g fat, 0 g saturated fat, 2 g protein, 49 g carbohydrates, 2 g fiber

RASPBERRY SAUCE

Straining the pureed thawed fruit makes this sauce attractively translucent.

4 cups or 2 (10-ounce) packages frozen raspberries, thawed	½–1 teaspoon fresh lemon juice
1–2 tablespoons confectioners' sugar, to taste	

Place the raspberries in a fine strainer set over a bowl. Using a wooden spoon, push as much pulp as possible through the strainer. Discard the solids from the strainer. Mix the confectioners' sugar and lemon juice into the strained fruit. Tightly covered in the refrigerator, the sauce keeps for 3 days.

Makes about 1 cup, 8 servings

Per serving (2 tablespoons): 84 calories, 0 g fat, 0 g saturated fat, 2 g protein, 53 g carbohydrates, 3 g fiber

Fruit Salads for All Seasons

Fruit salads finish a meal with a light touch and help you eat an assortment of fruits—but these four salads are far too enticing to think of as health food. Each is distinctive because in Paris I worked with a chef who taught me to compose contrasting textures in every fruit salad and to include a refreshing liquid, or *soupe*, that enhances the flavors of the fruit. Each of these four is ideal for its season, but delightful any time. Using pre-cut fruit, hands-on preparation time for some of these recipes is as little as 10 minutes.

Spring
SPRING FRUIT SALAD WITH MINT SYRUP

In spring, nature surrounds us with shades of green. This dessert features them in a combination of honeydew melon, kiwi, green grapes, and Granny Smith apple. The mint in the syrup is as refreshing as a spring breeze.

¼	cup sugar	½	Granny Smith apple, peeled, cored, and cut lengthwise into thin slices
4	mint sprigs		
2	cups honeydew melon cut into 1" × ½" pieces	4	sprigs spearmint, optional for garnish
2	kiwifruit, peeled and cut crosswise into 8 slices each		
1	cup seedless green grapes, halved lengthwise		

1. In a small saucepan, combine the sugar with ½ cup water. Cook over medium heat, stirring occasionally, until the sugar dissolves, about 2 minutes. Cook until the syrup is clear, 1 minute. Off the heat, add the mint. Cover and set aside to steep for 30 minutes. Remove the mint and discard. Allow the syrup to cool to room temperature. The cooled syrup can be covered and refrigerated for 24 hours.

(continued)

2. In a mixing bowl, combine the fruit. Pour in the mint syrup. With a fork, toss gently to combine. Serve immediately or cover and refrigerate for up to 24 hours. Toss gently before serving in small glass bowls or dessert dishes, including a generous amount of liquid. Garnish with mint sprigs, if using.

Makes 6 servings

Per serving (for 6 servings): 92 calories, 0 g fat, 0 g saturated fat, 1 g protein, 23 g carbohydrates, 2 g fiber

Summer

TROPICAL FRUIT SALAD
WITH WHITE TEA SYRUP

Mango, red papaya, and pineapple give this fruit salad the colors of a summer sunset. The dessert also finishes with a flavor glow thanks to a fresh chile that harmonizes with the tropical flavors.

½	cup cold water	1½	cups red papaya cut into ¾" cubes
1	bag white tea, preferably with lemongrass flavor	1	cup thinly sliced fresh pineapple
2	tablespoons raw or turbinado sugar	1	carambola (star fruit), cut into ¼" slices
1	long red chile pepper, thinly sliced	1	ripe medium mango (see Mango Methods, right)

1. In a small saucepan, boil the water. Off the heat, add the tea bag, cover, and steep for 3 minutes. Remove and discard the tea bag. Add the sugar and 3 slices chile pepper. Simmer over medium heat, stirring occasionally, until the sugar dissolves and the syrup is clear, about 2 minutes. Cool the syrup to room temperature, removing the chile pepper if you want just a hint of heat.

2. In a mixing bowl, combine the papaya, pineapple, carambola, and mango. Add the tea syrup. With a fork, toss gently to combine. Serve immediately in a large bowl or in small glass bowls. Or cover and refrigerate for up to 6 hours. Toss gently before serving. Garnish with a few thin slices from the chile pepper just before serving, if desired.

Makes 6 servings

Per serving: 61 calories, 0 g fat, 0 g saturated fat, 1 g protein, 16 g carbohydrates, 2 g fiber

● **SERVE WITH**

Asian dishes like Peanut Chicken Stir-Fry (page 152) and Thai Shrimp Curry with Broccoli, Carrots, and Green Peas (page 184), or following an outdoor barbecue with ribs and grilled chicken

● **MANGO METHODS**

Holding mango in one hand, run a knife around fruit at its widest point, cutting to the pit. With your fingers, pull skin off the top half. Over a bowl, slice fruit lengthwise, inserting knife at an angle and twisting blade to release the slices. When half the fruit is sliced, turn it over, peel and slice the other half.

Autumn
AUTUMN FRUIT SALAD IN CIDER

● **SERVE WITH**

Good at a weekend brunch, this is also elegant enough to serve at a dinner party.

The thinly sliced fruit in this mélange floats in a generous soupe of apple cider. The cider gives the salad a fall flavor and adds more nutrients than juice. While apples and pears are always available, they taste best when they are just picked.

1	kiwifruit, peeled, halved vertically, and thinly sliced crosswise	1	Gala apple, halved vertically
		1	ripe Bosc pear, peeled and halved vertically
1	cup golden pineapple chunks, thinly sliced with the grain	6	paper-thin lemon slices
		3	cups sweet apple or pear cider
½	ripe banana, thinly sliced	¼	teaspoon vanilla extract
½	cup small red seedless grapes, halved	1–2	tablespoons superfine sugar

1. In a large glass serving bowl, combine the kiwi, pineapple, banana, and grapes. Using a melon baller, core the apple and pear halves. Cut off the neck of the pear and reserve for another use. Cut the apple and pear crosswise into the thinnest possible slices and add them to the other fruit.

2. Add the lemon slices, cider, and vanilla. With your hands, gently turn the fruit to mix. Add 1 to 2 tablespoons sugar, according to your taste. Let the salad sit for 15 minutes to allow the flavors to meld. The salad can be covered and refrigerated for up to 4 hours, but it should be served the day it is made. Serve it cool, not cold, in individual dessert bowls, including a generous amount of the liquid.

Makes 8 servings

Per serving: 106 calories, 0 g fat, 0 g saturated fat, 1 g protein, 27 g carbohydrates, 2 g fiber

Winter

BERRIES AND RED GRAPES IN SPICED RED WINE

The bright berries, citrus, and wine in this sangria-like salad make a festive dessert. Its spices, reminiscent of those in mulled wine, improve the flavor of the fruit available in winter. Use pomegranate wine from Armenia or a fruity Beaujolais.

½	cup sugar		1	cup fresh blueberries
3	strips (2" × ½") lemon zest		½	cup fresh raspberries
3	strips (2" × ½") lime zest		½	cup fresh blackberries
3	strips (2" × 1") orange zest		½	cup pomegranate or other light red wine
1	(3") stick cinnamon			
1	whole star anise			
1½	cups large seedless red grapes, halved			

ANOTHER WAY

If blackberries are not available, increase the amount of raspberries to 1 cup. Do not use frozen fruit.

1. In a heavy medium saucepan, combine the sugar, lemon, lime, and orange zests, cinnamon, star anise, and ½ cup water. Cook over medium heat until the sugar has dissolved and the syrup boils, 4 minutes. Cover, remove from the heat, and steep for 30 minutes. Remove the spices and zest, reserving the zest. Cool the syrup to room temperature. The syrup can be covered and refrigerated for up to 24 hours.

2. In a clear glass serving bowl, combine the grapes, blueberries, raspberries, blackberries, syrup, and wine. Using a small, sharp knife, cut the reserved citrus zest crosswise into very thin strips. Sprinkle the zest over the salad. Cover with plastic wrap and refrigerate for 1 hour to let the flavors meld, or up to 24 hours.

3. Toss gently and serve in individual dessert bowls, including a generous amount of the syrup.

Makes 4 servings

Per serving: 202 calories, 1 g fat, 0 g saturated fat, 1 g protein, 46 g carbohydrates, 4 g fiber

BLOOD ORANGE
AND CRANBERRY PARFAIT

● BEST INGREDIENT

Blood oranges are in season from January through April. When they are not available, use a juicy Valencia instead.

Consider using an organic orange since you eat the peel.

● ANOTHER WAY

Serve the remaining cranberry-orange mixture as a relish with turkey or chicken.

Here, a little cream and sugar transform an orange—rind, pith, and all—into a conversation-stopping dessert. Serve it in tall glasses at a dinner party, or in smaller ones at a buffet.

1	blood orange, quartered	1	tablespoon orange-flavored
6	tablespoons sugar		liqueur, such as Grand
1½	cups fresh or frozen cranberries		Mariner
¾	cup well-chilled heavy cream	½	pint red raspberries (or a
1	tablespoon confectioners' sugar		4.4-ounce container)

1. Remove and discard the peel from one of the orange quarters. Chop each quarter into 4 pieces. Pulse the orange with the sugar in a food processor until coarsely chopped. Add the cranberries and pulse until the mixture resembles cranberry relish. Turn the mixture into a bowl. The mixture keeps in a container in the refrigerator for 3 days.

2. Drain ⅔ cup of the orange mixture in a strainer until it measures ½ cup. Place in a mixing bowl and reserve the remaining mixture (see Another Way, left).

3. Whip the cream until stiff. Mix in the sugar and liqueur. Mix ¼ cup of the whipped cream into the orange mixture, blending well.

4. For each parfait, spoon 1 tablespoon of the whipped cream into the bottom of each of 4 tall champagne flutes or other tall, narrow glasses. Add 1 tablespoon berry-cream mixture then 3 raspberries. Add 2 tablespoons whipped cream, then 2 tablespoons berry-cream. Top with a dollop of whipped cream and 4 raspberries. The parfaits can be covered with plastic wrap and refrigerated for up to 2 hours. Let sit at room temperature for 15 minutes before serving.

Makes 4 servings

Per serving: 296 calories, 17 g fat, 10 g saturated fat, 2 g protein, 35 g carbohydrates, 4 g fiber

BLACKBERRY SHORTCAKES WITH GINGER CREAM

A warm filling gives this familiar dessert a new twist. With blackberries now available much of the year, I particularly like serving this dish in winter.

● **FOOD FACT**
Blackberries provide nearly 4 grams of fiber per serving.

SHORTCAKES

1	cup + 2 tablespoons unbleached all-purpose flour
2	tablespoons granulated sugar
1	tablespoon baking powder
1	teaspoon ground cinnamon
¼	teaspoon salt
⅓	cup cold unsalted butter, cut into ¼" pieces
½	cup buttermilk
½	teaspoon vanilla extract
½	teaspoon turbinado sugar

BERRIES AND CREAM

¾	cup fresh orange juice
¼	cup sugar
2	(4.4-ounce) boxes blackberries
½	cup well-chilled heavy cream
1–2	teaspoons confectioners' sugar
	Pinch of ground ginger

1. Place a rack in the center of the oven. Preheat the oven to 400°F.

2. **FOR THE SHORTCAKES**: In a mixing bowl, combine all the flour, sugar, baking powder, cinnamon, and salt. Using a pastry cutter or fork, cut in the butter until the mixture resembles coarse cornmeal. Add the buttermilk and vanilla. Using the fork or a rubber spatula, gently toss until the mixture forms a moist, loose dough; do not overmix. Turn the dough out onto a lightly floured work surface. Gently shape it into a 4" square. Using a sharp knife, trim the edges to make them neat, then cut the dough into 4 squares.

3. Place the shortcakes on an ungreased baking sheet, 6" apart. Sprinkle the tops with the turbinado sugar. Bake 15 to 18 minutes, or until the shortcakes are puffed and golden. Transfer to a rack and cool completely.

(continued)

4. **FOR THE BERRIES AND CREAM:** Chill a small mixing bowl and beaters in the refrigerator for 10 minutes. Meanwhile, heat the juice and sugar in a large skillet over medium heat until the sugar dissolves and the mixture boils. Continue cooking until the liquid is reduced to ½ cup. Off the heat, add the blackberries, swirling the pan to bathe them in the hot liquid. Set aside.

5. Pour the cream into the chilled bowl and beat with a hand mixer at medium speed until foamy, 1 minute. Increase the speed to high and sprinkle in the confectioners' sugar and ginger. Continue beating until the cream forms soft peaks, 2 minutes.

6. Split the shortcakes in half horizontally. Place each bottom, cut side up, on a dessert plate. Top with one-quarter of the berry mixture. Add the cake top, tilting it to one side. Dollop some of the whipped cream, partly alongside and partly on the open bottom. Serve immediately.

Makes 4

Per shortcake: 505 calories, 27 g fat, 17 g saturated fat, 7 g protein, 60 g carbohydrates, 5 g fiber

BLACK BEAN BROWNIES

These are the fudgiest brownies ever and they are gluten-free! Best eaten right from the fridge, their velvet texture comes, in part, from pureed black beans, which also enhances the intensity of their chocolate flavor. I bake these brownies in generous rounds using a muffin-top pan, but using a square baking pan is fine (see Another Way, right).

1	cup canned black beans, rinsed and drained	1	cup sugar
¾	cup (1½ sticks) unsalted butter		Pinch of salt
3	ounces unsweetened chocolate	1	teaspoon vanilla extract
3	large eggs, at room temperature	1½	cups chopped walnuts, divided

● **ANOTHER WAY**

The brownies may also be baked in an 8" square baking pan for 45 to 50 minutes. Cool and then cut into 16 pieces.

● **BEST INGREDIENT**

Some canned black beans are softer than others, like those from Whole Foods' 365 Organic brand or Westbrae. Softer beans are best in this recipe.

1. Place a rack in the center of the oven. Preheat the oven to 350°F. Coat a 12-cup muffin-top tin with cooking spray.

2. Puree the beans in a food processor until smooth. Measure out ¾ cup. Reserve the rest of the bean puree to use in a soup, dip, or other dish.

3. In a heavy, medium saucepan over low heat, melt the butter and chocolate, stirring occasionally. This can also be done in a microwave oven. Set aside until cooled to room temperature.

4. In a bowl, using a hand mixer on medium speed, beat the eggs. Add the sugar and salt. Beat on high speed until the mixture is ivory colored and glossy, about 5 minutes. When the beaters are lifted, drips should linger on the surface for a few seconds before disappearing. Beat in the chocolate mixture until well combined. Beat in the bean puree and vanilla extract. Mix in half the walnuts. Spoon the batter into the prepared pan, filling each cup to the rim. Sprinkle the remaining walnuts over the tops, pressing them lightly into the batter.

(continued)

5. Bake for about 20 minutes, or until the tops are crusty and crinkly and a knife inserted in the center comes out clean. Cool completely in the pan. Run a thin knife around the edges of the cups. Cover with foil and refrigerate 6 hours to overnight. Carefully invert to release the round brownies. Serve chilled.

Makes 12

Per brownie: 332 calories, 26 g fat, 11 g saturated fat, 6 g protein, 24 g carbohydrates, 3 g fiber

SPICED FIG BARS

Crammed with as much whole grain, fiber, and phytonutrients as commercially made bars, this oat treat tastes much better.

1	cup fresh orange juice	1½	cups quick-cooking oats (not instant)
1	cup chopped dried Turkish figs		
¼	cup chopped pitted dates	1	cup unbleached all-purpose flour
¼	cup dried cranberries	⅔	cup packed brown sugar
½	cup chopped walnuts	¼	teaspoon salt
½	teaspoon ground cinnamon	⅓	cup cold unsalted butter, cut into ½" pieces
⅛	teaspoon ground cloves		
⅛	teaspoon ground mace	1	large egg white

● **BEST TECHNIQUE**

The flavor of anise cookies gets even better when they sit overnight.

1. Preheat the oven to 350°F. Coat an 8" square baking pan with cooking spray and set aside.

2. In a medium nonreactive saucepan, bring the orange juice, figs, dates, and cranberries to a boil over medium-high heat. Reduce the heat and simmer until the liquid has been absorbed. Transfer to a bowl. Mix in the nuts, cinnamon, cloves, and mace and set aside to cool.

3. Pulse the oats, flour, sugar, and salt in a food processor until the mixture is gritty. Add the butter and pulse until the mixture resembles coarse meal. Add the egg white and pulse until the mixture looks like wet sand.

4. Press half the oat mixture to cover the pan bottom. Spread the filling over the crust. Sprinkle on the remaining oat mixture and gently press until it is compact, especially around the edges.

5. Bake for 25 minutes, or until the top feels firm and is starting to brown around the edges. Cool in the pan. Using a sharp knife, make 2 cuts in one direction. Rotate the pan 90° and make 3 cuts. In an airtight container, these bars keep up to 1 week.

Makes 12

Per serving: 273 calories, 9 g fat, 4 g saturated fat, 4 g protein, 45 g carbohydrates, 4 g fiber

SICILIAN ALMOND COOKIES

● **BEST INGREDIENT**
For the almond paste, the best choices are Love'n Bake and Solo brands. Odense is too sweet and makes a very wet dough.

You find these chewy, flourless cookies at every Italian bakery. In Sicily, numerous bakers have reminded me to use only almond paste, never marzipan, which is too soft.

1	(10-ounce) can almond paste	2	large egg whites
¾	cup confectioners' sugar	1½	cups raw pine nuts

1. Preheat the oven to 350°F. Line 2 baking sheets with parchment paper.

2. In a medium mixing bowl, break up the almond paste into 1" pieces using your fingers. Add the sugar and blend with a hand mixer on low speed until combined, about 3 minutes. One at a time, add the egg whites, beating at medium speed until the first is blended in before adding the second. Cover with plastic wrap and refrigerate the dough for 1 hour.

3. Place the pine nuts in a shallow, wide bowl. Moisten your fingers very lightly with cold water. Shape a piece of the almond mixture into a loose 1" ball and place on the nuts. Flatten the dough lightly into a 1½" round pillow. Turning the dough gently, coat it with nuts on all sides, including the bottom. Place on a prepared baking sheet. Repeat with the remaining dough, spacing the cookies 2" apart.

4. Bake for 20 minutes, or until lightly golden. Cool on the sheets for 5 minutes, then transfer to a wire rack and cool completely. The warm cookies get firmer as they cool.

Makes 24

Per cookie: 133 calories, 9 g fat, 1 g saturated fat, 3 g protein, 11 g carbohydrates, 1 g fiber

GREEN TEA SHORTBREAD

Making the dough for this buttery shortbread takes 10 minutes. Baking it makes your house smell heavenly all day. Presented in a round tin, the shortbread makes a good hostess gift. It ships well, too.

¾	cup unbleached all-purpose flour	¼	cup superfine or granulated sugar
1	teaspoon powdered matcha green tea	6	tablespoons unsalted butter, chilled and cut in small pieces
⅛	teaspoon salt		

1. Preheat the oven to 325°F.

2. In a small bowl, combine the flour, tea, and salt. Place the sugar in a food processor. If using granulated sugar, whirl it for 1 minute to turn it into superfine. Add the butter and pulse until the mixture looks like pebbles. Add the dry ingredients and pulse until a coarse, loosely granular dough forms.

3. Turn the dough into an ungreased 8" round cake pan. With your fingers, quickly work in any powdery bits then press the dough into an even layer in the pan.

4. Bake for 15 minutes. Make a border by pressing the flat bottom of the tines of a fork in a circle around the outside of the dough. With the tips of the tines, prick the dough all over. Using a sharp knife, score the dough into 8 wedges.

5. Return the shortbread to the oven and bake for 20 to 25 minutes, or until golden. Do not let it brown. Cool in the pan on a rack for 10 minutes. Rescore the wedges and run a knife around the edge of the shortbread to loosen it. Invert the pan and gently unmold the shortbread. Cool and break into wedges. Serve warm or at room temperature. The shortbread keeps in an airtight container for 5 days.

Makes 8 pieces

Per piece: 143 calories, 9 g fat, 5 g saturated fat, 1 g protein, 15 g carbohydrates, 1 g fiber

PUMPKIN-DATE TEA CAKES

● **BEST INGREDIENT**

Be sure to use plain pureed pumpkin, not sweetened pie filling.

● **BEST METHOD**

The shallow cups of a muffin-top tin give you a cake with lots of crusty, browned top.

Little round spice cakes, these are just the right size to satisfy your sweet tooth. Their nutty topping makes them pretty enough to serve with afternoon tea, but enjoy them any time.

1	cup unbleached all-purpose flour	1	cup canned pumpkin
½	cup whole wheat pastry flour	¾	cup granulated sugar
½	teaspoon baking soda	1	large egg
½	teaspoon baking powder	3	tablespoons canola oil
1	teaspoon ground cinnamon	3	tablespoons apple cider or juice
¼	teaspoon ground cloves	¾	cup chopped dates
¼	teaspoon ground nutmeg	½	cup pecans, chopped
		3	tablespoons dark brown sugar

1. Preheat the oven to 400°F. Coat a 12-cup muffin-top tin with cooking spray and set aside.

2. In a mixing bowl, blend together the all-purpose flour, whole wheat flour, baking soda, baking powder, cinnamon, cloves, and nutmeg, using a hand mixer on low speed. In another bowl, use the mixer to combine the pumpkin, granulated sugar, egg, oil, and cider or juice. Add the pumpkin mixture to the dry ingredients and mix just until blended; do not overmix. By hand, stir in the dates.

3. Fill the cups of the prepared pan to just below the rim. In a small bowl, combine the pecans and brown sugar. Sprinkle the mixture over the top of the batter. Bake for 15 to 18 minutes, or until the tea cakes are golden on top and browned around the edges. Cool 3 minutes in the tin on a rack. Turn the tea cakes out on the rack and cool completely.

Makes 12

Per muffin top: 224 calories, 8 g fat, 1 g saturated fat, 3 g protein, 38 g carbohydrates, 3 g fiber

CHOCOLATE CUPCAKES
WITH CINNAMON FROSTING

The dark intensity of these tender, light cupcakes will surprise you. With their spicy frosting, they may be the best treat ever.

1	cup unbleached all-purpose flour	¼	cup Dutch process cocoa powder
¾	cup sugar	1	large egg, lightly beaten
½	teaspoon baking soda	¼	cup regular or light buttermilk
¼	teaspoon salt	½	teaspoon vanilla extract
½	cup lukewarm water		Cinnamon Frosting (page 284)
¼	cup canola oil		Grated dark chocolate, optional, for garnish

1. Preheat the oven to 375°F. Drop paper liners into a 12-cup muffin tin and set aside.

2. In a mixing bowl, whisk the flour, sugar, baking soda, and salt together. In another mixing bowl, whisk together the water, oil, and cocoa until the cocoa dissolves. Add to the dry ingredients and whisk until almost blended. Add the egg, buttermilk, and vanilla and whisk until the batter is smooth.

3. Spoon the batter into the muffin tin, filling the cups two-thirds full. Bake for 20 to 25 minutes, or until the tops of the cupcakes spring back when pressed lightly in the center. Cool in the pan for 3 minutes, then turn out on a rack to cool completely. Unfrosted and wrapped individually in plastic, these cupcakes keep in an airtight tin for up to 3 days.

4. Using a small spatula or the back of a spoon, spread 1½ tablespoons of the frosting over each cupcake. If using, sprinkle with grated chocolate. The frosting becomes firm as it sits.

Makes 12

Per cupcake: 236 calories, 10 g fat, 2 g saturated fat, 2 g protein, 40 g carbohydrates, 1 g fiber

CINNAMON FROSTING

● **ANOTHER WAY**

Use this to frost Chocolate Gingerbread (page 296) or spread thinly on warm toast.

This topping tastes so good that it may disappear before it gets onto the cupcakes.

1¼	cups confectioners' sugar	1	teaspoon ground cinnamon
⅓	cup packed brown sugar		Pinch of salt
3	tablespoons unsalted butter, softened	1–2	tablespoons reduced-fat (2%) milk
½	teaspoon vanilla extract		

Sift the confectioners' sugar into a mixing bowl. Mix in the brown sugar, butter, vanilla, cinnamon, salt, and 1 tablespoon of the milk. Add more milk, 1 teaspoon at a time until the frosting is thick but spreadable. Cover with plastic wrap, pressing the plastic onto the frosting and set aside for 30 minutes to let the flavors meld. This frosting keeps for 4 days, covered, in the refrigerator. Bring to room temperature before using.

Makes 1¼ cups, 12 servings

Per serving (heaping 1½ tablespoons): 100 calories, 3 g fat, 2 g saturated fat, 0 g protein, 19 g carbohydrates, 0 g fiber

BLUEBERRY BANANA BREAD

You get wild blueberries two ways in this moist loaf. The frozen berries are succulent while the dried ones add intense flavor. Lemon zest, a touch of butter, and the sparkling, crusty top add to its appeal.

2¼	cups unbleached all-purpose flour	¼	cup regular or light buttermilk
1	teaspoon baking powder	1	large egg
1	teaspoon baking soda	2	tablespoons unsalted butter, melted
½	teaspoon salt	1	teaspoon grated lemon zest
1	cup mashed ripe bananas, about 3 bananas	1	cup frozen wild blueberries
½	cup reduced-fat plain yogurt	½	cup dried wild blueberries
⅓	cup packed brown sugar	1	tablespoon raw sugar

1. Preheat the oven to 375°F. Coat an 8½" × 4½" × 2½" loaf pan with cooking spray and set aside.

2. In a mixing bowl, sift together the flour, baking powder, baking soda, and salt. In another bowl, combine the bananas, yogurt, brown sugar, buttermilk, egg, butter, and lemon zest. Whisk to blend. Add the dry ingredients and mix until they are just blended. Stir in the frozen and dried berries. Turn the batter into the prepared pan and smooth the top. Sprinkle on the raw sugar.

3. Bake for 40 to 45 minutes, or until a bamboo skewer inserted into the center comes out clean. Cool the cake in the pan on a rack for 5 minutes. Unmold and cool the loaf completely on the rack. Cut it into ¾" slices and serve.

Makes 10 servings

Per serving: 224 calories, 3 g fat, 2 g saturated fat, 5 g protein, 45 g carbohydrates, 3 g fiber

● **FOOD FACT**

Bananas are a good source of fiber and phytosterols that can help reduce cholesterol.

● **BEST INGREDIENT**

Raw and turbinado sugars have a light caramel flavor because they retain some molasses, which also adds minerals.

WALNUT CHOCOLATE STRUDELS WITH CINNAMON HONEY SYRUP

● **BEST INGREDIENTS**

I find the phyllo from the Fillo Factory, sold at natural food stores (including Whole Foods) and www. fillofactory.com, handles best.

Green & Black's Organic Hot Chocolate Drink resembles fine grains of chocolate and has just the right sweetness. Ghirardelli ground chocolate combines cocoa powder with sugar.

These individual pastries resemble golden Asian spring rolls. Filled with chopped nuts and chocolate, they are served with honey syrup fragrant with cinnamon. Together, the crisp pastry and hot syrup provide the best of strudel and baklava without cloying sweetness.

STRUDELS

12	sheets phyllo dough (12" x 17"), preferably whole-wheat or spelt
2	cups walnuts, coarsely chopped
¼	cup superfine sugar
¼	cup hot chocolate drink mix or ground chocolate
2	tablespoons cold water
6	tablespoons unsalted butter, melted

SYRUP

½	cup sugar
¾	cup cold water
2	tablespoons wildflower honey
1½	teaspoons fresh lemon juice
1	(2") cinnamon stick
1	whole clove
8	fresh whole strawberries or mint sprigs, optional, for garnish

1. **FOR THE STRUDELS:** Thaw the phyllo, if frozen, or bring it to room temperature following package directions. Place a rack in the center of the oven. Preheat the oven to 375°F.

2. Pulse the walnuts and sugar in a food processor until finely chopped. Transfer the mixture to a mixing bowl. Add the hot chocolate mix or ground chocolate. Stir to mix. Add the water and stir until the filling holds its shape when pressed into a small clump. Form the filling into sixteen 2" × 1" finger-size logs, using about 2 tablespoons for each. Set aside on a plate.

3. Unroll the phyllo and cover with a dish towel. Place one sheet on a work surface and coat with melted butter. Repeat, adding 3 more sheets. Cut the stacked phyllo into six 8½" × 4" pieces. Repeat 2 times, making a total of 18 rectangles of stacked phyllo. Place the short end of one rectangle toward you.

Set the filling 1" above the bottom. Bring up the bottom of the phyllo over it. Fold in the two long sides and roll tightly away from you, making a roll. Set the strudel seam side down on a large ungreased baking sheet and brush the top with butter. Repeat, making 16 strudels in all. Discard the remaining phyllo.

4. Bake the strudels until golden, 20 minutes. Do not worry if some of the filling leaks out. Using a wide spatula, transfer the strudels to a rack and cool completely. The baked strudels will keep, loosely covered with foil, for 24 hours at room temperature.

5. **FOR THE SYRUP.** In a small, heavy saucepan combine the sugar, water, honey, lemon juice, cinnamon stick, and clove. Bring to a boil over medium heat and simmer for 10 minutes. Remove the spices.

6. To serve, spoon 2 tablespoons hot syrup onto 8 dessert plates. Add 2 strudels. If using, garnish with a strawberry or mint sprig.

Makes 8 servings

Per serving: 453 calories, 28 g fat, 7 g saturated fat, 7 g protein, 49 g carbohydrates, 4 g fiber

SERIOUSLY LEMON MERINGUE PIE

I like meringue pie where the filling is so tart your tongue tingles and the meringue is sweet, smooth velvet. For the pie shell, use your favorite commercial brand. If your pie should weep, a problem that plagues even experienced bakers, tell guests what Martha says: "It tastes great anyway."

FILLING

1	cup granulated sugar
1¼	cups cold water
4	large eggs, separated
⅓	cup cornstarch
	Grated zest of 2 lemons
¾	cup fresh lemon juice
¼	teaspoon salt
3	tablespoons unsalted butter, chilled and cut into ¼" pieces

MERINGUE

3	tablespoons sifted confectioners' sugar
1	tablespoon superfine sugar
	Pinch of salt
1	large egg white, at room temperature
½	teaspoon cream of tartar
¼	teaspoon vanilla extract
1	(9") pie shell, baked

1. Place a rack in the center of the oven. Preheat the oven to 325°F.

2. **FOR THE FILLING**: In a heavy nonreactive saucepan, combine the sugar, water, egg yolks, cornstarch, lemon zest, lemon juice, and salt. Whisk until well blended. Cook over medium heat, whisking constantly, until the mixture simmers, 7 to 8 minutes. Continue whisking for 1 minute. Remove from the heat and gradually whisk in the butter. Set aside.

3. **FOR THE MERINGUE**: In a small bowl, combine the confectioners' sugar, superfine sugar, and salt. Set aside. In another immaculately clean mixing bowl, combine all 5 egg whites. Using a hand mixer, beat on medium speed until the whites are frothy. Add the cream of tartar and increase the speed to medium-high. Beat until the whites form stiff peaks and look glossy but not dry. One tablespoon at a time, add the sugar mixture, mixing for 30 seconds

(continued)

between each addition. Add the vanilla and beat until the meringue is thick and shiny, about 1 minute.

4. Spoon the warm lemon filling into the baked pie shell. Using a tablespoon, drop mounds of the meringue in a ring around the edge of the filling, then mound the rest in the center of the pie. With the back of the spoon, swirl the meringue, making sure it seals against the crust all around and pressing gently to eliminate any air pockets.

5. Bake for 15 to 18 minutes, or until the meringue is golden brown. Cool the pie on a rack. Keep at room temperature and serve the day it is made.

Makes 8 servings

Per serving: 337 calories, 14 g fat, 6 g saturated fat, 5 g protein, 50 g carbohydrates, 0 g fiber

SOUTHERN SWEET POTATO PIE

Inspired by the legendary Southern chef and author Edna Lewis, renowned for her homestyle yet refined cooking, the filling in this pie is nicely spiced and lightly sweetened. Its creamy texture goes perfectly with its untraditional whole wheat crust.

1½	cups mashed baked sweet potatoes	½	teaspoon vanilla extract
		¼	teaspoon salt
2	large eggs, at room temperature, separated	⅛	teaspoon ground nutmeg
		1	cup reduced-fat (2%) milk, at room temperature
¼	cup sugar		
2	tablespoons unsalted butter, melted	1	(9") whole wheat pie shell, frozen or your favorite recipe
¾	teaspoon ground cinnamon		

● **BEST TECHNIQUE**

Baking sweet potatoes brings out their natural sweetness. Using the baked potatoes in this pie lets you add less sugar to the filling.

Replacing the heavy cream usually used in the filling with lightly beaten egg whites keeps it velvety yet considerably lower in fat.

1. Place a rack in the center of the oven. Preheat the oven to 350°F.

2. In a mixing bowl whisk the sweet potatoes, egg yolks, sugar, butter, cinnamon, vanilla, salt, and nutmeg together. Add the milk and whisk until well blended. In a smaller bowl, whisk the egg whites until foamy. Add them to the filling, whisking until blended in. Pour the filling into the pie shell.

3. Bake for 45 minutes, or until the filling is well set except in the center and a toothpick inserted into the center has some grainy filling clinging to it. Cool the pie completely on a rack. Cover with plastic wrap and refrigerate 6 hours to overnight. Serve within 24 hours to avoid a soggy crust.

Makes 8 servings

Per serving: 337 calories, 14 g fat, 6 g saturated fat, 5 g protein, 50 g carbohydrates, 0 g fiber

MY MOM'S ONE-CRUST APPLE PIE

The way my mother made her apple pie has always seemed unique. Once we convinced her to stop making a bottom crust since the flood of juices from the fruit always turned it soggy, she used only a top crust, flaky and crisp and domed over a heap of apples. I follow her way, too, in using so little sugar that the filling tastes like a perfect baked apple.

● **BEST INGREDIENT**

Using a variety of apples gives a pie the best flavor. Choose from Winesap, Rome, Jonathan, Ida Red, and Golden Delicious.

● **BEST TECHNIQUE**

Making the dough for flaky pie crust is an art. Doing it with whole wheat flour took serious experimenting. The secret is using a combination of butter and trans fat–free shortening, both chilled icy-cold. Spectrum Organics All-Vegetable Shortening works best. Then, rather than sealing the crust against the pie plate, let it float on top of the apples so their juices have room to bubble and concentrate.

● **ANOTHER WAY**

To make pumpkin pie spice, combine ½ teaspoon ground cinnamon, ¼ teaspoon ground cardamom, ⅛ teaspoon ground ginger, pinch of ground cloves, and a few gratings of nutmeg.

CRUST

1	cup unbleached all-purpose flour
½	cup whole wheat pastry flour
1	tablespoon sugar
½	teaspoon salt
3	tablespoons cold unsalted butter, cut into small pieces
2	tablespoons trans fat–free vegetable shortening, chilled
3–4	tablespoons ice water

FILLING

3½	pounds apples
1	tablespoon unsalted butter
2	tablespoons sugar
1	teaspoon pumpkin pie spice (see Another Way, left)
	Grated zest of 1 lemon

1. **FOR THE CRUST:** Whirl the all-purpose flour, whole wheat flour, sugar, and salt in a food processor to combine them. Scatter on the butter over the flour and pulse until almost blended, 15 to 20 times. Coarsely chop the shortening and add to the bowl, pulsing until the mixture resembles sand, with some larger pieces of shortening remaining. Add 2 tablespoons of the water and blend. One teaspoon at a time, add more water until the dough almost holds together. Turn the dough onto a piece of waxed paper. Press into a 6" disk, wrap, and chill for 30 minutes.

2. Preheat the oven to 425°F. Coat a 9" ovenproof glass pie dish with cooking spray.

3. **FOR THE FILLING:** Peel, quarter, and core the apples. Cut each quarter into 3 wedges. There will be about 12 cups.

4. In a large skillet, melt the butter over medium heat. Add the apples and sugar. Cook until the apples are moist, about 4 minutes. Sprinkle on the spice. Add the zest and gently mix to combine. Heap the apples into the prepared dish.

5. Roll out the dough between 2 sheets of waxed paper to an 11½" circle. Drape the dough over the apples. Fold the edges inside the pie plate so the dough sits like a cap over the apples. With a sharp knife, cut four 1½" slits and four 1" slits in the center of the dough.

6. Bake for 20 minutes. Reduce the heat to 375°F and bake for 40 minutes, or until the crust is browned and the apples soft but not mushy. Cool on a rack. Serve warm.

Makes 8 servings

Per serving: 277 calories, 9 g fat, 5 g saturated fat, 3 g protein, 49 g carbohydrates, 6 g fiber

PEAR AND SWEET POTATO CRUMBLE

● **BEST INGREDIENT**

Raw sugar from Hawaii is coarse crystals with a slight molasses taste. Supposedly, the molasses also provides minerals that are removed from white sugar.

● **ANOTHER WAY**

If desired, serve a scoop of vanilla frozen yogurt with the warm crumble.

The creamy texture of the potatoes alongside ripe Bartlett pears is a lovely surprise in this homey dessert. Keeping it minimally sweet lets you better enjoy its interplay of spices and citrus. Raw sugar sprinkled on top makes the crust sparkle.

FILLING

1⅔	cups orange juice, divided
⅓	cup packed brown sugar
1	tablespoon cornstarch
1	tablespoon chopped preserved ginger
1	pound orange-fleshed sweet potatoes, peeled and cut into 1" pieces
1½	pounds Bartlett pears, peeled, cored, and cut into 1" pieces

TOPPING

⅔	cup unbleached all-purpose flour
1	teaspoon ground cinnamon
¼	teaspoon ground allspice
¼	teaspoon salt
⅓	cup unsalted butter, chilled and cut into pieces
⅔	cup old-fashioned rolled oats
⅓	cup raw sugar

1. Preheat the oven to 375°F. Coat an 8" square baking dish with cooking spray and set aside.

2. **FOR THE FILLING**: Grease an 8" square baking dish with butter or coat with cooking spray and set aside. In a mixing bowl, combine ⅓ cup of the juice with the brown sugar, cornstarch, and ginger.

3. Pour the remaining juice into a medium saucepan. Add the sweet potatoes. Bring to a boil over medium-high heat. Reduce the heat and simmer until the potatoes are tender, 5 minutes. Using a slotted spoon, transfer the sweet potatoes to the bowl with the juice mixture. Discard the cooking liquid. Add the pears and mix with a rubber spatula to coat the fruit. Turn the filling into the prepared baking dish.

4. **FOR THE TOPPING:** Whirl the flour, cinnamon, allspice, and salt in a food processor until combined. Scatter the butter over the flour mixture. Pulse until the mixture looks like moist sand, about 30 seconds. Add the oats and raw sugar and whirl for 5 seconds. Sprinkle the topping evenly over the filling. Do not press it down.

5. Bake 40 minutes, or until the juices bubble and the topping darkens evenly in color. Cool the crumble on a rack for 20 minutes. Serve warm.

Makes 6 servings

Per serving: 420 calories, 11 g fat, 6 g saturated fat, 5 g protein, 78 g carbohydrates, 7 g fiber

CHOCOLATE GINGERBREAD
WITH LEMON YOGURT FROSTING

● BEST INGREDIENT

The fat content in buttermilk makes little difference in baking recipes but using one without gums like guar or carrageenan is important. I like Organic Valley, made with just milk and enzymes.

● BEST TECHNIQUE

Baked goods made with oil are often dense and dry. My technique using chilled oil and cold eggs gives them exceptional lightness and a moist crumb that makes you think "butter."

If you like intense desserts that go light on fat, this casual cake is for you. Like most spiced dishes and chocolate desserts, it tastes best after its flavors mellow for a day. The wait also allows time to make the topping, which is one of the yummiest frostings ever.

1½	cups unbleached all-purpose flour	2	cold, large eggs
2	teaspoons Dutch-process cocoa powder	⅓	cup canola oil, chilled
		½	cup packed dark brown sugar
1¼	teaspoons ground cinnamon	½	cup regular or light buttermilk
1	teaspoon ground ginger	¼	cup unsulfured molasses
1	teaspoon baking soda	¼	cup buckwheat or wildflower honey
½	teaspoon salt		Lemon Yogurt Frosting (opposite)
¼	teaspoon ground pepper	½	lemon
	Pinch of ground cloves		

1. Preheat the oven to 350°F. Coat a 9" square baking pan with butter and set the pan aside.

2. Into a mixing bowl, sift together the flour, cocoa, cinnamon, ginger, baking soda, salt, pepper, and cloves. In a larger bowl, whisk the eggs until beaten. Add the oil and whisk until the mixture resembles homemade mayonnaise, about 30 seconds. Whisk in the sugar until it dissolves, 1 minute. The mixture will resemble caramel sauce. Whisk in the buttermilk, molasses, and honey until blended, 30 seconds. Add the dry ingredients, mixing with a rubber spatula until thoroughly combined.

3. Pour the batter into the prepared pan. Rap it on the counter to eliminate air bubbles. Bake for 30 to 35 minutes, or until the sides pull away from the pan and the top springs back when lightly pressed in the center. Unmold, place right side up on a rack, and cool completely. Wrap in foil and let sit at room temperature overnight to let the flavors mellow and texture settle.

4. Place the cake on a serving platter. Dollop the frosting on top. Using a spatula, spread it evenly over the top. Holding a rasp in one hand and the lemon half in the other, grate the zest from the lemon over the cake. The cake keeps for 3 days, wrapped in foil.

Makes 9 servings

Per serving: 346 calories, 11 g fat, 2 g saturated fat, 8 g protein, 55 g carbohydrates, 1 g fiber

LEMON YOGURT FROSTING

In my experience, only Dannon yogurt works for this recipe because it contains no gums or other additives and has the perfect creamy texture when drained. In addition to the gingerbread, use it to fill and frost other cakes and cupcakes.

3	cups reduced-fat lemon yogurt	1	teaspoon fresh lemon juice
1	tablespoon confectioners' sugar	¼	teaspoon vanilla extract

● **BEST TECHNIQUE**

Drain the yogurt for at least 16 hours, even if it looks dry. This assures that the yogurt is thoroughly drained so it does not make the cake soggy.

1. Place the yogurt in a yogurt cheese maker, or a large coffee brewing cone lined with a paper filter, and set over a bowl. Spoon in the yogurt. Cover loosely with a plastic bag, refrigerate, and drain until there is 1 cup of yogurt that resembles light cream cheese, 16 to 18 hours.

2. Transfer the drained yogurt to the bowl of a mini food processor. Add the sugar, lemon juice, and vanilla. Whirl until smooth. This frosting can be refrigerated in a covered container for 4 to 6 hours. Stir well before using.

Makes 1 cup, 8 servings

Per serving (2 tablespoons): 82 calories, 1 g fat, 1 g saturated fat, 5 g protein, 14 g carbohydrates, 0 g fiber

LEMON YOGURT CHEESECAKE WITH SOUR CHERRY SAUCE

● **BEST INGREDIENT**

Arrowroot powder produces a smoother result than cornstarch as a thickener.

● **ANOTHER WAY**

For a walnut crust, replace the graham crackers with 1 cup ground walnuts mixed with 2 tablespoons sugar.

This ethereally light, decidedly tangy cheesecake was inspired by a Turkish recipe. Flatter than typical cheesecakes, it keeps very well. If the top cracks, the Sour Cherry Sauce spooned over the cheesecake conceals this nicely.

½	cup low-fat graham cracker crumbs (4 double crackers)	½	cup sugar
		2	large eggs
1½	cups reduced-fat (2%) plain Greek yogurt	1	tablespoon arrowroot powder or cornstarch
1	cup reduced-fat (2%) cottage cheese	1	teaspoon grated lemon zest
½	cup reduced-fat cream cheese		Sour Cherry Sauce (opposite)

1. Place a rack in the center of the oven. Preheat the oven to 350°F. Coat an 8½" springform pan with cooking spray. Sprinkle the cracker crumbs in an even layer to cover the bottom of the pan and set aside.

2. Whirl the yogurt, cottage cheese, and cream cheese in a food processor until smooth. Add the sugar, eggs, arrowroot powder, and zest and whirl just until blended. Overblending develops air bubbles. Gently pour the batter into the pan, taking care not to disturb the crumbs. Rap the pan sharply on the countertop 4 times to knock out air bubbles.

3. Bake for 45 to 50 minutes, or until the cake starts to pull away from the side of the pan and is barely set in the center. Cool it on a rack completely. Cover with foil and refrigerate for 8 hours to overnight.

4. To serve, cut the cake into 12 wedges and place on dessert plates. Serve with cherries from the sauce spread around the cake and then some of the syrup on top.

Makes 12 servings

Per serving: 208 calories, 4 g fat, 2 g saturated fat, 7 g protein, 37 g carbohydrates, 1 g fiber

SOUR CHERRY SAUCE

Besides the lemon cheesecake, this fruited syrup is good on pancakes and waffles, yogurt, or Buckwheat Polenta Cakes (page 324).

(page 324)

1	cup sugar	1	(24-ounce) jar sour cherries, drained, liquid reserved
1	(4") cinnamon stick		
2	cloves	¼	cup dry red wine

● **BEST INGREDIENT**
Many stores carry sour cherries in a jar. Look for those with minimal added sugar and no preservatives.

1. In a large, deep saucepan, combine the sugar with 2 cups water. Cook over medium heat until the sugar has dissolved. Add the cinnamon and cloves and boil gently until the liquid is syrupy, about 10 minutes. Add the drained cherries and cook for 3 minutes. Using a slotted spoon, remove the cherries and set aside.

2. Boil the syrup until it has the consistency of maple syrup, about 5 minutes. Add 1 cup of the reserved cherry juice and the wine. Boil until the syrup has reduced to 2 cups, about 15 minutes. Set it aside to cool to room temperature. Remove and discard the cinnamon stick and cloves. Return the cherries to the syrup. The cooled sauce may be covered tightly and refrigerated for up to 2 weeks. Reheat gently before serving.

Makes 4 cups, 12 servings

Per serving (⅓ cup): 89 calories, 0 g fat, 0 g saturated fat, 0 g protein, 22 g carbohydrates, 1 g fiber

CHOCOLATE CRANBERRY TORTE

● **ANOTHER WAY**
The chocolate and butter can also be melted in the top part of double boiler set over simmering water.

A recipe I found 25 years ago in a newsletter for chocolate lovers, this lavish dessert proves chocolate and cranberries make an exquisite couple. The glossy top of this almost flourless cake hints at the berries inside. Valrhona Guanaja or Ghirardelli 70 percent extra bittersweet are ideal choices. Avoid Scharffen Berger for this recipe; its acidity fights with the cranberries.

1	tablespoon all-purpose flour +¼ cup sifted all-purpose flour	½	cup + 1 tablespoon ground almonds, sifted
7	ounces dark chocolate (70% cocoa), chopped	3	large eggs, separated
		½	cup sugar
5	tablespoons unsalted butter	¼	teaspoon almond extract
1	(16-ounce) can jelled cranberry sauce with whole berries	¼	teaspoon salt

1. Set a rack in the bottom third of the oven. Preheat the oven to 350°F. Coat a 9" springform pan with cooking spray, then coat with the 1 tablespoon flour, shaking out the excess. Set the pan aside.

2. In a heatproof measuring cup or bowl, combine the chocolate and butter. Microwave on medium until the butter melts, about 30 seconds. Remove and stir until smooth. Set aside to cool slightly.

3. Turn the cranberry sauce into a small bowl. Using a fork, mash gently to loosen the mixture. In another small bowl, combine the ½ cup almonds with the ¼ cup sifted flour.

4. In a large bowl, using an electric mixer, combine the egg yolks with the sugar. Beat on medium speed until the mixture forms a ribbon that stays on top of the batter for 3 seconds, 4 to 5 minutes. Reduce the speed to low. Beat in the flour mixture just to incorporate it. Blend in the chocolate mixture. By hand, mix in the cranberry sauce and almond extract. Wash and dry the beaters.

(continued)

5. In another bowl, beat the egg whites on medium speed until foamy. Add the salt and increase the speed to medium-high. Beat until the whites form stiff peaks but do not look dry, 3 to 4 minutes. Scoop them over the chocolate mixture. Using a rubber spatula, gently fold them into the batter. Do not overmix. Spread the batter in the prepared pan.

6. Bake for 55 to 60 minutes, or until the torte is set in the center when gently shaken. Cool the torte completely in the pan set on a rack. Cover with foil and refrigerate until chilled, at least 3 hours or up to 1 day.

7. Remove the collar of the pan. Sprinkle the remaining 1 tablespoon ground almonds over the torte. Cut into 10 wedges.

Makes 10 servings

Per serving: 320 calories, 18 g fat, 9 g saturated fat, 5 g protein, 41 g carbohydrates, 3 g fiber

PEANUT BUTTER TRUFFLES

These chocolate-coated delights conceal two secrets: velvety peanut butter and a wonderful crunch. Dipping the nutty centers is so easy that kids can help—but make sure they do not eat more than they dip.

¾	cup smooth natural peanut butter	2	ounces dark chocolate (70% cocoa), such as Ghirardelli
¼	cup marshmallow cream	2	ounces dark chocolate (62% cocoa), such as Scharffen Berger
¼	cup confectioners' sugar		
½	teaspoon vanilla extract		
½	cup crisp brown rice cereal	4	teaspoons unsalted butter

● **BEST INGREDIENT**

The acidic intensity of Ghirardelli's Extra Bittersweet Chocolate (70%) paired with vanilla and caramel notes in Scharffen Berger's Semi-Sweet Dark Chocolate are perfect against the peanut filling in these truffles.

1. In a mixing bowl, use a wooden spoon to combine the peanut butter, marshmallow cream, sugar, and vanilla until the mixture is smooth and resembles a pliable dough. Using your hands, work in the cereal. Form the mixture into 1" balls, rolling them between your palms until smooth. Arrange the balls in one layer on a baking sheet.

2. In a double boiler over hot water, melt the chocolates and butter. Set a wire rack over a baking sheet. One at a time, roll the peanut butter balls in the melted chocolate, using a fork and teaspoon to turn them until completely coated, then set them on the rack. Chill the truffles in the refrigerator to set the chocolate. Transfer to a tightly sealed container and refrigerate for up to 5 days. Serve cold.

Makes 24

Per truffle: 84 calories, 6 g fat, 2 g saturated fat, 2 g protein, 6 g carbohydrates, 1 g fiber

NUTTY POPCORN BUNDT RING

● **FOOD FACT**

Popcorn is a whole grain and a good source of fiber.

● **BEST INGREDIENT**

Kosher marshmallows, made with gelatin from fish, have a chewier texture that I prefer over the usual kind.

Dried fruit and nuts are mixed with popcorn then pressed into a tube cake pan to make this addictive, stunning confection. Use fat-free hot-air or microwave popcorn, or the plain, unsalted organic popcorn in a bag from a natural food store.

18	cups unsalted, air-popped popcorn	2	tablespoons raw sunflower seeds
¾	cup almonds		
½	cup dried sour cherries	4	tablespoons unsalted butter
⅓	cup dry roasted peanuts	1	(10.5-ounce) bag miniature marshmallows, preferably kosher
⅓	cup raisins		
2	tablespoons sesame seeds		

1. Coat a 10" tube cake pan, 2 large mixing bowls, and a heat-proof rubber spatula liberally with oil or cooking spray and set aside.

2. In each of the 2 bowls, combine half the popcorn, almonds, cherries, peanuts, raisins, sesame seeds, and sunflower seeds. Place the butter and marshmallows in a saucepan and melt them over medium heat, stirring occasionally with a spatula.

3. Pour half of the hot marshmallow mixture over the popcorn mixture in each bowl. Carefully use the spatulas to mix until the popcorn, fruit, and nuts are coated and clumpy. The mixture will be very hot at first so do not touch it until it is cool enough not to burn you. Cover your hands with a greased plastic bag and press the sticky mixture into the prepared pan, adding more in clumps and working quickly. Lean very hard to pack it down firmly until it all fits into the pan.

4. Cover with plastic wrap and chill until firm, 2 hours to overnight. To unmold, work the long blade of a knife around between the popcorn and pan, including around the tube, several times, then invert the pan over a plate.

5. To serve, slice the cake with a serrated knife, or tear it apart into chunks.

Makes 12 servings

Per serving: 280 calories, 12 g fat, 4 g saturated fat, 6 g protein, 40 g carbohydrates, 5 g fiber

AVOCADO LEMON SHERBET

Avocado is used in desserts and drinks in many Asian and Latin American countries. Making this tart-sweet sherbet the American way, I include milk to make it nicely creamy. Make sure to use a ripe, rich Hass avocado.

● **FOOD FACT**

Monounsaturated fat in avocado gives dishes like this cholesterol-free richness.

1	large ripe Hass avocado, diced, about 1¾ cup	Grated zest and juice from 1 lemon
⅔	cup confectioners' sugar	Pinch of salt
1	cup reduced-fat (2%) milk	

1. Whirl the avocado, sugar, milk, zest, juice, and salt in a blender or a food processor until pureed.

2. Transfer the mixture to a container. Cover and refrigerate until well chilled, 4 hours to overnight.

3. Freeze the mixture in an ice cream maker according to the manufacturer's instructions. Transfer the sherbet to a covered container and place in the freezer to harden, 4 to 6 hours. Serve within 24 hours.

Makes 8 servings

Per serving: 108 calories, 5 g fat, 1 g saturated fat, 2 g protein, 15 g carbohydrates, 2 g fiber

GINGER POMEGRANATE GRANITA

● **BEST TECHNIQUE**
To make ginger juice, grate fresh ginger on a rasp or very fine grater. Then, over a small bowl, squeeze the pulp between your fingers to release the juice.

● **BEST INGREDIENT**
For the best purple color, I use Pom's Wonderful pomegranate juice.

This sparkling ice made with pomegranate juice is refreshing and reviving, especially during hot weather, but it tastes good enough to serve all year. The finished granita should be thin, crunchy flakes.

2	cups pomegranate juice, at room temperature	2	teaspoons ginger juice (see Best Technique, left)
½	cup superfine sugar		

1. In a mixing bowl, combine the pomegranate juice, sugar, and ginger juice. Whisk until the sugar dissolves, 2 to 3 minutes. Pour the mixture into an 8" square metal pan.

2. Place the granita in the freezer, uncovered, until it is partially frozen, 3 to 6 hours, depending on your freezer. With a spatula, scrape the mixture into loose, slushy shreds.

3. Scrape and mound the granita into six glass dessert dishes.

Makes 6 servings

Per serving: 111 calories, 0 g fat, 0 g saturated fat, 0 g protein, 28 g carbohydrates, 0 g fiber

FROZEN BLUEBERRY YOGURT POPS

Tangy-sweet, these yogurt treats, flecked with pureed blueberries and studded with whole wild ones, are a good casual dessert or snack. Making them takes 5 minutes and saves you dollars compared to ready-made pops.

1	cup reduced-fat vanilla yogurt	1	teaspoon lemon juice
1	cup fresh or frozen blueberries	4	tablespoons wild blueberries
1	tablespoon light corn syrup, preferably organic		

1. Whirl the yogurt, fresh or frozen blueberries, corn syrup, and lemon juice together in a blender or food processor until smooth, 1 minute. Pour the mixture into four ¼-cup ice pop molds. Add 1 tablespoon of wild blueberries to each mold, using the handle of a spoon to distribute them evenly. Seal the molds or cover the top with foil.

2. Freeze the pops for 30 minutes. Insert a wooden stick into each mold. Cover with foil, making slits in the foil for the sticks, if necessary. Freeze until the pops are solid, 4 hours to overnight. These pops are best when eaten within 24 hours.

Makes 4

Per pop: 92 calories, 1 g fat, 1 g saturated fat, 3 g protein, 19 g carbohydrates, 1 g fiber

CHAPTER ELEVEN

BREAKFASTS AND DRINKS

[
THREE BREAKFAST BRUSCHETTA

Blueberry and Ricotta Bruschetta 314

Apple, Cheddar, and Raisin Bruschetta 315

Triple Strawberry Bruschetta 316
]

Melon and Orange Yogurt Bowl 310, Peaches and Cream Breakfast Sundae 311,

Morning Fruit and Cheese Plate 312, Chocolate Cinnamon Toast 313, Nutty Fiber Mix 317,

Everyday Irish Oatmeal 318, Strawberry Smash 319, Creamy Chai Oatmeal 320, Pear and Walnut Muesli 321,

Japanese Winter Cereal 322, Maple Buckwheat with Wild Blueberries* 323,

Buckwheat Polenta Cakes with Warm Apricot Glaze* 324, Big Chocolate Breakfast Cookies 326,

Peanut Butter and Jelly Muffins 328, Blue Corncakes with Mixed Berry Compote 330,

Turkey Breakfast Sausage 332, Sour Cherry Marmalade 333, Citrus Charge-Up 334, Strawberry Surprise 335,

Sweet Potato Smoothie 336, Peanut Butter Milkshake 338, Raspberry Watermelon Cooler 339,

Cherry Lime Ricky 340, Tropical White Tea Spritzer 341, Iced Mocha Espresso 342, Almond Chai 343,

Spiced Cafe au Lait 344, Hot Cocolat 345, Ginger Mint Tea 346

*Gluten-free and whole grain

MELON AND ORANGE YOGURT BOWL

● **FOOD FACT**

Some yogurt brands today contain inulin, a prebiotic form of fiber. Besides encouraging good bacteria in your gut, it helps you absorb carbohydrates more slowly and keeps blood sugar levels more even.

When you want yogurt and fruit, this one-bowl breakfast includes an orange, which is preferable to drinking juice. It also gives you omega-3s.

1	(6-ounce) container reduced-fat peach yogurt	⅓	cup frozen blueberries
1	small navel orange	2	teaspoons shelled hemp seed or Nutty Fiber Mix (page 317)
½	cup diced cantaloupe		

Spoon the yogurt into a pasta bowl. To peel the orange, slice off the top and bottom of the fruit. Standing the fruit on its flat bottom on a work surface, work a knife down the side, following the curved shape of the orange to remove the peel and white pith in strips. Cut the orange crosswise into ½" slices. Arrange the slices in a ring around the edge of the dish. Spoon the melon and berries into the center. Sprinkle on the hemp seeds or fiber mix. Serve immediately.

Makes 1 serving

Per serving: 328 calories, 5 g fat, 1 g saturated fat, 9 g protein, 66 g carbohydrates, 7 g fiber

PEACHES AND CREAM BREAKFAST SUNDAE

This makes a nice change from yogurt with fruit for breakfast. Frozen peaches usually taste better than fresh, are reliable year-round, and are easy to keep on hand.

1	teaspoon unsalted butter	⅔	cup part-skim ricotta cheese
2	tablespoons fresh orange juice	1	teaspoon fresh lime juice
2	tablespoons brown sugar	2	tablespoons Nutty Fiber Mix
½	teaspoon vanilla extract		(page 317)
¼	teaspoon ground cinnamon	2	large strawberries
½	(16-ounce) bag frozen sliced peaches		

● **BEST TECHNIQUE**

Save any liquid remaining in the pan to spoon over yogurt, oatmeal, or fresh fruit.

1. In a medium skillet over medium heat, melt the butter. Off the heat, add the orange juice, sugar, vanilla, and cinnamon to the pan. Return to the heat, stirring with a wooden spoon to dissolve the sugar.

2. Add the peaches. When the mixture bubbles, cover and cook 4 minutes. Stir to help the fruit cook evenly. Re-cover and cook until the peaches are al dente, 5 minutes. Set aside 5 minutes to let the fruit cool somewhat.

3. In a bowl, combine the cheese and lime juice. Stir to blend.

4. Divide the fruit between 2 cereal bowls. Mound the ricotta in the center on top of the peaches. Spoon over 2 tablespoons of the pan juices, sprinkle with the fiber mix, and top with a strawberry. Serve immediately.

Makes 2 servings

Per serving: 257 calories, 9 g fat, 5 g saturated fat, 11 g protein, 33 g carbohydrates, 2 g fiber

MORNING FRUIT
AND CHEESE PLATE

● **ANOTHER WAY**

Without the cheese, this fruit plate makes an elegant start or finish for brunch.

Arranging cut fruit and cottage cheese nicely on a plate creates a beautiful still life. Children particularly like this as a meal.

⅓	cup fresh orange juice	8	large red grapes, halved
1½	teaspoons orange liqueur, optional	¾	cup fresh blueberries
½	small cantaloupe, cut into 4 wedges	1	large navel orange, peeled and cut crosswise into 10 slices
4	large strawberries, hulled and halved	2	cups low-fat cottage cheese
1	kiwifruit, peeled and cut into 8 slices	4	mint sprigs

1. Divide the orange juice, and liqueur if using, among 4 white or clear shallow bowls or deep salad plates.

2. Pare away the melon rind and lay a cantaloupe wedge on one side of each plate, on its side like a half moon, facing the center. Grouping each fruit and leaving room in the center, add to each plate 2 strawberry halves, cut side up, 2 kiwi slices, overlapped, 4 grape halves, 8 to 10 blueberries, and 2 orange slices, overlapped (discard the top and bottom slices). Mound ½ cup of the cheese in the center of each plate and add a mint sprig.

Makes 4 servings

Per serving: 173 calories, 2 g fat, 1 g saturated fat, 14 g protein, 29 g carbohydrates, 3 g fiber

CHOCOLATE CINNAMON TOAST

Using whole wheat bread adds nutritional power to this old-fashioned favorite and helps you meet the day's recommended requirements for whole grain and fiber. A touch of chocolate enhances the cinnamon's edge.

1	tablespoon packed light brown sugar	⅛	teaspoon ground cinnamon
¼	teaspoon natural unsweetened cocoa powder	2	slices whole wheat bread
		1	tablespoon unsalted butter, softened

1. In a small bowl, combine the brown sugar, cocoa, and cinnamon, using your fingers to blend them.

2. Toast the bread. Spread half the butter on each slice of hot toast. Sprinkle half the cinnamon-sugar mixture on top. Cut the toast diagonally in half and serve.

Makes 1 serving

Per serving: 307 calories, 14 g fat, 8 g saturated fat, 8 g protein, 39 g carbohydrates, 5 g fiber

Three Breakfast Bruschetta

Each of these bruschetta provides protein, fruit, complex carbs, and whole grain. A quick breakfast, they also make an energy-boosting snack at midmorning. Each recipe makes one serving, but putting together two or more is a snap.

 # BLUEBERRY AND RICOTTA BRUSCHETTA

● **ANOTHER WAY**

To take a bruschetta for a midmorning snack, wrap it in plastic and put it in an insulated container with an ice pack. Eat it within 3 hours.

Blueberries and nuts plus creamy ricotta and whole grain bread turn this into a lovely breakfast of bread and cheese.

1	slice sprouted wheat or multigrain bread	¼	cup part-skim ricotta cheese
2	teaspoons wild blueberry fruit spread	1	tablespoon dried blueberries
		1	heaping teaspoon toasted sliced almonds

1. Grill or toast the bread.

2. Cover the bread with the fruit spread. Top with the cheese, dried blueberries, and almonds. Serve immediately, or see Another Way (left).

Makes 1

Per bruschetta: 239 calories, 7 g fat, 3 g saturated fat, 12 g protein, 32 g carbohydrates, 5 g fiber

APPLE, CHEDDAR, AND RAISIN BRUSCHETTA

Many artisanal bakeries make a crusty whole grain walnut-raisin bread that is ideal for this bruschetta. Alternatively, use the packaged raisin bread supermarkets carry; you can sometimes even find a whole wheat version.

1	slice walnut-raisin or cinnamon-raisin bread	¼	Jonagold or Golden Delicious apple, cored and sliced
1	tablespoon apple butter		
1½	ounces 50% fat mild Cheddar cheese, thinly sliced		

● **ANOTHER WAY**

This bruschetta makes a good late-day snack, or even a light meal when accompanied by a handful of walnuts.

1. Grill or toast the bread.

2. Cover the bread with the apple butter. Arrange the cheese slices to cover the bread. Place the apple slices over the cheese. Serve immediately, or see Another Way (opposite).

Makes 1

Per bruschetta: 286 calories, 8 g fat, 5 g saturated fat, 15 g protein, 46 g carbohydrates, 8 g fiber

TRIPLE STRAWBERRY BRUSCHETTA

● **ANOTHER WAY**

Dollop any remaining yogurt cheese on sliced peaches for a midmorning snack.

Draining the yogurt for this bruschetta turns it into yogurt cheese. Set this up the night before. Kids usually pick this as their favorite.

1	(6-ounce) container reduced-fat strawberry yogurt without gums or inulin	4	teaspoons strawberry fruit spread
		4	large fresh strawberries, hulled
2	(¾") slices Italian whole wheat or semolina bread with sesame seeds		

1. Using a yogurt cheese maker or strainer lined with a paper coffee filter, drain the yogurt 8 hours or up to overnight in the refrigerator, until it resembles whipped cream cheese. There will be ⅓ cup.

2. Grill or toast the bread.

3. Cover each slice of the bread with 2 teaspoons fruit spread and spread on 2 tablespoons of the yogurt.

4. Make 4 vertical cuts in each strawberry, slicing from the bottom almost to the top. Press lightly to fan out the cut berries. Place them on top of the bruschetta. Serve immediately or see Another Way (page 314).

Makes 2

Per bruschetta: 198 calories, 2 g fat, 1 g saturated fat, 8 g protein, 38 g carbohydrates, 3 g fiber

NUTTY FIBER MIX

This fiber-rich topping for cereal, pancakes, or yogurt tastes better than bran. It also provides important omega-3s.

2	tablespoons sliced raw almonds	1	tablespoon raw sunflower seeds
1	tablespoon raw pumpkin seeds	1–2	tablespoons ground flax seeds
1	tablespoon unhulled sesame seeds		

Whirl the almonds, pumpkin seeds, sesame seeds, and sunflower seeds in a mini food processor, pulsing until finely chopped. Add the flax seeds, using 1 tablespoon for a lighter topping or 2 tablespoons for a nuttier flavor. The topping keeps in the refrigerator for 4 days in a sealed container.

Makes ½ cup, 4 servings

Per serving (2 tablespoons): 66 calories, 5 g fat, 1 g saturated fat, 2 g protein, 2 g carbohydrates, 1 g fiber

EVERYDAY IRISH OATMEAL

● **BEST TECHNIQUE**

For a creamier consistency, cover the oats as they simmer.

Oatmeal lovers know that Irish steel-cut oats taste best, but cooking them takes 30 minutes, time few of us have in the morning. Soaking them overnight cuts this to a mere 5 to 10 minutes, depending on whether you like them chewy or more tender.

¼	teaspoon salt	Brown sugar or maple syrup, optional
¼	cup steel-cut oats	Sliced banana, optional
	Cold milk, optional	Strawberry Smash (opposite), optional
	Dried blueberries or raisins, optional	

1. The night before serving, in a small saucepan, boil 1 cup water. Add the salt. Mix in the oats. Remove from heat, cover the pot, and set aside overnight.

2. In the morning, stir and set the pot over medium-high heat. Cook, uncovered, until the oatmeal boils. Reduce the heat and simmer until the oatmeal is chewy, 5 minutes, or tender, 10 minutes. Cover and let sit off the heat for 1 minute. Serve hot with your choice of toppings, if desired: cold milk, dried blueberries or raisins, brown sugar or maple syrup, sliced banana, or strawberry smash.

Makes 1 serving

Per serving (without toppings): 148 calories, 3 g fat, 1 g saturated fat, 5 g protein, 27 g carbohydrates, 4 g fiber

STRAWBERRY SMASH

Mixing fresh berries with maple syrup draws out their juice. Use this succulent, rosy topping on warm oatmeal or plain yogurt to satisfy your sweet tooth while piling on antioxidants.

1	pint fresh strawberries, hulled and halved	2	tablespoons grade A light maple syrup

Place the strawberries in the bowl of a food processor. Add the maple syrup. Pulse 5 or 6 times to coarsely chop the fruit. Use within 2 hours.

Makes 1 cup, 4 servings

Per serving (¼ cup): 49 calories, 0 g fat, 0 g saturated fat, 0 g protein, 12 g carbohydrates, 1 g fiber

CREAMY CHAI OATMEAL

This hot cereal begins with freshly brewed tea steeped with spices. Making the chai takes the same 3 minutes as brewing a cup of tea. Sliced banana, flax, and a dusting of cocoa powder nearly double the fiber from the oats.

2	cups cold water		¼	teaspoon salt
2	bags black tea		1	cup quick-cooking oats (not instant)
¼	teaspoon ground cinnamon			
¼	teaspoon ground ginger		2–4	tablespoons honey
⅛	teaspoon ground allspice		2	tablespoons ground flax seeds, optional
⅛	teaspoon ground cardamom			
	Pinch of ground cloves		1	banana, sliced
	Freshly ground pepper			Unsweetened natural cocoa powder
1	cup reduced-fat (1%) milk			

1. In a medium, nonreactive saucepan, bring the water to a boil. Add the tea bags, cinnamon, ginger, allspice, cardamom, cloves, and 4 or 5 grinds pepper. Remove from the heat, cover, and steep for 3 minutes. Remove the tea bags.

2. Add the milk to the chai. Bring to a boil over medium-high heat. Add the salt and stir in the oats. When the mixture boils, reduce the heat and simmer for 4 minutes. Remove from the heat, cover, and set aside for 1 minute. The oats will be creamy but slightly chewy. Mix in 2 tablespoons of the honey.

3. Divide the oatmeal between 2 bowls. Sprinkle with the flax seeds, if desired, and top with the sliced banana. If desired, drizzle an additional 1 tablespoon honey over each serving. Add a generous sprinkle of cocoa powder, using a sugar shaker or fine tea strainer. Serve immediately.

Makes 2 servings

Per serving: 339 calories, 5 g fat, 1 g saturated fat, 11 g protein, 67 g carbohydrates, 7 g fiber

PEAR AND WALNUT MUESLI

The cool freshness of muesli is ideal for warm weather. It also makes the good-ness of oats portable for breakfast or as an afternoon snack. Muesli usually includes dried fruit, nuts, shredded peeled apple, and yogurt, but this one calls for a pear and buttermilk, which is lighter. Be sure to use a fragrant, ripe pear or your muesli will taste bland.

½	cup quick-cooking oats (not instant)	¼	cup raisins, preferably Red Flame
1	cup regular or light buttermilk	1	teaspoon cocoa nibs
½	teaspoon salt	1	tablespoon granola or ⅛ teaspoon
1	ripe Bartlett pear, shredded		instant espresso coffee
½	cup chopped walnuts		powder, optional
3	dried Calimyrna figs, chopped		

In mixing bowl, combine the oats, buttermilk, and salt. Stir to blend. Add the pear, nuts, figs, and raisins, mixing until the muesli is well combined. Cover and refrigerate for 4 hours or up to overnight. The muesli keeps, tightly covered in the refrigerator, for 2 days. Stir and top with cocoa nibs and granola or coffee powder and serve.

Makes 2 servings

Per serving: 506 calories, 23 g fat, 3 g saturated fat, 13 g protein, 70 g carbohydrates, 11 g fiber

● **BEST TECHNIQUE**
Pears ripen off the tree, so leave green Bartletts at room temperature until aromatic and golden.

● **FOOD FACT**
Pears are as fiber-full as apples. They also contain flavonoids and phytosterols that protect your heart.

JAPANESE WINTER CEREAL

I discovered furikake, a condiment the Japanese usually use to season rice, when it was sprinkled on oatmeal, along with raisins and sesame seeds, at a macrobiotic bed and breakfast. I have enjoyed it sprinkled on my morning porridge ever since. Try it on this blend of whole grains and raisins, and see if you like it.

¼ cup quick-cooking wild rice

¼ cup steel-cut oats

½ teaspoon salt

¼ cup quick-cooking barley

¼ cup quinoa, rinsed and drained

½ cup raisins

Japanese furikake

1. In a medium saucepan, bring 4 cups water to a boil. Add the wild rice, oats, and salt. Reduce the heat, cover, and simmer for 20 minutes.

2. Add the barley and quinoa. Leaving the cover ajar, boil gently, stirring 3 or 4 times, until most of the liquid has been absorbed and all the grains are tender, 22 to 25 minutes. Mix in the raisins. Cover and set aside for 5 minutes.

3. Divide the cereal among 3 bowls. Sprinkle generously with the furikake. Serve immediately.

Makes 3 servings

Per serving: 283 calories, 2 g fat, 0 g saturated fat, 8 g protein, 61 g carbohydrates, 6 g fiber

MAPLE BUCKWHEAT
WITH WILD BLUEBERRIES

I call this a grown-up version of cream of wheat because of its smooth and soothing consistency—although it is wheat- and gluten-free. The more you mix it, the more the blueberries turn this hot cereal a delicate lavender.

½	cup reduced-fat (2%) milk	⅓	cup fresh or frozen wild blueberries
¼	teaspoon salt		
3	tablespoons cream of buckwheat	1	tablespoon black sesame seeds or 2 teaspoons toasted sliced almonds
2	tablespoons oat bran cereal		
1	tablespoon grade A maple syrup		

● **BLUE FOOD**

If your children like blue food, this may help them eat a whole grain breakfast.

1. In a small, heavy saucepan, combine the milk with ¾ cup water. Bring to a boil over medium-high heat. Add the salt.

2. While whisking vigorously, slowly add the buckwheat and then the oat bran. Reduce the heat and cook at a gentle simmer, stirring often, until the cereal resembles polenta, about 10 minutes. Remove from the heat and stir in the maple syrup. Cover and let the cereal stand for 1 minute.

3. Scoop the hot cereal into a bowl. Gently mix in the blueberries. Sprinkle on the sesame seeds or nuts. Serve immediately.

Makes 1 serving

Per serving: 410 calories, 10 g fat, 2 g saturated fat, 14 g protein, 68 g carbohydrates, 9 g fiber

BUCKWHEAT POLENTA CAKES WITH WARM APRICOT GLAZE

Polenta reheated in butter until it is crisp outside and still soft inside is a quick alternative to pancakes. It is so good that you may want to plan for leftovers when making buckwheat polenta for dinner.

1	tablespoon unsalted butter	Warm Fruit Glaze (opposite;
1	tablespoon canola oil	made with apricot fruit spread)
	Crisp Buckwheat Polenta (page 198), cut into 4 pieces	

Melt the butter in the oil in a medium skillet over medium high heat. Add the pieces of Buckwheat Polenta and cook until they are browned and crisp on the bottom, 5 minutes. Turn and cook until crisp on the other side, about 4 minutes. Place each piece on a plate. Spoon one-quarter of the Warm Fruit Glaze over each serving. Serve immediately.

Makes 4 servings

Per serving: 308 calories, 11 g fat, 3 g saturated fat, 4 g protein, 55 g carbohydrates, 2 g fiber

WARM FRUIT GLAZE

Use this tart-sweet topping in place of syrup on polenta, pancakes, and waffles. The better the quality of fruit spread you use, the better the glaze will taste.

¾   cup apricot or peach fruit spread   1   tablespoon fresh lemon juice
¼   cup apple juice

Place the fruit spread in a small saucepan over medium heat. Cook, stirring occasionally, until melted, about 2 minutes. Mix in the apple juice and lemon juice. Serve warm.

Makes 1 cup, 4 servings

Per serving (¼ cup): 13 calories, 0 g fat, 0 g saturated fat, 0 g protein, 32 g carbohydrates, 0 g fiber

BIG CHOCOLATE BREAKFAST COOKIES

What could beat a big chocolate cookie for breakfast? These are soft and crammed with antioxidants from dried fruits and nuts, along with oats, cocoa, and apple sauce to provide solid nutrition. They even include a touch of coffee.

⬤ **SERVE WITH**

Vanilla yogurt or a hard-cooked egg along with two cookies makes a full, balanced breakfast.

⬤ **BEST TECHNIQUE**

My technique for chilling the canola oil gives baked goods body and the moistness of butter, but without its saturated fat.

⅔	cup unbleached all-purpose flour	1	teaspoon instant espresso coffee powder, regular or decaffeinated
⅓	cup natural unsweetened cocoa powder	1	teaspoon vanilla extract
1	teaspoon baking soda	1	cup quick-cooking oats (not instant)
1½	teaspoons ground cinnamon		
½	teaspoon ground allspice	1	cup coarsely chopped walnuts
¼	teaspoon salt	½	cup dried blueberries
⅓	cup canola oil, chilled	½	cup dried sour cherries
1	cold large egg	½	cup raisins
¾	cup sugar	2	tablespoons ground flax seeds, optional
1½	cups natural unsweetened apple sauce		

1. Place the racks in the upper and lower thirds of the oven. Preheat the oven to 350°F. Line 2 baking sheets with parchment paper and set aside.

2. Into a mixing bowl, sift the flour with the cocoa, baking soda, cinnamon, allspice, and salt. In a larger bowl, whisk the cold oil and egg until they resemble homemade mayonnaise, 15 to 20 strokes. Beat in the sugar. Add half the dry ingredients and whisk to combine. When some lumps still remain, mix in the apple sauce, coffee powder, and vanilla. Add the remaining dry ingredients and whisk to combine. Stir in the oats, nuts, blueberries, cherries, raisins, and flax seeds if using.

3. Drop the dough, a scant ¼ cup at a time, onto the lined baking sheets, making 8 cookies on each sheet.

4. Bake for 15 minutes. Switch the position of the baking sheets in the oven and rotate them 180°. Bake 5 minutes longer, or until the centers spring back when pressed with your finger. Cool cookies for 2 minutes on the pan, then transfer to a rack and cool completely. Repeat with the remaining batter to make about 6 more cookies. The cookies keep for up to 1 week in a tightly covered container.

Makes 22

Per serving (2 cookies): 334 calories, 15 g fat, 2 g saturated fat, 5 g protein, 47 g carbohydrates, 6 g fiber

PEANUT BUTTER AND JELLY MUFFINS

These muffins with a heart of raspberry jam, include all the benefits of whole wheat, peanut butter, and fruit. Think of them for a midmorning or afternoon snack containing protein, complex carbs, the good fat you want, and fiber. Wrapped in aluminum foil, they are good to go, and will keep for a day at room temperature. But best of all, they are delicious.

1	cup unbleached all-purpose flour	½	cup packed brown sugar
1	cup whole wheat pastry flour	2	large eggs
1½	teaspoons baking powder	1	cup buttermilk
½	teaspoon baking soda	1	teaspoon vanilla extract
½	cup smooth natural peanut butter	½	cup raspberry jam
		6	tablespoons salted dry roasted peanuts, coarsely chopped

1. Preheat the oven to 400°F. Coat a 12-cup muffin tin with cooking spray and set aside.

2. In a bowl, sift together the all-purpose flour, whole wheat flour, baking powder, and baking soda. Set aside.

3. In a mixing bowl, use a hand mixer on medium-low to combine the peanut butter with the sugar until well blended. One at a time, add the eggs, beating well after each addition. Alternating, mix in one-third of the dry ingredients, then one-half of the buttermilk. Repeat, including the vanilla with the last addition of buttermilk, and finish with the remaining dry ingredients, making each addition before the last is completely blended in. The batter will be very stiff.

4. Using 1½ tablespoons batter, cover the bottom of each muffin cup, spreading out to the edge. Place 2 teaspoons of the jam in the center of each muffin. Cover with about 2½ tablespoons batter, bringing it out to the edge to seal in

the jam. The cups should be about two-thirds full. Sprinkle 1½ teaspoons of the peanuts over each muffin.

5. Bake for 20 minutes, or until the muffins are puffed and golden, not browned. Cool 5 minutes on a rack in the tin. Turn the muffins out onto the rack and cool completely.

Makes 12

Per muffin: 259 calories, 9 g fat, 1 g saturated fat, 7 g protein, 37 g carbohydrates, 2 g fiber

BLUE CORNCAKES
WITH MIXED BERRY COMPOTE

● **BEST INGREDIENT**

Blue cornmeal is made from corn grown only by Native Americans in the Southwest. Look for it in natural food stores and at www. amazon.com.

● **FOOD FACT**

Blue corn is higher in protein and fiber than other varieties of corn.

Made mainly from blue cornmeal, these petite pancakes are crisp outside and creamy as polenta inside. They are best served piping hot straight from the griddle, so make sure everyone is gathered at the table and waiting. Compote usually means cooked fruit, but here, letting the berries sit makes them just as tender without using heat, which diminishes their antioxidant content.

COMPOTE

1	(4.4-ounce) container or ½ pint raspberries
1	pint strawberries, hulled and halved or quartered
¾	cup frozen wild blueberries
3	tablespoons sugar

1	teaspoon sugar
½	teaspoon baking soda
½	teaspoon salt
4	tablespoons (½ stick) + 1 teaspoon cold unsalted butter
1	large egg
2	cups regular or light buttermilk
	Maple syrup, optional

CORNCAKES

1⅓	cups blue cornmeal
¼	cup sifted unbleached all-purpose flour

1. **FOR THE COMPOTE:** In a wide, shallow bowl, combine the raspberries, strawberries, blueberries, and sugar. Set aside for 30 minutes to let the berries soften.

2. **FOR THE CORNCAKES:** In a mixing bowl, whisk together the cornmeal, flour, sugar, baking soda, and salt. Whisk to blend. Cut the 4 tablespoons butter into ½" pieces and add to the dry ingredients. Using a pastry cutter or sturdy fork, blend the butter into the mixture. Beat the egg with the buttermilk until combined and pour into the dry ingredients. Whisk just until the batter is blended; do not overmix.

3. Heat a griddle or large skillet over medium-high heat until hot. Coat with about ¼ teaspoon of the butter. For each corncake, spoon 2 heaping table-spoons of the batter onto the griddle, allowing room for spreading. Cook until the bottoms are dark brown and the edges look dull, about 3 minutes. Turn the corncakes and cook until the other sides are well browned, 2 to 3 minutes. Serve immediately or keep in a 200°F oven while cooking the rest of the pancakes, buttering the grill as needed.

4. Place 3 pancakes on each of 6 plates. Top each serving with ⅓ cup com-pote. Pass maple syrup in a pitcher, if desired.

Makes 6 servings

Per serving (3 pancakes): 286 calories, 11 g fat, 6 g saturated fat, 7 g protein, 40 g carbohydrates, 6 g fiber

TURKEY BREAKFAST SAUSAGE

● **BEST INGREDIENT**

Lean ground turkey with 10 grams of fat per serving makes the juiciest sausage. Extra lean (5 grams of fat) and fat-free ground turkey breast make firmer, drier patties.

● **BEST TECHNIQUE**

If you have Bell's Seasoning left over from the holidays, add ¼ teaspoon along with the other seasonings and your sausages will taste even better.

A blend of seasonings makes these patties taste just like the breakfast sausage you buy, but with a fraction of the fat. Adding apple sauce keeps the lean turkey juicy.

1	pound lean ground turkey	½	teaspoon ground ginger
2	tablespoons natural	½	teaspoon salt
	unsweetened apple sauce	½	teaspoon freshly ground pepper
1½	teaspoons dried thyme		

1. In a mixing bowl, combine the turkey, apple sauce, thyme, ginger, salt, and pepper. Mix to blend. Using your hands, shape into eighteen 2" patties. If possible, set on a platter, cover with plastic wrap, and refrigerate 1 hour or up to overnight.

2. Coat a large skillet generously with cooking spray and set over medium-high heat. Add half the patties and cook, reducing the heat to prevent burning, until crusty brown, 5 minutes. Turn and cook until the patties are well browned on the bottom and no longer pink in the center, 4 to 5 minutes. Transfer the patties to a plate and keep warm. Repeat with the remaining patties.

Makes 6 servings

Per serving (3 patties): 86 calories, 1 g fat, 0 g saturated fat, 19 g protein, 1 g carbohydrates, 1 g fiber

SOUR CHERRY MARMALADE

I call this marmalade because it includes chunks of orange zest. It is so tart that you can also serve it with savory dishes, especially pork and turkey. The spread keeps for a month in the refrigerator when you spoon it into clean jars taken straight from the dishwasher and still hot, an easier method than dealing with canning.

2	cups orange juice	2	tablespoons fresh lemon juice
1	cup dried sour cherries	1	cup sugar
1	Valencia orange, halved		

1. Combine the orange juice and cherries in a bowl and soak until the cherries are plumped, 20 minutes.

2. Cut half the orange into thin slices then chop the slices. Place in a heavy stainless steel or other nonreactive medium saucepan. Squeeze the juice from the other orange half into the pot. Discard the orange half. Add the cherry mixture and lemon juice to the pot.

3. Bring the liquid to a boil over medium-high heat. Cover, reduce the heat, and simmer, stirring often with a wooden spoon, until the orange peel is pleasantly soft, 15 to 20 minutes.

4. While stirring, add the sugar slowly and gradually. Increase the heat and boil the mixture vigorously until it reaches the gel stage, 20 to 30 minutes. Remove it from the heat and test to be sure. (See Best Technique, right, for how to test.)

5. Skim off any foam and carefully transfer the hot marmalade into clean glass jars hot from the dishwasher. Cover tightly and set aside to cool completely to room temperature. If it is not gelled when cool, it will still taste great. Store in the refrigerator for up to 1 month.

Makes 2 (½-pint) jars

Per serving (2 tablespoons): 86 calories, 0 g fat, 0 g saturated fat, 1 g protein, 21 g carbohydrates, 2 g fiber

● **BEST TECHNIQUE**

To see if your marmalade is ready, use this gel test: Place 2 or 3 small plates in the freezer until chilled, at least 20 minutes. Spoon 1 teaspoon of the boiling marmalade onto a cold plate and return it to the freezer for 1 minute. Push the edge of the spread with your finger. When it has reached the gel stage, it will set and the surface will wrinkle when the edge is pushed. (See *Ball Complete Book for Home Preserving* or www.homecanning.com for more information.)

CITRUS CHARGE-UP

Lighter than a smoothie, this creamy drink is a perfect morning starter. Paired with whole grain toast and a hard-cooked egg, it makes a fine breakfast. I prefer using the fresh-squeezed grapefruit juice sold in some stores because it tastes sweeter than juice from a carton.

¾	cup pink grapefruit juice	1	(6-ounce) container or ¾ cup
1	small banana, frozen in 1" pieces		reduced-fat lemon yogurt

In a blender, combine the grapefruit juice, banana, and yogurt. Blend until smooth. Serve immediately.

Makes 2 servings

Per serving: 144 calories, 1 g fat, 1 g saturated fat, 5 g protein, 30 g carbohydrates, 1 g fiber

STRAWBERRY SURPRISE

The surprise in this rosy drink is beans pureed with fruit. They make a smoothie that is a light meal and one of the best ways to sneak 13 grams of fiber into your day. If blood orange juice, sold in bottles and cartons, is not available, use regular orange juice.

● **ANOTHER WAY**

Using frozen berries makes a thick, ice-cold drink; fresh berries make one that is more liquid and cool.

1½	cups frozen whole strawberries or halved fresh strawberries	½	cup blood orange juice
1	small banana, sliced	1	teaspoon pure vanilla extract
½	cup kidney beans, rinsed and drained	¼	teaspoon grated fresh ginger

In a blender, combine the strawberries, banana, beans, orange juice, vanilla, and ginger. Blend until smooth. Serve immediately in a large glass.

Makes 1 serving

Per serving: 344 calories, 2 g fat, 1 g saturated fat, 10 g protein, 76 g carbohydrates, 13 g fiber

SWEET POTATO SMOOTHIE

● **ANOTHER WAY**

If pumpkin pie spice is not available, use ⅛ teaspoon ground cinnamon plus pinches of ground allspice, ginger, and nutmeg.

A great midafternoon pickup, this drink tastes like sweet potato pie à la mode. When baking sweet potatoes, I usually make an extra one so I can enjoy this smoothie the next day.

½	cup reduced-fat (2%) milk	1	tablespoon maple syrup
½	cup baked sweet potato, about 1 medium	¼	teaspoon pumpkin pie spice
¼	cup reduced-fat vanilla frozen yogurt		

In a blender, combine the milk, sweet potato, frozen yogurt, maple syrup, and spice. Blend until smooth and foamy. Serve immediately.

Makes 1 serving

Per serving: 355 calories, 5 g fat, 3 g saturated fat, 11 g protein, 67 g carbohydrates, 4 g fiber

PEANUT BUTTER MILKSHAKE

This retro indulgence shows why a milkshake makes a good midafternoon or after school treat.

¾	cup reduced-fat (2%) milk	3	tablespoons smooth natural peanut butter
⅓	banana, sliced	1	teaspoon unsulfured molasses

In a blender, combine the milk, banana, peanut butter, and molasses. Blend until smooth. Serve immediately.

Makes 1 serving

Per serving: 440 calories, 28 g fat, 5 g saturated fat, 17 g protein, 33 g carbohydrates, 4 g fiber

RASPBERRY WATERMELON COOLER

On a hot day, this frosty drink may even beat lemonade for pure refreshment. Usually raspberries are pureed in a blender and then strained, but here just straining them makes a clearer, more vivid drink.

7	cups cubed seedless watermelon	3	(2" × 1") strips lemon zest
1	(12-ounce) package thawed frozen raspberries	3	tablespoons sugar Mint sprigs, optional, for garnish

● **BEST TECHNIQUES**

The finer the strainer, the clearer the watermelon juice will be.

If you have a powerful blender, make all 3 coolers at once: Place all the watermelon cubes, 1½ cups watermelon juice, the raspberry puree, the lemon strips and the sugar in the blender. Blend until smooth. Divide among 3 tall glasses.

1. Place the watermelon in a blender and puree until smooth. Strain through a fine strainer into a bowl to extract about 5 cups of juice. Discard the solids. Pour 3 cups of the juice into 3 ice cube trays and freeze. The cubes may be unmolded and stored in the freezer in a resealable plastic bag for up to 3 days. Refrigerate the remaining 2 cups juice for up to 2 days. Reserve any extra juice for another use.

2. Puree the raspberries in a strainer, pressing them with the back of a wooden spoon to get ¾ cup puree. Discard the pulp and seeds left in the strainer.

3. For each cooler, place in a blender 8 frozen watermelon juice cubes, ½ cup of the reserved watermelon juice, ¼ cup raspberry puree, 1 strip lemon zest, and 1 tablespoon sugar. Blend until smooth. Pour into a glass and serve immediately. Garnish with a sprig of mint, if using.

Makes 3 servings

Per serving: 96 calories, 0 g fat, 0 g saturated fat, 1 g protein, 24 g carbohydrates, 2 g fiber

CHERRY LIME RICKY

Replacing the artificially flavored cherry syrup that soda jerks use with tart cherry juice gives this fizzy soda fountain drink new benefits. Sweet cherry juice makes a less citrus-tasting, even more fruity drink.

½	cup tart cherry juice	Ice
	Juice of 1 lime	Club soda
¼	cup Simple Syrup (below)	Lime slice, optional

In a 16-ounce glass, combine the cherry juice, lime juice, and syrup and stir. Fill the glass with ice. Top off with club soda. Add a straw and hang a lime slice on the rim of the glass, if using.

Makes 1 serving

Per serving: 144 calories, 0 g fat, 0 g saturated fat, 0 g protein, 37 g carbohydrates, 0 g fiber

SIMPLE SYRUP

The ideal sweetener for cold drinks, simple syrup blends instantly with liquids. Use it for iced tea, iced coffee, or fruit juice spritzers. It keeps indefinitely in the refrigerator. Making it takes less than 5 minutes.

1	cup cold water	½	cup sugar

In a small saucepan, combine the water and sugar. Over medium heat, cook until the sugar dissolves and the syrup is clear, about 3 minutes.

Makes 1½ cups

TROPICAL WHITE TEA SPRITZER

Pineapple juice balances the austere flavor of white tea, and a hint of thyme adds depth to this frosty tropical brew. Agave syrup, made from the same cactus as tequila, enhances its fruit flavors.

1	bag white tea		Ice
2	tablespoons agave syrup or Simple Syrup (opposite)		Club soda
3	or 4 sprigs thyme	1	pineapple spear and 3 or 4 sprigs thyme, optional
¼	cup pineapple juice		

● **ANOTHER WAY**

To prepare in larger batches, use 4 tea bags for every 3 cups of hot water.

● **FOOD FACT**

White tea is low in caffeine and contains the highest level of antioxidants of any tea. I recommend the kind known as White Peony for this drink.

1. In a small saucepan, bring 1 cup water almost to a boil. Remove from the heat and add the teabag. Cover and steep for 3 minutes. Remove the bag, squeezing it well, and discard. Cool the tea to room temperature, or refrigerate in a covered container until chilled.

2. Place the syrup in a 16-ounce glass. Add the thyme. Using the back of a soup spoon, press and mash the sprigs against the side of the glass for 30 seconds. Remove and discard the thyme, leaving any leaves that remain in the syrup.

3. Pour in the tea and pineapple juice. Stir to dissolve the syrup. Fill the glass three-fourths full with ice cubes. Top off the glass with club soda. Serve immediately, garnished with the pineapple spear and thyme sprigs, if using.

Makes 1 serving

Per serving: 156 calories, 0 g fat, 0 g saturated fat, 0 g protein, 41 g carbohydrates, 1 g fiber

ICED MOCHA ESPRESSO

● BEST INGREDIENT

Ground chocolate is a blend of cocoa powder, powdered chocolate, and sugar. Ghirardelli's ground chocolate is a good choice for this drink.

● BEST TECHNIQUE

If you do not have an espresso coffee maker, brew espresso-blend coffee in a Melitta-style coffee maker.

This is industrial-strength refreshment. It tastes crisp and intense, with just enough sweetness to temper the coffee's bitterness. You can make the chocolate base in quantity and keep it chilled for 24 hours, but the coffee should be freshly brewed. Use decaffeinated coffee if you wish.

3	tablespoons ground chocolate		Ice
½	cup hot water	1	tablespoon heavy cream or whole
¼	cup brewed espresso coffee,		milk, optional
	room temperature or chilled		

In a measuring cup, dissolve the chocolate in the hot water. Pour into a 16-ounce glass. Add the espresso. Stir to blend. Fill the glass with ice. If using, spoon the cream or milk carefully over the drink. Serve immediately, preferably with a straw.

Makes 1 serving

Per serving: 37 calories, 1 g fat, 1 g saturated fat, 1 g protein, 6 g carbohydrates, 1 g fiber

ALMOND CHAI

Chai should be spicy and sweet. This one is dairy-free, using almond milk, which is available in aseptic boxes in natural food stores and many supermarkets. Use either plain or vanilla flavor.

3	pods green cardamom, cracked	1	teaspoon black peppercorns
1	(3") stick cinnamon	1	(2") strip orange zest
2	whole cloves	2	bags black tea
½	teaspoon coriander seeds	1	cup almond milk
½	teaspoon fennel seeds	3	tablespoons wildflower honey

1. In a medium saucepan, combine the cardamom, cinnamon, cloves, coriander, fennel, peppercorns, and orange zest with 2 cups water. Bring to a boil over medium heat. Reduce the heat, cover, and simmer for 5 minutes. Remove from the heat, add the teabags, and steep for 5 minutes.

2. Remove the tea bags, squeezing them well, and discard. Cover the pot and let the flavorings infuse for 25 minutes longer.

3. Strain the chai to remove the spices and zest, and return to the pot. Add the almond milk and honey. Heat over medium heat until steaming, but do not boil. Divide among 4 small mugs and serve.

Makes 4 servings

Per serving: 61 calories, 1 g fat, 0 g saturated fat, 0 g protein, 16 g carbohydrates, 0 g fiber

SPICED CAFE AU LAIT

The flavors of cinnamon and star anise infused in hot milk turn mellow break-fast-blend coffee into an exotic escape. To fully enjoy its aroma, serve this coffee French-style, in wide drinking bowls.

1	cup reduced-fat (2%) milk, plain soy milk, or almond milk	1	whole star anise
2	(3") cinnamon sticks	1	cup freshly brewed coffee

1. In a small saucepan, heat the milk over medium heat until it starts to steam. Remove from the heat and add the cinnamon and star anise. Cover and set aside to infuse for 10 minutes.

2. Remove the spices and return the pot to medium heat, stirring occasionally so it does not form a skin, until the milk is steaming hot, 2 minutes. Set out 2 drinking bowls. Holding the coffee pot in one hand and the pot of milk in the other, pour from both at the same time, dividing the coffee and milk between the two bowls. Serve immediately.

Makes 2 servings

Per serving: 62 calories, 2 g fat, 2 g saturated fat, 4 g protein, 6 g carbohydrates, 0 g fiber

HOT COCOLAT

Dark chocolate and coconut are a heavenly combination. Together they make this hot chocolate luxurious and dairy-free.

¼   cup natural unsweetened cocoa
        powder
1   cup light coconut milk

2   (1-ounce) squares dark chocolate
        (62–67% cocoa), chopped

Place the cocoa powder in a small saucepan. Gradually add ½ cup water while whisking constantly until the cocoa is dissolved. Set the pan over medium heat and cook until the mixture starts to bubble around the edges, 2 minutes. Add the coconut milk. Remove from the heat and add the chocolate, stirring until it melts. Return the pot to medium heat and cook until the mixture is steaming hot, about 1 minute. Divide between 2 mugs and serve.

Makes 2 servings

Per serving: 274 calories, 19 g fat, 13 g saturated fat, 5 g protein, 27 g carbohydrates, 6 g fiber

GINGER MINT TEA

● **ANOTHER WAY**

When you have a cold, add a pinch of cayenne pepper to help clear your nose and fight the bug.

Warming ginger and soothing mint are an ideal remedy when your tummy feels unhappy. Adding honey makes them even more soothing. I recommend this on a damp, chilly day, and anytime your spirit and body need cheering up.

2	cups cold water		Juice of 1 lemon
1"	fresh ginger, cut into 4 slices	2	tablespoons honey, or to taste
6	(4") sprigs spearmint		

1. In a small saucepan, combine the water, ginger, and spearmint. Set over medium-high heat. When the water boils, reduce the heat to medium-low, cover, and simmer for 5 minutes. Remove from the heat and steep for 20 minutes.

2. Rinse two mugs in hot water and dry them. Remove the ginger and mint and discard. Add the lemon juice to the tea. Divide the tea between the 2 warmed mugs and sweeten each with 1 tablespoon honey, or more to taste. Serve immediately.

Makes 2 servings

Per serving: 70 calories, 0 g fat, 0 g saturated fat, 0 g protein, 19 g carbohydrates, 0 g fiber

Index

Underscored page references indicate boxed text. **Boldfaced** page references indicate photographs.

A

Almonds
  Almond Chai, 343
  Blueberry and Ricotta
    Bruschetta, 314
  Chocolate Cranberry Torte,
    300–302, **301**
  Dukka, 77
  good to know facts, 44
  health benefits, 43–44
  Maple Buckwheat with Wild
    Blueberries, 323
  Nutty Fiber Mix, 317
  Nutty Popcorn Bundt Ring, 304
  selecting, 44
  serving ideas, 44
  Sicilian Almond Cookies, 280
  Spanish Smoked Almonds, 89
  storing, 44
Antioxidants, 3, 17
Appetizers and starters
  Black Bean and Nectarine Salsa,
    80
  Black Olive Caviar in Endive,
    85
  Chinese Tea Eggs, 84
  Chocolate-Glazed Peanuts, 91
  Citrus-Marinated Shrimp,
    86–87, **87**
  Curried Chickpeas, 90
  Feta Dip with Confetti
    Vegetables, 72
  Ginger Chicken Meatballs, 88
  Hot Bean Dip, 75
  Lemon Pesto Dip with Red
    Pepper and Cherry
    Tomatoes, 70–71, **71**
  Pita Chips with Dukka, 76–77
  Roasted Red Pepper and Walnut
    Spread, 74
  Rosemary-Marinated Olives, 78,
    79
  Salmon-Stuffed Eggs, 82, **83**

  Smoked Salmon and Goat
    Cheese Crostini with
    Fennel Gremolata, 81
  Spanish Smoked Almonds, 89
  Three-Onion Dip with Broccoli,
    73
Apples
  Apple, Cheddar, and Raisin
    Bruschetta, 315
  Apple Ratatouille, 243
  Autumn Fruit Salad in Cider, 272
  good to know facts, 18
  health benefits, 17–18
  Kumquat-Apple Chutney, 258
  Melted Swiss, Smoked Turkey,
    and Apple Panini, 191
  My Mom's One-Crust Apple Pie,
    292–93
  Persian Chicken with Sour
    Cherries, 155
  Russian Cabbage and Apple
    Soup, 108–9
  selecting, 18
  serving ideas, 18
  Spring Fruit Salad with Mint
    Syrup, 269–70, **270**
  storing, 18
  Turkey Waldorf Salad, 136, **137**
Apricots
  Red Lentil and Apricot Soup,
    100–101, **101**
  Warm Apricot Glaze, 325
Arugula
  Chopped Arugula Salad with
    Edamame and Avocado, 125
  Goat Cheese, Sun-Dried
    Tomato, and Arugula
    Panini, 190
Asian-style dishes
  Asian Chicken and Pineapple
    Soup, 114–16, **115**
  Chinese Tea Eggs, 84
  Ginger Chicken Meatballs, 88
  Ginger Vinaigrette, 140

  Japanese Winter Cereal, 322
  Lemon Sesame Chicken, 154
  Orange-Glazed Japanese
    Squash, 252–53
  Peanut Chicken Stir-Fry, 152–53
  Peanut Fried Rice, 200
  Red Curried Cauliflower, 237
  Singapore Noodles, 207
  Teriyaki Salmon Steaks, 168
  Thai Shrimp Curry with
    Broccoli, Carrots, and
    Green Peas, 184–85
  Tropical Fruit Salad with White
    Tea Syrup, **270**, 271
Asparagus
  Asparagus with Egg Milanese,
    214, **215**
Avocados
  Avocado Cream, 176
  Avocado Lemon Sherbet, 305
  Avocado-Mango Salsa, 180, **181**
  Chicken with Pear and Avocado,
    150–51, **151**
  Chopped Arugula Salad with
    Edamame and Avocado, 125
  good to know facts, 9
  health benefits, 8
  selecting, 8
  serving ideas, 8
  slicing, 125
  storing, 8

B

Bacon
  pancetta, about, <u>104</u>
  Scrambled Egg Hash, 216
Bananas
  Autumn Fruit Salad in Cider, 272
  Blueberry Banana Bread, 285
  Citrus Charge-Up, 334
  Creamy Chai Oatmeal, 320
  Peanut Butter Milkshake, **337**, 338
  Strawberry Surprise, 335

Barley
    Japanese Winter Cereal, 322
    Wild Mushroom–Barley Soup,
        110
Basil
    Fresh Herb Vinaigrette, 141
    good to know facts, 52
    health benefits, 51
    Lemon Pesto Dip with Red
        Pepper and Cherry
        Tomatoes, 70–71, **71**
    Mediterranean Onions, 247
    serving ideas, 51–52
    storing, 78
Beans. *See also* Black beans;
        Kidney beans; Soy beans
    Baked Beans on Toast, 225
    Black and White Hoppin' John,
        228
    Chocolate Baked Beans, 224
    Curried Chickpeas, 90
    Greens Gumbo with Black-Eyed
        Peas, 106–7
    Hot Bean Dip, 75
    Roasted Broccoli, Green Beans,
        and Grape Tomatoes, 235
    quick-cooking method, 224
    selecting, 228
    storing, 228
    Tuscan Minestrone with
        Butternut Squash and Farro,
        104–5, **105**
Bean sprouts
    Lemon Sesame Chicken, 154
Beef
    Beef and Buckwheat Soup,
        112–13
    Cocoa-Crusted Beef Filet with
        Pomegranate Sauce, 162–63
    Five-Way Chili Spaghetti, 204–5,
        205
    Herb-Stuffed Flank Steak,
        160–61, **161**
    Three-Onion Pot Roast, 164
Beets
    Roasted Beet and Walnut Salad,
        132
Belgian endive
    Black Olive Caviar in Endive, 85
    Red Lettuce, Endive, and Red
        Grapefruit Salad, 122, **123**
Bell peppers
    Apple Ratatouille, 243
    Chipotle Salmon Salad, 138

Curried Egg Salad with Spinach,
        134
Deviled Red Potatoes, 255
Feta Dip with Confetti
        Vegetables, 72
Four-Pepper Shrimp, 183
Golden Cauliflower and Tofu
        Curry, 226, **227**
good to know facts, 14
health benefits, 14
Lemon Pesto Dip with Red
        Pepper and Cherry
        Tomatoes, 70–71, **71**
Peanut Chicken Stir-Fry, 152–53
Peanut Fried Rice, 200
Roasted Red Pepper and Walnut
        Spread, 74
Roasted Red Pepper Gazpacho,
        117
roasting, 117
selecting, 14
serving ideas, 14
Singapore Noodles, 207
Spice-Rubbed Salmon Kebabs
        with Tzatziki Sauce,
        172–73, **173**
storing, 14
Tuna Muffuletta, 186–87, **187**
Berries. *See* Blackberries;
        Blueberries; Cranberries;
        Raspberries; Strawberries
Black beans
    Black and White Hoppin' John,
        228
    Black Bean and Nectarine Salsa,
        80
    Black Bean and Two-Berry Soup,
        119
    Black Bean Brownies, 277–78
    Black Bean Salad with Butternut
        Squash and Broccoli, 130,
        131
    good to know facts, 35
    health benefits, 34
    serving ideas, 34–35
Blackberries
    Berries and Red Grapes in
        Spiced Red Wine, 273
    Blackberry Shortcakes with
        Ginger Cream, 275–76
    Black Rice with Blackberries, 201
    good to know facts, 19
    health benefits, 19
    selecting, 19

serving ideas, 19
storing, 19
wild, picking, 18
Black-eyed peas
    Black and White Hoppin' John,
        228
    Greens Gumbo with Black-Eyed
        Peas, 106–7
Blueberries
    Berries and Red Grapes in
        Spiced Red Wine, 273
    Big Chocolate Breakfast
        Cookies, 326–27
    Black Bean and Two-Berry Soup,
        119
    Blueberry and Ricotta
        Bruschetta, 314
    Blueberry Banana Bread, 285
    Blue Corncakes with Mixed
        Berry Compote, 330–31
    Frozen Blueberry Yogurt Pops,
        308
    good to know facts, 20
    health benefits, 19–20
    Maple Buckwheat with Wild
        Blueberries, 323
    Melon and Orange Yogurt Bowl,
        310
    Morning Fruit and Cheese Plate,
        312
    Pork Tenderloin with Blueberry-
        Plum Sauce, 159
    selecting, 20
    serving ideas, 20
    storing, 20
    WBBJ Sandwich, 192
Breads and toast
    Apple, Cheddar, and Raisin
        Bruschetta, 315
    Blueberry and Ricotta
        Bruschetta, 314
    Chocolate Cinnamon Toast, 313
    Peanut Butter and Jelly Muffins,
        328–29, **329**
    Pita Chips with Dukka, 76–77
    Smoked Salmon and Goat
        Cheese Crostini with
        Fennel Gremolata, 81
    Triple Strawberry Bruschetta, 316
Breakfast dishes
    Apple, Cheddar, and Raisin
        Bruschetta, 315
    Big Chocolate Breakfast
        Cookies, 326–27

Blueberry and Ricotta
Bruschetta, 314
Blue Corncakes with Mixed
Berry Compote, 330–31
Buckwheat Polenta Cakes with
Warm Apricot Glaze,
324–25
Chocolate Cinnamon Toast, 313
Citrus Charge-Up, 334
Creamy Chai Oatmeal, 320
Everyday Irish Oatmeal, 318
Japanese Winter Cereal, 322
Maple Buckwheat with Wild
Blueberries, 323
Melon and Orange Yogurt Bowl,
310
Morning Fruit and Cheese Plate,
312
Nutty Fiber Mix, 317
Peaches and Cream Breakfast
Sundae, 311
Peanut Butter and Jelly Muffins,
328–29, **329**
Pear and Walnut Muesli, 321
Sour Cherry Marmalade, 333
Strawberry Smash, 319
Strawberry Surprise, 335
Triple Strawberry Bruschetta,
316
Turkey Breakfast Sausage, 332
Broccoli
Black Bean Salad with Butternut
Squash and Broccoli, 130,
131
California Salad with Citrus
Dressing, 124
Fusilli with Broccoli Bolognese,
202–3
good to know facts, 9
health benefits, 9
Macaroni and Cheese with
Broccoli, 206
Roasted Broccoli, Green Beans,
and Grape Tomatoes, 235
selecting, 9
serving ideas, 9
Steak-Cut Broccoli, 234
storing, 9
Thai Shrimp Curry with
Broccoli, Carrots, and
Green Peas, 184–85
Three-Onion Dip with Broccoli,
73
20-Minute Vegetable Soup, 93

Broccoli raab
Garlic Greens, 240
Tuscan Potatoes with Bitter
Greens, 254
Broth
Souped-Up Chicken Broth, 120
Wild Mushroom Broth, 111
Brownies
Black Bean Brownies, 277–78
Bruschetta
Apple, Cheddar, and Raisin
Bruschetta, 315
Blueberry and Ricotta
Bruschetta, 314
Triple Strawberry Bruschetta, 316
Brussels sprouts
Brussels Sprouts and Kale, 239
Buckwheat
about, 112
Beef and Buckwheat Soup,
112–13
Buckwheat Polenta Cakes with
Warm Apricot Glaze,
324–25
Crisp Buckwheat Polenta with
Mushroom Topping,
198–99
good to know facts, 30
health benefits, 30
Maple Buckwheat with Wild
Blueberries, 323
Pomegranate Tabbouleh, 197
serving ideas, 30
Burgers
Juicy Turkey Burgers, 145
Buttermilk
Buttermilk-Brined Pork Chops,
158
Spiced Buttermilk Dressing, 139

C
Cabbage
Michel's Kaleslaw, 129
Red Cabbage with Sour
Cherries, 244
Russian Cabbage and Apple
Soup, 108–9
Salmon Tacos with Avocado
Cream, 176–77
Cakes
Blueberry Banana Bread, 285
Chocolate Cranberry Torte,
300–302, **301**

Chocolate Cupcakes with
Cinnamon Frosting,
283–84, **284**
Chocolate Gingerbread with
Lemon Yogurt Frosting,
296–97
Pumpkin-Date Tea Cakes, 282
Calcium, 3
Cantaloupe
Iced Melon Soup, 118
Melon and Orange Yogurt Bowl,
310
Morning Fruit and Cheese Plate,
312
Capers
Lemon Kale with Capers, 238
removing excess salt from, 238
salt-preserved, buying, 238
Carrot juice
buying, 196
Popped Quinoa Pilaf, 196
Carrots
Pomegranate-Glazed Carrots,
230
Thai Shrimp Curry with
Broccoli, Carrots, and
Green Peas, 184–85
Cauliflower
Golden Cauliflower and Tofu
Curry, 226, **227**
Indian Roasted Cauliflower, 236
Red Curried Cauliflower, 237
Cereal
Creamy Chai Oatmeal, 320
Everyday Irish Oatmeal, 318
Japanese Winter Cereal, 322
Maple Buckwheat with Wild
Blueberries, 323
Pear and Walnut Muesli, 321
Chard
Greens Gumbo with Black-Eyed
Peas, 106–7
Cheddar cheese
Apple, Cheddar, and Raisin
Bruschetta, 315
Five-Way Chili Spaghetti, 204–5,
205
Grilled Cheddar and Tomato
Panini, 189
Macaroni and Cheese with
Broccoli, 206
Cheese
Apple, Cheddar, and Raisin
Bruschetta, 315

Cheese (cont.)
  Asparagus with Egg Milanese,
    214, **215**
  Baked Rigatoni with Butternut
    Squash and Turkey Sausage,
    210–11
  Baked Spinach and Feta, 241
  Blueberry and Ricotta
    Bruschetta, 314
  Feta Dip with Confetti
    Vegetables, 72
  Five-Way Chili Spaghetti, 204–5,
    205
  Goat Cheese, Sun-Dried
    Tomato, and Arugula
    Panini, 190
  Greek Pizzettes, 193
  Grilled Cheddar and Tomato
    Panini, 189
  Herb-Stuffed Flank Steak,
    160–61, **161**
  Kale Frittata, 220
  Lemon Yogurt Cheesecake with
    Sour Cherry Sauce, 298–99
  Macaroni and Cheese with
    Broccoli, 206
  Melted Swiss, Smoked Turkey,
    and Apple Panini, 191
  Morning Fruit and Cheese Plate,
    312
  Parmigiano-Reggiano, about,
    202
  Peaches and Cream Breakfast
    Sundae, 311
  Polenta Lasagna with Red Wine
    Lentils, 212
  Smoked Salmon and Goat
    Cheese Crostini with
    Fennel Gremolata, 81
  Spinach Lasagna with Creamy
    Tomato Sauce, 208–9
Cheesecakes
  Lemon Yogurt Cheesecake with
    Sour Cherry Sauce, 298–99
Cherries, sour. *See* Sour cherries
Cherry juice
  Cherry Lime Ricky, 340
Chicken
  Asian Chicken and Pineapple
    Soup, 114–16, **115**
  Chicken with Pear and Avocado,
    150–51, **151**
  Ginger Chicken Meatballs, 88
  Lemon Sesame Chicken, 154

  Mexican Molé Chicken Salad,
    135
  Peanut Chicken Stir-Fry, 152–53
  Persian Chicken with Sour
    Cherries, 155
  Souped-Up Chicken Broth, 120
Chickpeas
  Curried Chickpeas, 90
Chile peppers
  Black Rice with Blackberries,
    201
  chipotle chiles, about, 138
  Chipotle Salmon Salad, 138
  good to know facts, 59
  health benefits, 58
  serving ideas, 58–59
Chili
  Five-Way Chili Spaghetti, 204–5,
    205
  Turkey Meatball Chili, 148–49
Chocolate and cocoa
  Big Chocolate Breakfast
    Cookies, 326–27
  Black Bean Brownies, 277–78
  Brownie Dippers, **261**, 262
  Chocolate Baked Beans, 224
  Chocolate Cinnamon Toast,
    313
  Chocolate-Covered Pears with
    Espresso Sauce, 263–64
  Chocolate Cranberry Torte,
    300–302, **301**
  Chocolate Cupcakes with
    Cinnamon Frosting,
    283–84, **284**
  Chocolate Gingerbread with
    Lemon Yogurt Frosting,
    296–97
  Chocolate-Glazed Peanuts, 91
  Chocolate Soup with Brownie
    Dippers, 260–62, **261**
  good to know facts, 64
  health benefits, 62–63
  Hot Chocolat, 345
  Iced Mocha Espresso, 342
  Peanut Butter Truffles, 303
  Seasoned Cocoa Nib Powder,
    163
  selecting, 63
  serving ideas, 63
  storing, 63
  Walnut Chocolate Strudels with
    Cinnamon Honey Syrup,
    286–87

Chowder
  Manhattan Tuna Chowder,
    97
  Sweet Potato and Shrimp
    Chowder, 98
Chutney
  Coconut Chutney, 175
  Kumquat-Apple Chutney, 258
Cilantro
  Corn with Cilantro and Chives,
    231
  good to know facts, 52
  health benfits, 52
  serving ideas, 52
Cinnamon
  Cinnamon Frosting, 284
  good to know facts, 57
  health benefits, 56–57
  serving ideas, 57
  Walnut Chocolate Strudels with
    Cinnamon Honey Syrup,
    286–87
Citrus fruits. *See also* Grapefruit;
    Lemons; Limes; Oranges
  good to know facts, 21
  health benefits, 20–21
  sectioning, 122
  selecting, 21
  serving ideas, 21
  storing, 21
  zest, good to know facts, 60
  zest, health benefits from, 59
  zest, serving ideas, 60
Coconut
  dried unsweetened, buying,
    175
  Grilled Salmon with Coconut
    Chutney, 175
Coconut milk
  buying, 171
  Curry Cream Sauce, 170–71
  Hot Chocolat, 345
  Thai Shrimp Curry with
    Broccoli, Carrots, and
    Green Peas, 184–85
Coffee
  Chocolate-Covered Pears with
    Espresso Sauce, 263–64
  good to know facts, 65
  health benefits, 64
  Iced Mocha Espresso, 342
  serving ideas, 65
  Spiced Cafe au Lait, 344
  storing, 65

Collard greens
  BBQ Bean Soup, 103
  Cajun Eggs and Greens, 218–19
  Garlic Greens, 240
  good to know facts, 10
  Greens Gumbo with Black-Eyed
    Peas, 106–7
  health benefits, 10
  lean cooking method, 218
  selecting, 10
  serving ideas, 10
  storing, 10
  stripping tough stems from, 238
Condiments. *See also* Salsa
  Chili Onions, 246
  Coconut Chutney, 175
  Cranberries and Pearl Onions,
    257
  Curried Onions, 245
  Ginger Cranberry Relish, 256
  Kumquat-Apple Chutney, 258
  Mediterranean Onions, 247
  Mixed Berry Compote, 330–31
  Moroccan Tomato Compote,
    166–67
  Sour Cherry Marmalade, 333
  Walnut Butter, 192
Cookies and bars
  Big Chocolate Breakfast
    Cookies, 326–27
  Black Bean Brownies, 277–78
  Brownie Dippers, **261**, 262
  Green Tea Shortbread, 281
  Sicilian Almond Cookies, 280
  Spiced Fig Bars, 279
Corn
  Corn with Cilantro and Chives,
    231
  Greens Gumbo with Black-Eyed
    Peas, 106–7
  Nutty Popcorn Bundt Ring, 304
  Red Quinoa with Corn and
    Pecans, 194, **195**
Cornmeal
  Blue Corncakes with Mixed
    Berry Compote, 330–31
Cottage cheese
  Lemon Yogurt Cheesecake with
    Sour Cherry Sauce, 298–99
  Morning Fruit and Cheese Plate,
    312
Cranberries
  Blood Orange and Cranberry
    Parfait, 274

Chocolate Cranberry Torte,
    300–302, **301**
  Cranberries and Pearl Onions,
    257
  Cranberry-Pomegranate Salsa,
    143
  Ginger Cranberry Relish, 256
  good to know facts, 22
  health benefits, 21–22
  selecting, 22
  serving ideas, 22
  Spiced Fig Bars, 279
  storing, 22
Crostini
  Smoked Salmon and Goat
    Cheese Crostini with
    Fennel Gremolata, 81
Cucumbers
  Greek Pizzettes, 193
  Tzatziki Sauce, 172–73
Curry
  Curried Chickpeas, 90
  Curried Egg Salad with Spinach,
    134
  Curried Onions, 245
  Curry Cream Sauce, 170–71
  Golden Cauliflower and Tofu
    Curry, 226, **227**
  Red Curried Cauliflower, 237
  Singapore Noodles, 207
  Thai Shrimp Curry with
    Broccoli, Carrots, and
    Green Peas, 184–85

D

Dates
  California Salad with Citrus
    Dressing, 124
  Pumpkin-Date Tea Cakes, 282
  Spiced Fig Bars, 279
Desserts
  Autumn Fruit Salad in Cider, 272
  Avocado Lemon Sherbet, 305
  Berries and Red Grapes in
    Spiced Red Wine, 273
  Black Bean Brownies, 277–78
  Blackberry Shortcakes with
    Ginger Cream, 275–76
  Blood Orange and Cranberry
    Parfait, 274
  Blueberry Banana Bread, 285
  Chocolate-Covered Pears with
    Espresso Sauce, 263–64

Chocolate Cranberry Torte,
    300–302, **301**
  Chocolate Cupcakes with
    Cinnamon Frosting,
    283–84, **284**
  Chocolate Gingerbread with
    Lemon Yogurt Frosting,
    296–97
  Chocolate Soup with Brownie
    Dippers, 260–62, **261**
  Frozen Blueberry Yogurt Pops,
    308
  Ginger Pomegranate Granita,
    306, **307**
  Green Tea Shortbread, 281
  Honey-Baked Peaches with
    Raspberry Sauce, 267–68
  Lemon Yogurt Cheesecake with
    Sour Cherry Sauce,
    298–99
  My Mom's One-Crust Apple Pie,
    292–93
  Nutty Popcorn Bundt Ring, 304
  Peanut Butter Truffles, 303
  Pear and Sweet Potato Crumble,
    294–95
  Pumpkin-Date Tea Cakes, 282
  Red Grapefruit with Pumpkin
    Seed Praline, 265–66, **266**
  Seriously Lemon Pie, 288–90,
    289
  Sicilian Almond Cookies, 280
  Southern Sweet Potato Pie, 291
  Spiced Fig Bars, 279
  Spring Fruit Salad with Mint
    Syrup, 269–70, **270**
  Tropical Fruit Salad with White
    Tea Syrup, **270**, 271
  Walnut Chocolate Strudels with
    Cinnamon Honey Syrup,
    286–87
Dips and spreads
  Black Bean and Nectarine Salsa,
    80
  Feta Dip with Confetti
    Vegetables, 72
  Hot Bean Dip, 75
  Lemon Pesto Dip with Red
    Pepper and Cherry
    Tomatoes, 70–71, **71**
  Roasted Red Pepper and Walnut
    Spread, 74
  Three-Onion Dip with Broccoli,
    73

Drinks
    Almond Chai, 343
    Cherry Lime Ricky, 340
    Citrus Charge-Up, 334
    Ginger Mint Tea, 346
    Hot Chocolat, 345
    Iced Mocha Espresso, 342
    Peanut Butter Milkshake, **337**, 338
    Raspberry Watermelon Cooler, **337**, 339
    Simple Syrup for, 340
    Spiced Cafe au Lait, 344
    Strawberry Surprise, 335
    Sweet Potato Smoothie, 336, **337**
    Tropical White Tea Spritzer, 341

E

Edamame
    Chopped Arugula Salad with Edamame and Avocado, 125
Eggplant
    Apple Ratatouille, 243
    Golden Cauliflower and Tofu Curry, 226, **227**
Eggs
    Asparagus with Egg Milanese, 214, **215**
    Baked Beans on Toast, 225
    Cajun Eggs and Greens, 218–19
    Chinese Tea Eggs, 84
    Curried Egg Salad with Spinach, 134
    good to know facts, 41
    health benefits, 40–41
    Kale Frittata, 220
    Salmon-Stuffed Eggs, 82, **83**
    Scrambled Egg Hash, 216
    Scrambled Eggs with Pasta and Cherry Tomatoes, 217
    selecting, 41
    serving ideas, 41
    storing, 41
Endive
    Black Olive Caviar in Endive, 85
    Red Lettuce, Endive, and Red Grapefruit Salad, 122, **123**

F

Farmers markets, 4
Farro
    Tuscan Minestrone with Butternut Squash and Farro, 104–5, **105**

whole-grain farro pasta, about, <u>204</u>
Fennel
    Smoked Salmon and Goat Cheese Crostini with Fennel Gremolata, 81
Feta cheese
    Baked Spinach and Feta, 241
    Feta Dip with Confetti Vegetables, 72
    Greek Pizzettes, 193
Fiber, 17
Figs
    Pear and Walnut Muesli, 321
    Spiced Fig Bars, 279
Fish. *See also* Salmon
    Grilled Red Snapper with Avocado-Mango Salsa, 180, **181**
    Manhattan Tuna Chowder, 97
    Trout with Meyer Lemon Gremolata, 182
    Tuna Muffuletta, 186–87, **187**
Fish sauce, about, <u>116</u>
Flax seeds
    Big Chocolate Breakfast Cookies, 326–27
    Creamy Chai Oatmeal, 320
    Nutty Fiber Mix, 317
Frittatas
    Kale Frittata, 220
Frostings
    Cinnamon Frosting, 284
    Lemon Yogurt Frosting, 297
Fruits. *See also* Citrus fruits; *specific fruits*
    Autumn Fruit Salad in Cider, 272
    Berries and Red Grapes in Spiced Red Wine, 273
    health benefits, 17
    recommended daily intake, 17
    Spring Fruit Salad with Mint Syrup, 269–70, **270**
    Tropical Fruit Salad with White Tea Syrup, **270**, 271
Furikake
    about, <u>322</u>
    Japanese Winter Cereal, 322

G

Garam masala, preparing, <u>100</u>
Garlic
    Garlic Greens, 240
    good to know facts, 61

health benefits, 60
serving ideas, 60
Steak-Cut Broccoli, 234
Ginger
    Blackberry Shortcakes with Ginger Cream, 275–76
    Chocolate Gingerbread with Lemon Yogurt Frosting, 296–97
    Ginger Chicken Meatballs, 88
    Ginger Cranberry Relish, 256
    Ginger Lentils, 223
    Ginger Mashed Sweet Potatoes, 248
    Ginger Mint Tea, 346
    Ginger Pomegranate Granita, 306, **307**
    Ginger Vinaigrette, 140
    good to know facts, 61–62
    health benefits, 61
    Kumquat-Apple Chutney, 258
    serving ideea, 61
Glazes
    Warm Apricot Glaze, 325
Goat cheese
    Goat Cheese, Sun-Dried Tomato, and Arugula Panini, 190
    Herb-Stuffed Flank Steak, 160–61, **161**
    Polenta Lasagna with Red Wine Lentils, 212
    Smoked Salmon and Goat Cheese Crostini with Fennel Gremolata, 81
Grains. *See also* Buckwheat; Oats; Quinoa; Rice
    Blue Corncakes with Mixed Berry Compote, 330–31
    health benefits, 29–30
    Japanese Winter Cereal, 322
    selecting, <u>198</u>
    storing, <u>198</u>
    Tuscan Minestrone with Butternut Squash and Farro, 104–5, **105**
    whole wheat, about, 33
    Wild Mushroom–Barley Soup, 110
Granita
    Ginger Pomegranate Granita, 306, **307**
Grapefruit
    Citrus Charge-Up, 334
    good to know facts, 21

health benefits, 20–21
Red Grapefruit with Pumpkin
 Seed Praline, 265–66, **266**
Red Lettuce, Endive, and Red
 Grapefruit Salad, 122, **123**
sectioning, <u>122</u>
selecting, 21
serving ideas, 21
storing, 21
Warm Pineapple-Grapefruit
 Salsa, 156–57
zest from, 59–60
Grapes
 Autumn Fruit Salad in Cider,
  272
 Berries and Red Grapes in
  Spiced Red Wine, 273
 Morning Fruit and Cheese Plate,
  312
 Spring Fruit Salad with Mint
  Syrup, 269–70, **270**
 Turkey Waldorf Salad, 136, **137**
Green beans
 Roasted Broccoli, Green Beans,
  and Grape Tomatoes, 235
Greens. *See also* Cabbage; Collard
  greens; Kale; Spinach
 California Salad with Citrus
  Dressing, 124
 Chopped Arugula Salad with
  Edamame and Avocado, 125
 Garlic Greens, 240
 Goat Cheese, Sun-Dried
  Tomato, and Arugula
  Panini, 190
 Greek Pizzettes, 193
 Greens Gumbo with Black-Eyed
  Peas, 106–7
 Red Lettuce, Endive, and Red
  Grapefruit Salad, 122, **123**
 Tuscan Potatoes with Bitter
  Greens, 254

H

Herbs, 51–56. *See also* Basil;
  Cilantro; Mint
 about, 50–51
 buying, 51, <u>78</u>
 cooking with, 51
 Dried Tomato–Mint Salsa, 171
 Fresh Herb Vinaigrette, 141
 Herb-Stuffed Flank Steak,
  160–61, **161**
 medicinal uses of, 50

Mediterranean Onions, 247
 oregano, about, 53–54
 parsley, about, 54–55
 Parsley and Grape Tomato Salad,
  127
 Pomegranate Tabbouleh, 197
 rosemary, about, 55
 Rosemary-Marinated Olives, 78,
  79
 selecting, <u>78</u>
 storing, 51, <u>78</u>
 substituting dried for fresh, 51
 thyme, about, 55–56
 Tropical White Tea Spritzer,
  341
 Turkey Breakfast Sausage, 332
 Turkey Oreganato, 144
Honey
 Honey-Baked Peaches with
  Raspberry Sauce, 267–68
 Walnut Chocolate Strudels with
  Cinnamon Honey Syrup,
  286–87
Honeydew
 Spring Fruit Salad with Mint
  Syrup, 269–70, **270**
Hors d'oeuvres. *See* Appetizers and
  starters

I

Insulin resistance, 3
Italian-style dishes
 Apple, Cheddar, and Raisin
  Bruschetta, 315
 Apple Ratatouille, 243
 Asparagus with Egg Milanese,
  214, **215**
 Baked Rigatoni with Butternut
  Squash and Turkey Sausage,
  210–11
 Blueberry and Ricotta
  Bruschetta, 314
 Curried Chickpeas, 90
 Fusilli with Broccoli Bolognese,
  202–3
 Kale Frittata, 220
 Lemon Pesto Dip with Red
  Pepper and Cherry
  Tomatoes, 70–71, **71**
 Polenta Lasagna with Red Wine
  Lentils, 212
 Rosemary-Marinated Olives, 78,
  79
 Sicilian Almond Cookies, 280

Smoked Salmon and Goat
  Cheese Crostini with
  Fennel Gremolata, 81
 Spinach Lasagna with Creamy
  Tomato Sauce, 208–9
 Triple Strawberry Bruschetta,
  316
 Tuscan Minestrone with
  Butternut Squash and Farro,
  104–5, **105**
 Tuscan Potatoes with Bitter
  Greens, 254

K

Kale
 Brussels Sprouts and Kale, 239
 Garlic Greens, 240
 good to know facts, 10
 Greens Gumbo with Black-Eyed
  Peas, 106–7
 health benefits, 10
 Kale Frittata, 220
 Lemon Kale with Capers, 238
 Michel's Kaleslaw, 129
 selecting, 10
 serving ideas, 10
 storing, 10
 stripping tough stems from, <u>238</u>
Kidney beans
 BBQ Bean Soup, 103
 Five-Way Chili Spaghetti, 204–5,
  205
 good to know facts, 35
 health benefits, 34
 Kidney Beans with Potatoes and
  Dill, 221
 Red Bean and Walnut Soup, 102
 serving ideas, 34–35
 Strawberry Surprise, 335
 20-Minute Vegetable Soup, 93
Kiwifruit
 Autumn Fruit Salad in Cider,
  272
 good to know facts, 23
 health benefits, 22
 Morning Fruit and Cheese Plate,
  312
 selecting, 23
 serving ideas, 23
 Spring Fruit Salad with Mint
  Syrup, 269–70, **270**
 storing, 23
Kumquats
 Kumquat-Apple Chutney, 258

L

Lasagna
Polenta Lasagna with Red Wine Lentils, 212
Spinach Lasagna with Creamy Tomato Sauce, 208–9
Legumes. *See also* Beans; Lentils
health benefits, 34
recommended daily intake, 34
selecting, <u>78</u>, <u>228</u>
storing, <u>78</u>, <u>228</u>
Lemons
Avocado Lemon Sherbet, 305
Citrus-Marinated Shrimp, 86–87, 87
good to know facts, 21
health benefits, 20–21
Lemon Kale with Capers, 238
Lemon Sesame Chicken, 154
Lemon Yogurt Cheesecake with Sour Cherry Sauce, 298–99
Lemon Yogurt Frosting, 297
Marinated Tomato Salad, 128
Meyer Lemon Gremolata, 182
selecting, 21
Seriously Lemon Pie, 288–90, **289**
serving ideas, 21
storing, 21
zest from, 59–60
Lentils
Ginger Lentils, 223
good to know facts, 35
health benefits, 35
Polenta Lasagna with Red Wine Lentils, 212
Red Lentil and Apricot Soup, 100–101, **101**
Red Wine Lentils, 222
selecting, <u>228</u>
serving ideas, 35
storing, <u>228</u>
Lettuce
California Salad with Citrus Dressing, 124
Greek Pizzettes, 193
Red Lettuce, Endive, and Red Grapefruit Salad, 122, **123**
Limes
Cherry Lime Ricky, 340
Citrus Salmon Cakes, 174
good to know facts, 21
health benefits, 20–21
selecting, 21

serving ideas, 21
storing, 21
zest from, 59–60
Lycopene, 15–16

M

Main dishes (eggs, beans, soy)
Asparagus with Egg Milanese, 214, **215**
Baked Beans on Toast, 225
Black and White Hoppin' John, 228
Cajun Eggs and Greens, 218–19
Chocolate Baked Beans, 224
Ginger Lentils, 223
Golden Cauliflower and Tofu Curry, 226, **227**
Kale Frittata, 220
Kidney Beans with Potatoes and Dill, 221
Red Wine Lentils, 222
Scrambled Egg Hash, 216
Scrambled Eggs with Pasta and Cherry Tomatoes, 217
Main dishes (meat)
Buttermilk-Brined Pork Chops, 158
Cocoa-Crusted Beef Filet with Pomegranate Sauce, 162–63
Herb-Stuffed Flank Steak, 160–61, **161**
Jerk Pork Chops with Warm Pineapple-Grapefruit Salsa, 156–57
Pork Tenderloin with Blueberry-Plum Sauce, 159
Three-Onion Pot Roast, 164
Main dishes (meatless)
Asparagus with Egg Milanese, 214, **215**
Baked Beans on Toast, 225
Black and White Hoppin' John, 228
Chocolate Baked Beans, 224
Ginger Lentils, 223
Goat Cheese, Sun-Dried Tomato, and Arugula Panini, 190
Golden Cauliflower and Tofu Curry, 226, **227**
Greek Pizzettes, 193
Grilled Cheddar and Tomato Panini, 189

Kale Frittata, 220
Macaroni and Cheese with Broccoli, 206
Polenta Lasagna with Red Wine Lentils, 212
Red Wine Lentils, 222
Scrambled Eggs with Pasta and Cherry Tomatoes, 217
Spinach Lasagna with Creamy Tomato Sauce, 208–9
WBBJ Sandwich, 192
Main dishes (pasta)
Baked Rigatoni with Butternut Squash and Turkey Sausage, 210–11
Five-Way Chili Spaghetti, 204–5, **205**
Fusilli with Broccoli Bolognese, 202–3
Macaroni and Cheese with Broccoli, 206
Singapore Noodles, 207
Spinach Lasagna with Creamy Tomato Sauce, 208–9
Main dishes (poultry)
Chicken with Pear and Avocado, 150–51, **151**
Juicy Turkey Burgers, 145
Lemon Sesame Chicken, 154
Mexican Molé Chicken Salad, 135
Peanut Chicken Stir-Fry, 152–53
Persian Chicken with Sour Cherries, 155
Turkey and Spinach Mini-Meat Loaves, 146–47, **147**
Turkey Cutlets with Cranberry-Pomegranate Salsa, 143
Turkey Meatball Chili, 148–49
Turkey Oreganato, 144
Turkey Waldorf Salad, 136, **137**
Main dishes (salads)
Chipotle Salmon Salad, 138
Mexican Molé Chicken Salad, 135
Turkey Waldorf Salad, 136, **137**
Main dishes (sandwiches)
Goat Cheese, Sun-Dried Tomato, and Arugula Panini, 190
Greek Pizzettes, 193
Grilled Cheddar and Tomato Panini, 189

Melted Swiss, Smoked Turkey, and Apple Panini, 191
WBBJ Sandwich, 192
Main dishes (seafood)
Chipotle Salmon Salad, 138
Citrus Salmon Cakes, 174
Four-Pepper Shrimp, 183
Grilled Red Snapper with Avocado-Mango Salsa, 180, **181**
Grilled Salmon with Coconut Chutney, 175
Perfect Poached Salmon with Two Sauces, 170–71
Potato-Crusted Salmon, 169
Roasted Salmon, Grape Tomatoes, and Leeks with Sparkling Wine Sauce, 178–79
Roasted Salmon with Moroccan Tomato Compote, 166–67
Salmon Tacos with Avocado Cream, 176–77
Spice-Rubbed Salmon Kebabs with Tzatziki Sauce, 172–73, **173**
Teriyaki Salmon Steaks, 168
Thai Shrimp Curry with Broccoli, Carrots, and Green Peas, 184–85
Trout with Meyer Lemon Gremolata, 182
Tuna Muffuletta, 186–87, **187**
Mangoes
Avocado-Mango Salsa, 180, **181**
good to know facts, 24
health benefits, 23
selecting, 23
serving ideas, 23–24
skinning and cutting up, _271_
storing, 23
Tropical Fruit Salad with White Tea Syrup, **270**, 271
Maple syrup
Maple Buckwheat with Wild Blueberries, 323
Maple Mustard Dressing, 126
Strawberry Smash, 319
Marshmallows
kosher, about, _249_
Marshmallow Sweet Potatoes for Grown-Ups, 249
Nutty Popcorn Bundt Ring, 304
Meat. _See_ Beef; Pork

Meatballs
Ginger Chicken Meatballs, 88
Turkey Meatball Chili, 148–49
Meat loaf
Turkey and Spinach Mini-Meat Loaves, 146–47, **147**
Melon
Iced Melon Soup, 118
Melon and Orange Yogurt Bowl, 310
Morning Fruit and Cheese Plate, 312
Raspberry Watermelon Cooler, **337**, 339
Mint
Dried Tomato–Mint Salsa, 171
Fresh Herb Vinaigrette, 141
Ginger Mint Tea, 346
good to know facts, 53
health benefits, 53
serving ideas, 53
Spring Fruit Salad with Mint Syrup, 269–70, **270**
Mirin, about, _88_
Muffins
Peanut Butter and Jelly Muffins, 328–29, **329**
Mushrooms
good to know facts, 11
health benefits, 10, 11
Meyer Lemon Gremolata, 182
Mushroom Kebabs, 242
Mushroom Topping, 199
Peanut Fried Rice, 200
selecting, 11
serving ideas, 11
storing, 11
taste and texture, 11
Wild Mushroom–Barley Soup, 110
Wild Mushroom Broth, 111

N

Nectarines
Black Bean and Nectarine Salsa, 80
Noodles
Singapore Noodles, 207
Nuts. _See also_ Almonds; Peanuts; Walnuts
health benefits, 43
Pumpkin-Date Tea Cakes, 282

Red Quinoa with Corn and Pecans, 194, **195**
Sicilian Almond Cookies, 280
toasting, _74_

O

Oats
Big Chocolate Breakfast Cookies, 326–27
Creamy Chai Oatmeal, 320
Everyday Irish Oatmeal, 318
good to know facts, 31
health benefits, 31
Japanese Winter Cereal, 322
Pear and Sweet Potato Crumble, 294–95
Pear and Walnut Muesli, 321
serving ideas, 31
Spiced Fig Bars, 279
Oils. _See_ Olive oil
Olive oil
extra-virgin, about, 49
good to know facts, 50
health benefits, 49
selecting, 49
serving ideas, 50
storing, 49
Olives
Black Olive Caviar in Endive, 85
Rosemary-Marinated Olives, 78, **79**
Tuna Muffuletta, 186–87, **187**
Omega-3 fatty acids, 37, 40, 45
Onions
about, 11–12
Chili Onions, 246
Cranberries and Pearl Onions, 257
Curried Egg Salad with Spinach, 134
Curried Onions, 245
good to know facts, 12
health benefits, 12
Mediterranean Onions, 247
primer on, _107_
selecting, _107_
serving ideas, 12, _245_
spring onions, about, _107_
storage onions, about, _107_
storing, _107_
taste and texture, 12
Three-Onion Dip with Broccoli, 73
Three-Onion Pot Roast, 164

Oranges
    Blood Orange and Cranberry
        Parfait, 274
    Citrus Dressing, 124
    Citrus-Marinated Shrimp,
        86–87, **87**
    Ginger Cranberry Relish, 256
    good to know facts, 21
    health benefits, 20–21
    Melon and Orange Yogurt Bowl,
        310
    Morning Fruit and Cheese Plate,
        312
    Orange-Glazed Japanese
        Squash, 252–53
    sectioning, 122
    selecting, 21
    serving ideas, 21
    Sour Cherry Marmalade, 333
    storing, 21
    Strawberry Surprise, 335
    zest from, 59–60
Oregano
    good to know facts, 54
    health benefits, 53–54
    Mediterranean Onions, 247
    Pomegranate Tabbouleh, 197
    serving ideas, 54
    Turkey Oreganato, 144

P

Pancakes
    Blue Corncakes with Mixed
        Berry Compote, 330–31
Pancetta, about, 104
Parmesan cheese
    Asparagus with Egg Milanese,
        214, **215**
    Parmigiano-Reggiano, about,
        202
Parsley
    Dried Tomato–Mint Salsa, 171
    good to know facts, 55
    health benefits, 54
    Parsley and Grape Tomato Salad,
        127
    Pomegranate Tabbouleh, 197
    serving ideas, 54–55
    storing, 78
Pasta
    Baked Rigatoni with Butternut
        Squash and Turkey Sausage,
        210–11

Five-Way Chili Spaghetti, 204–5,
    205
Fusilli with Broccoli Bolognese,
    202–3
Macaroni and Cheese with
    Broccoli, 206
Scrambled Eggs with Pasta and
    Cherry Tomatoes, 217
Singapore Noodles, 207
Spinach Lasagna with Creamy
    Tomato Sauce, 208–9
whole-grain farro pasta, about,
    204
Peaches
    Honey-Baked Peaches with
        Raspberry Sauce, 267–68
    Peaches and Cream Breakfast
        Sundae, 311
Peanut butter
    Peanut Butter and Jelly Muffins,
        328–29, **329**
    Peanut Butter Milkshake, **337**,
        338
    Peanut Butter Truffles, 303
    Peanut Tomato Soup, 96
Peanuts
    Chocolate-Glazed Peanuts, 91
    good to know facts, 45
    health benefits, 44–45
    Nutty Popcorn Bundt Ring,
        304
    Peanut Chicken Stir-Fry,
        152–53
    Peanut Fried Rice, 200
    selecting, 45
    serving ideas, 45
    storing, 45
Pears
    Autumn Fruit Salad in Cider,
        272
    Chicken with Pear and Avocado,
        150–51, **151**
    Chocolate-Covered Pears with
        Espresso Sauce, 263–64
    Pear and Root Vegetable Soup,
        99
    Pear and Sweet Potato Crumble,
        294–95
    Pear and Walnut Muesli, 321
Peas
    Singapore Noodles, 207
    Thai Shrimp Curry with
        Broccoli, Carrots, and
        Green Peas, 184–85

Pecans
    Pumpkin-Date Tea Cakes, 282
    Red Quinoa with Corn and
        Pecans, 194, **195**
Peppers. *See* Bell peppers; Chile
    peppers
Phyllo dough
    buying, 286
    Walnut Chocolate Strudels with
        Cinnamon Honey Syrup,
        286–87
Phytochemicals, 3, 17
Pies
    My Mom's One-Crust Apple Pie,
        292–93
    Seriously Lemon Pie, 288–90,
        289
    Southern Sweet Potato Pie, 291
Pineapple
    Asian Chicken and Pineapple
        Soup, 114–16, **115**
    Autumn Fruit Salad in Cider,
        272
    Tropical Fruit Salad with White
        Tea Syrup, **270**, 271
    Tropical White Tea Spritzer, 341
    Upside-Down Pineapple Sweet
        Potatoes, 250–51, **251**
    Warm Pineapple-Grapefruit
        Salsa, 156–57
Pine nuts
    Sicilian Almond Cookies, 280
Plums
    Pork Tenderloin with Blueberry-
        Plum Sauce, 159
Polenta
    Buckwheat Polenta Cakes with
        Warm Apricot Glaze,
        324–25
    Polenta Lasagna with Red Wine
        Lentils, 212
Pomegranates (and juice)
    Cocoa-Crusted Beef Filet with
        Pomegranate Sauce, 162–63
    Cranberry-Pomegranate Salsa,
        143
    Ginger Pomegranate Granita,
        306, **307**
    good to know facts, 66
    health benefits, 65–66
    Pomegranate-Glazed Carrots,
        230
    Pomegranate Walnut
        Vinaigrette, 141

Pork Tenderloin with Blueberry-
Plum Sauce, 159
Red Bean and Walnut Soup, 102
selecting, 66
serving ideas, 66
storing, 66
Popcorn
Nutty Popcorn Bundt Ring,
304
Pork
Buttermilk-Brined Pork Chops,
158
Cajun Eggs and Greens, 218–19
internal cooking temperature,
158
Jerk Pork Chops with Warm
Pineapple-Grapefruit Salsa,
156–57
pancetta, about, 104
Pork Tenderloin with Blueberry-
Plum Sauce, 159
Scrambled Egg Hash, 216
Spanish chorizo, about, 98
Sweet Potato and Shrimp
Chowder, 98
Potatoes. See also Sweet potatoes
Deviled Red Potatoes, 255
instant mashed, buying, 146
Kidney Beans with Potatoes and
Dill, 221
Potato-Crusted Salmon, 169
purple, buying, 133
Purple Potato Salad with
Smoked Salmon, 133
Scrambled Egg Hash, 216
Turkey and Spinach Mini-Meat
Loaves, 146–47, 147
Tuscan Potatoes with Bitter
Greens, 254
Poultry. See Chicken; Turkey
Probiotics, 41–42
Pumpkin
Pumpkin-Date Tea Cakes, 282
Pumpkin seeds
Dukka, 77
good to know facts, 47
health benefits, 46
Nutty Fiber Mix, 317
Pumpkin Seed Praline, 265–66,
266
selecting, 46
serving ideas, 47
storing, 47
toasting, 154

Quinoa
good to know facts, 32
health benefits, 31–32
Japanese Winter Cereal, 322
Popped Quinoa Pilaf, 196
red, about, 194
Red Quinoa with Corn and
Pecans, 194, 195
serving ideas, 32

Raisins
Apple, Cheddar, and Raisin
Bruschetta, 315
Big Chocolate Breakfast
Cookies, 326–27
Golden Cauliflower and Tofu
Curry, 226, 227
good to know facts, 25
health benefits, 24
Japanese Winter Cereal, 322
Kumquat-Apple Chutney, 258
Nutty Popcorn Bundt Ring,
304
Pear and Walnut Muesli, 321
selecting, 24
serving ideas, 25
storing, 25
Raspberries
Berries and Red Grapes in
Spiced Red Wine, 273
Black Bean and Two-Berry Soup,
119
Blood Orange and Cranberry
Parfait, 274
Blue Corncakes with Mixed
Berry Compote, 330–31
good to know facts, 26
health benefits, 25
Honey-Baked Peaches with
Raspberry Sauce, 267–68
Raspberry Sauce, 268
Raspberry Watermelon Cooler,
337, 339
selecting, 25
serving ideas, 26
storing, 25–26
Red snapper
Grilled Red Snapper with
Avocado-Mango Salsa, 180,
181

Relish
Ginger Cranberry Relish, 256
Rice
Black and White Hoppin' John,
228
Black Rice with Blackberries,
201
Four-Pepper Shrimp, 183
good to know facts, 33
health benfits, 32
Japanese Winter Cereal, 322
Peanut Fried Rice, 200
serving ideas, 33
Ricotta cheese
Blueberry and Ricotta
Bruschetta, 314
Peaches and Cream Breakfast
Sundae, 311
Polenta Lasagna with Red Wine
Lentils, 212
Rosemary
good to know facts, 55
health benefits, 55
Rosemary-Marinated Olives, 78,
79
serving ideas, 55

Salad dressings
Citrus Dressing, 124
Fresh Herb Vinaigrette, 141
Ginger Vinaigrette, 140
Maple Mustard Dressing, 126
Pomegranate Walnut
Vinaigrette, 141
Spiced Buttermilk Dressing, 139
Salads (fruit)
Autumn Fruit Salad in Cider, 272
Berries and Red Grapes in
Spiced Red Wine, 273
Spring Fruit Salad with Mint
Syrup, 269–70, 270
Tropical Fruit Salad with White
Tea Syrup, 270, 271
Salads (main-dish)
Chipotle Salmon Salad, 138
Mexican Molé Chicken Salad,
135
Turkey Waldorf Salad, 136, 137
Salads (side-dish)
Black Bean Salad with Butternut
Squash and Broccoli, 130,
131

Salads (side-dish) *(cont.)*
  California Salad with Citrus
    Dressing, 124
  Chopped Arugula Salad with
    Edamame and Avocado,
    125
  Curried Egg Salad with Spinach,
    134
  Marinated Tomato Salad, 128
  Michel's Kaleslaw, 129
  Parsley and Grape Tomato Salad,
    127
  Pomegranate Tabbouleh, 197
  Purple Potato Salad with
    Smoked Salmon, 133
  Red Lettuce, Endive, and Red
    Grapefruit Salad, 122, **123**
  Roasted Beet and Walnut Salad,
    132
  Spinach Salad with Maple
    Mustard Dressing, 126
Salmon
  Atlantic, about, 177
  Chipotle Salmon Salad, 138
  Citrus Salmon Cakes, 174
  good to know facts, 38–39
  Grilled Salmon with Coconut
    Chutney, 175
  health benefits, 37–38
  Pacific, species of, 177
  Perfect Poached Salmon with
    Two Sauces, 170–71
  Potato-Crusted Salmon, 169
  Purple Potato Salad with
    Smoked Salmon, 133
  Roasted Salmon, Grape
    Tomatoes, and Leeks with
    Sparkling Wine Sauce,
    178–79
  Roasted Salmon with Moroccan
    Tomato Compote, 166–67
  Salmon-Stuffed Eggs, 82, **83**
  Salmon Tacos with Avocado
    Cream, 176–77
  selecting, 38
  serving ideas, 38
  Smoked Salmon and Goat
    Cheese Crostini with
    Fennel Gremolata, 81
  Spice-Rubbed Salmon Kebabs
    with Tzatziki Sauce,
    172–73, **173**
  storing, 38
  Teriyaki Salmon Steaks, 168

Salsa
  Avocado-Mango Salsa, 180, **181**
  Black Bean and Nectarine Salsa,
    80
  Cranberry-Pomegranate Salsa,
    143
  Dried Tomato–Mint Salsa, 171
  Salsa, 176
  Warm Pineapple-Grapefruit
    Salsa, 156–57
Sandwiches
  Goat Cheese, Sun-Dried
    Tomato, and Arugula
    Panini, 190
  Greek Pizzettes, 193
  Grilled Cheddar and Tomato
    Panini, 189
  grilling, tips for, 190
  Melted Swiss, Smoked Turkey,
    and Apple Panini, 191
  Tuna Muffuletta, 186–87, **187**
  WBBJ Sandwich, 192
Sauces. *See also* Salsa
  Cranberries and Pearl Onions,
    257
  Curry Cream Sauce, 170–71
  Moroccan Tomato Compote,
    166–67
  Raspberry Sauce, 268
  Sour Cherry Sauce, 299
  Strawberry Smash, 319
  Tzatziki Sauce, 172–73
Sausages, pork
  Cajun Eggs and Greens,
    218–19
  Spanish chorizo, about, 98
  Sweet Potato and Shrimp
    Chowder, 98
Sausages, turkey
  Baked Rigatoni with Butternut
    Squash and Turkey Sausage,
    210–11
  Turkey Breakfast Sausage, 332
Scallions
  about, 107
  Three-Onion Dip with Broccoli,
    73
  Three-Onion Pot Roast, 164
Seafood. *See* Fish; Shrimp
Seeds. *See also* Flax seeds;
    Pumpkin seeds; Sesame
    seeds; Sunflower seeds
  health benefits, 43
  toasting, 154

Sesame seeds
  Dukka, 77
  good to know facts, 48
  health benefits, 47
  Lemon Sesame Chicken, 154
  Maple Buckwheat with Wild
    Blueberries, 323
  Nutty Fiber Mix, 317
  Nutty Popcorn Bundt Ring, 304
  selecting, 47
  serving ideas, 47
  storing, 47
  toasting, 154
Shallots
  about, 107
  Three-Onion Dip with Broccoli,
    73
Shellfish. *See* Shrimp
Sherbet
  Avocado Lemon Sherbet, 305
Shortcakes
  Blackberry Shortcakes with
    Ginger Cream, 275–76
Shrimp
  Citrus-Marinated Shrimp,
    86–87, **87**
  Four-Pepper Shrimp, 183
  Singapore Noodles, 207
  Sweet Potato and Shrimp
    Chowder, 98
  Thai Shrimp Curry with
    Broccoli, Carrots, and
    Green Peas, 184–85
Side dishes
  Apple Ratatouille, 243
  Baked Spinach and Feta, 241
  Black Rice with Blackberries, 201
  Brussels Sprouts and Kale, 239
  Chili Onions, 246
  Corn with Cilantro and Chives,
    231
  Cranberries and Pearl Onions,
    257
  Crisp Buckwheat Polenta with
    Mushroom Topping,
    198–99
  Curried Onions, 245
  Deviled Red Potatoes, 255
  Garlic Greens, 240
  Ginger Cranberry Relish, 256
  Ginger Mashed Sweet Potatoes,
    248
  Green and Yellow Squash
    Ribbons, 232, **233**

Indian Roasted Cauliflower, 236
Kumquat-Apple Chutney, 258
Lemon Kale with Capers, 238
Marshmallow Sweet Potatoes for
    Grown-Ups, 249
Mediterranean Onions, 247
Mushroom Kebabs, 242
Orange-Glazed Japanese
    Squash, 252–53
Peanut Fried Rice, 200
Pomegranate-Glazed Carrots,
    230
Pomegranate Tabbouleh, 197
Popped Quinoa Pilaf, 196
Red Cabbage with Sour
    Cherries, 244
Red Curried Cauliflower, 237
Red Quinoa with Corn and
    Pecans, 194, **195**
Roasted Broccoli, Green Beans,
    and Grape Tomatoes, 235
Steak-Cut Broccoli, 234
Tuscan Potatoes with Bitter
    Greens, 254
Upside-Down Pineapple Sweet
    Potatoes, 250–51, **251**
Side dish salads
    Black Bean Salad with Butternut
        Squash and Broccoli, 130,
        131
    California Salad with Citrus
        Dressing, 124
    Chopped Arugula Salad with
        Edamame and Avocado,
        125
    Curried Egg Salad with Spinach,
        134
    Marinated Tomato Salad, 128
    Michel's Kaleslaw, 129
    Parsley and Grape Tomato Salad,
        127
    Pomegranate Tabbouleh, 197
    Purple Potato Salad with
        Smoked Salmon, 133
    Red Lettuce, Endive, and Red
        Grapefruit Salad, 122, **123**
    Roasted Beet and Walnut Salad,
        132
    Spinach Salad with Maple
        Mustard Dressing, 126
Soups
    Asian Chicken and Pineapple
        Soup, 114–16, **115**
    BBQ Bean Soup, 103

Beef and Buckwheat Soup,
    112–13
Black Bean and Two-Berry Soup,
    119
Chocolate Soup with Brownie
    Dippers, 260–62, **261**
Greens Gumbo with Black-Eyed
    Peas, 106–7
Iced Melon Soup, 118
Manhattan Tuna Chowder, 97
Peanut Tomato Soup, 96
Pear and Root Vegetable Soup, 99
Red Bean and Walnut Soup, 102
Red Lentil and Apricot Soup,
    100–101, **101**
Roasted Red Pepper Gazpacho,
    117
Roasted Tomato Soup, 94–95
Russian Cabbage and Apple
    Soup, 108–9
Souped-Up Chicken Broth, 120
Sweet Potato and Shrimp
    Chowder, 98
Tuscan Minestrone with
    Butternut Squash and Farro,
    104–5, **105**
20-Minute Vegetable Soup, 93
Wild Mushroom–Barley Soup,
    110
Wild Mushroom Broth, 111
Sour cherries
    Big Chocolate Breakfast
        Cookies, 326–27
    good to know facts, 27
    health benefits, 26
    jarred, buying, 299
    Nutty Popcorn Bundt Ring, 304
    Persian Chicken with Sour
        Cherries, 155
    Red Cabbage with Sour
        Cherries, 244
    selecting, 26
    serving ideas, 27
    Sour Cherry Marmalade, 333
    Sour Cherry Sauce, 299
    storing, 27
Southwestern-style dishes
    BBQ Bean Soup, 103
    Black Bean and Nectarine Salsa,
        80
    Chili Onions, 246
    Hot Bean Dip, 75
    Mexican Molé Chicken Salad,
        135

Salmon Tacos with Avocado
    Cream, 176–77
Turkey Meatball Chili, 148–49
Soy beans
    Black and White Hoppin' John,
        228
    Chopped Arugula Salad with
        Edamame and Avocado, 125
    good to know facts, 36–37
    health benefits, 36
    serving ideas, 36
Spices, 56–59. *See also specific*
    spices
    about, 50–51
    buying, 51
    Cajun Spice, 219
    cooking with, 51
    Dukka, 77
    garam masala, preparing, 100
    medicinal uses of, 50
Spinach
    Baked Spinach and Feta, 241
    Curried Egg Salad with Spinach,
        134
    good to know facts, 13
    health benefits, 13
    Mexican Molé Chicken Salad,
        135
    selecting, 13
    serving ideas, 13
    Spinach Lasagna with Creamy
        Tomato Sauce, 208–9
    Spinach Salad with Maple
        Mustard Dressing, 126
    storing, 13
    Turkey and Spinach Mini-Meat
        Loaves, 146–47, **147**
Squash, summer
    Apple Ratatouille, 243
    Feta Dip with Confetti
        Vegetables, 72
    Golden Cauliflower and Tofu
        Curry, 226, **227**
    Green and Yellow Squash
        Ribbons, 232, **233**
Squash, winter
    Baked Rigatoni with Butternut
        Squash and Turkey Sausage,
        210–11
    Black Bean Salad with Butternut
        Squash and Broccoli, 130,
        131
    good to know facts, 17
    health benefits, 16

Squash, winter *(cont.)*
    Orange-Glazed Japanese
        Squash, 252–53
    Pumpkin-Date Tea Cakes, 282
    selecting, 17
    serving ideas, 17
    storing, 17
    Tuscan Minestrone with
        Butternut Squash and Farro,
        104–5, **105**
    varieties of, <u>253</u>
Strawberries
    Blue Corncakes with Mixed
        Berry Compote, 330–31
    good to know facts, 28
    health benefits, 27
    Morning Fruit and Cheese Plate,
        312
    selecting, 28
    serving ideas, 28
    storing, 28
    Strawberry Smash, 319
    Strawberry Surprise, 335
    Triple Strawberry Bruschetta, 316
Sunflower seeds
    good to know facts, 48
    health benefits, 48
    Nutty Fiber Mix, 317
    Nutty Popcorn Bundt Ring, 304
    selecting, 48
    serving ideas, 48
    storing, 48
Sweet potatoes
    Ginger Mashed Sweet Potatoes,
        248
    glycemic index, 14
    Golden Cauliflower and Tofu
        Curry, 226, **227**
    good to know facts, 15
    health benefits, 15
    Marshmallow Sweet Potatoes for
        Grown-Ups, 249
    orange varieties (yams), about,
        15
    Pear and Root Vegetable Soup,
        99
    Pear and Sweet Potato Crumble,
        294–95
    selecting, 15
    serving ideas, 15
    Southern Sweet Potato Pie, 291
    storing, 15
    Sweet Potato and Shrimp
        Chowder, 98

Sweet Potato Smoothie, 336, **337**
    Upside-Down Pineapple Sweet
        Potatoes, 250–51, **251**
Swiss chard
    Greens Gumbo with Black-Eyed
        Peas, 106–7
Swiss cheese
    Kale Frittata, 220
    Melted Swiss, Smoked Turkey,
        and Apple Panini, 191

T

Tacos
    Salmon Tacos with Avocado
        Cream, 176–77
Tea
    Almond Chai, 343
    Chinese Tea Eggs, 84
    Creamy Chai Oatmeal, 320
    good to know facts, 67
    Green Tea Shortbread, 281
    health benefits, 66–67
    selecting, 67
    serving ideas, 67
    storing, 67
    Tropical Fruit Salad with White
        Tea Syrup, **270**, 271
    Tropical White Tea Spritzer, 341
Thermometers, digital, <u>158</u>
Thyme
    good to know facts, 56
    health benefits, 56
    Mediterranean Onions, 247
    serving ideas, 55–56
    Tropical White Tea Spritzer, 341
    Turkey Breakfast Sausage, 332
Tofu
    Golden Cauliflower and Tofu
        Curry, 226, **227**
    pan-crisping, <u>226</u>
    pressing, <u>226</u>
    Spinach Lasagna with Creamy
        Tomato Sauce, 208–9
    varieties of, 36–37
Tomatoes
    Apple Ratatouille, 243
    Baked Rigatoni with Butternut
        Squash and Turkey Sausage,
        210–11
    BBQ Bean Soup, 103
    Dried Tomato–Mint Salsa, 171
    Feta Dip with Confetti
        Vegetables, 72

Five-Way Chili Spaghetti, 204–5,
        205
    Fusilli with Broccoli Bolognese,
        202–3
    Goat Cheese, Sun-Dried
        Tomato, and Arugula
        Panini, 190
    good to know facts, 16
    Grilled Cheddar and Tomato
        Panini, 189
    health benefits, 15–16
    Lemon Pesto Dip with Red
        Pepper and Cherry
        Tomatoes, 70–71, **71**
    lycopene in, 15–16
    Manhattan Tuna Chowder, 97
    Marinated Tomato Salad, 128
    Moroccan Tomato Compote,
        166–67
    Mushroom Kebabs, 242
    Parsley and Grape Tomato Salad,
        127
    Peanut Tomato Soup, 96
    Red Wine Lentils, 222
    Roasted Broccoli, Green Beans,
        and Grape Tomatoes,
        235
    Roasted Red Pepper Gazpacho,
        117
    Roasted Salmon, Grape
        Tomatoes, and Leeks with
        Sparkling Wine Sauce,
        178–79
    Roasted Tomato Soup, 94–95
    Salsa, 176
    Scrambled Eggs with Pasta and
        Cherry Tomatoes, 217
    selecting, 16
    serving ideas, 16
    Spice-Rubbed Salmon Kebabs
        with Tzatziki Sauce,
        172–73, **173**
    Spinach Lasagna with Creamy
        Tomato Sauce, 208–9
    storing, 16
    Turkey Meatball Chili, 148–49
Tortillas
    Salmon Tacos with Avocado
        Cream, 176–77
Trout
    Trout with Meyer Lemon
        Gremolata, 182
Truffles
    Peanut Butter Truffles, 303

Tuna
  Manhattan Tuna Chowder, 97
  Tuna Muffuletta, 186–87, **187**
Turkey
  Baked Rigatoni with Butternut
    Squash and Turkey Sausage,
    210–11
  buying, at deli counter, 136
  Fusilli with Broccoli Bolognese,
    202–3
  good to know facts, 40
  health benefits, 39
  internal cooking temperature,
    158
  Juicy Turkey Burgers, 145
  Melted Swiss, Smoked Turkey,
    and Apple Panini, 191
  selecting, 39
  serving ideas, 39–40
  storing, 39
  Turkey and Spinach Mini-Meat
    Loaves, 146–47, **147**
  Turkey Breakfast Sausage, 332
  Turkey Cutlets with Cranberry-
    Pomegranate Salsa, 143
  Turkey Meatball Chili, 148–49
  Turkey Oreganato, 144
  Turkey Waldorf Salad, 136, **137**
Turmeric
  good to know facts, 58
  health benefits, 57
  serving ideas, 58

U

Umami
  description, 11
  sources of, 116

V

Vegetables. *See also specific*
    vegetables
  fiber in, 8
  health benefits, 7–8
  Pear and Root Vegetable Soup,
    99
  recommended daily intake, 8

Tuscan Minestrone with
    Butternut Squash and Farro,
    104–5, **105**
  20-Minute Vegetable Soup, 93
Vinaigrettes
  Fresh Herb Vinaigrette, 141
  Ginger Vinaigrette, 140
  Pomegranate Walnut
    Vinaigrette, 141
Vitamins, 17

W

Walnuts
  Big Chocolate Breakfast
    Cookies, 326–27
  Black Bean Brownies, 277–78
  California Salad with Citrus
    Dressing, 124
  good to know facts, 46
  health benefits, 45–46
  Pear and Walnut Muesli, 321
  Pomegranate Tabbouleh,
    197
  Red Bean and Walnut Soup,
    102
  Roasted Beet and Walnut Salad,
    132
  Roasted Red Pepper and Walnut
    Spread, 74
  selecting, 46
  serving ideas, 46
  Spiced Fig Bars, 279
  storing, 46
  toasting, 74
  Turkey Waldorf Salad, 136,
    137
  Walnut Butter, 192
  Walnut Chocolate Strudels with
    Cinnamon Honey Syrup,
    286–87
Watermelon
  good to know facts, 29
  health benefits, 28
  Iced Melon Soup, 118
  Raspberry Watermelon Cooler,
    337, 339
  selecting, 29

  serving ideas, 29
  storing, 29
Whole wheat
  good to know facts, 33
  health benefits, 33
  serving ideas, 33
Wine, red
  Berries and Red Grapes in
    Spiced Red Wine, 273
  good to know facts, 68
  health benefits, 68
  Red Wine Lentils, 222
  selecting, 68
  serving ideas, 68
  storing, 68

Y

Yogurt
  Citrus Charge-Up, 334
  Frozen Blueberry Yogurt Pops,
    308
  good to know facts, 42
  health benefits, 41–42
  Lemon Yogurt Cheesecake with
    Sour Cherry Sauce,
    298–99
  Lemon Yogurt Frosting, 297
  Melon and Orange Yogurt Bowl,
    310
  selecting, 42
  serving ideas, 42
  storing, 42
  Sweet Potato Smoothie, 336, **337**
  Triple Strawberry Bruschetta,
    316
  Tzatziki Sauce, 172–73

Z

Zucchini
  Apple Ratatouille, 243
  Feta Dip with Confetti
    Vegetables, 72
  Golden Cauliflower and Tofu
    Curry, 226, **227**
  Green and Yellow Squash
    Ribbons, 232, **233**

Conversion Chart

These equivalents have been slightly rounded to make measuring easier.

Volume Measurements

U.S.	Imperial	Metric
¼ tsp	–	1 ml
½ tsp	–	2 ml
1 tsp	–	5 ml
1 Tbsp	–	15 ml
2 Tbsp (1 oz)	1 fl oz	30 ml
¼ cup (2 oz)	2 fl oz	60 ml
⅓ cup (3 oz)	3 fl oz	80 ml
½ cup (4 oz)	4 fl oz	120 ml
⅔ cup (5 oz)	5 fl oz	160 ml
¾ cup (6 oz)	6 fl oz	180 ml
1 cup (8 oz)	8 fl oz	240 ml

Weight Measurements

U.S.	Metric
1 oz	30 g
2 oz	60 g
4 oz (¼ lb)	115 g
5 oz (⅓ lb)	145 g
6 oz	170 g
7 oz	200 g
8 oz (½ lb)	230 g
10 oz	285 g
12 oz (¾ lb)	340 g
14 oz	400 g
16 oz (1 lb)	455 g
2.2 lb	1 kg

Length Measurements

U.S.	Metric
¼"	0.6 cm
½"	1.25 cm
1"	2.5 cm
2"	5 cm
4"	11 cm
6"	15 cm
8"	20 cm
10"	25 cm
12" (1')	30 cm

Pan Sizes

U.S.	Metric
8" cake pan	20 × 4 cm sandwich or cake tin
9" cake pan	23 × 3.5 cm sandwich or cake tin
11" × 7" baking pan	28 × 18 cm baking tin
13" × 9" baking pan	32.5 × 23 cm baking tin
15" × 10" baking pan	38 × 25.5 cm baking tin (Swiss roll tin)
1½ qt baking dish	1.5 liter baking dish
2 qt baking dish	2 liter baking dish
2 qt rectangular baking dish	30 × 19 cm baking dish
9" pie plate	22 × 4 or 23 × 4 cm pie plate
7" or 8" springform pan	18 or 20 cm springform or loose-bottom cake tin
9" × 5" loaf pan	23 × 13 cm or 2 lb narrow loaf tin or pâté tin

Temperatures

Fahrenheit	Centigrade	Gas
140°	60°	–
160°	70°	–
180°	80°	–
225°	105°	¼
250°	120°	½
275°	135°	1
300°	150°	2
325°	160°	3
350°	180°	4
375°	190°	5
400°	200°	6
425°	220°	7
450°	230°	8
475°	245°	9
500°	260°	–